D1602815

# ➤ OUR ➤
# DOLPHIN ANCESTORS

"For years we have been hoping that a book on the subject of human/dolphin kinship would be written by someone with the credentials to treat this special relationship with our aquatic cousins with the seriousness the subject requires. Frank Joseph has produced a masterful treatment of this ancient family bond between dolphin and human that will intrigue, provoke, and satisfy the most exacting critic of the challenging aquatic ape theory that links our species as one."

BRAD AND SHERRY STEIGER, AUTHORS OF
*REAL VISITORS, VOICES FROM BEYOND,*
*AND PARALLEL DIMENSIONS*

"A meticulously researched investigation of dolphins, with reference to ancient and modern encounters, that offers an exciting possibility for the future survival of humanity and the planet."

DAVID JONES,
EDITOR OF *NEW DAWN MAGAZINE*

"Renowned author Frank Joseph's newest probe into Earth's ancient mysteries uncovers a major connection between people and dolphins, something that people close to the sea have often observed in myth and legend. He looks deeply into our common origins and into startling physiological features that we share uniquely. His amazing description of how dolphins can communicate and even heal people demonstrates the interconnectedness and interdependence of life, which humanity is only now beginning to grasp."

VON BRASCHLER,
AUTHOR OF *7 SECRETS OF TIME TRAVEL*

"The amazing Frank Joseph reveals an entirely new link between dolphins and humans and raises questions that, if answered, could resolve some of the most deadly problems on this beleaguered planet and just might save our profoundly troubled species. This book is a truly unforgettable journey."

JEFF RENSE,
SYNDICATED NATIONAL TALK SHOW HOST

"Mesmerizing as the dolphins themselves! Only Frank Joseph, with his expansive global knowledge of history and true origins, could bring this masterpiece together. It is so well researched that it truly calls for a re-education of the public. I was captivated!"

DIANA PALM,
AUTHOR OF *SETTING SPIRITS FREE*

"Joseph explains our biological characteristics that support an early aquatic phase of human development as an 'aquatic ape.' The facts are convincing, evolutionary theory is correctly applied, and the implications are fascinating. This thesis deserves media exposure and inclusion in academic curricula."

JAY STUART WAKEFIELD,
BIOLOGIST AND ARCHAEOLOGICAL RESEARCHER

# — OUR —
# DOLPHIN
# ANCESTORS

## *Keepers of Lost Knowledge*
## *and Healing Wisdom*

## Frank Joseph

Bear & Company
Rochester, Vermont • Toronto, Canada

Bear & Company
One Park Street
Rochester, Vermont 05767
www.BearandCompanyBooks.com

Text stock is SFI certified

Bear & Company is a division of Inner Traditions International

Copyright © 2016 by Frank Joseph

All rights reserved. No part of this book may be reproduced or utilized in any form
or by any means, electronic or mechanical, including photocopying, recording, or by
any information storage and retrieval system, without permission in writing from the
publisher.

**Library of Congress Cataloging-in-Publication Data**
Joseph, Frank.
  Our dolphin ancestors : keepers of lost knowledge and healing wisdom / Frank
Joseph.
    pages cm
  Includes bibliographical references and index.
  ISBN 978-1-59143-231-9 (pbk.)  ISBN 978-1-59143-232-6 (e-book)
  1. Dolphins. 2. Human-animal communication. I. Title.
  QL737.C432J67 2016
  599.53—dc23

                                            2015028812

Printed and bound in the United States by Lake Book Manufacturing, Inc.
The text stock is SFI certified. The Sustainable Forestry Initiative® program promotes
sustainable forest management.

10  9  8  7  6  5  4  3  2  1

Text design and layout by Virginia Scott Bowman
This book was typeset in Garamond Premier Pro with Book Antiqua used as the
display typeface

To send correspondence to the author of this book, mail a first-class letter to the
author c/o Inner Traditions • Bear & Company, One Park Street, Rochester, VT
05767, and we will forward the communication, or contact the author directly at
**www.ancientamerican.com**.

# Contents

INTRODUCTION

# The Eye
# of the Dolphin

*It's the dolphin's eyes that get me. They're full of wisdom.
It's like they're looking straight at your soul, and know
everything about you. I think they can tune into you and
your problems. I think they're a sophisticated animal that
is further up the evolutionary ladder.*

ADRIAN HARRIS, REPORTER FOR
THE *BRISBANE JOURNAL*

In December 2013, my wife, Laura, and I were aboard a 55,819-
ton cruise ship, sailing through the Gulf of Mexico from Key West,
Florida—the southernmost landfall in the United States—to Honduras.
MS *Ryndam*'s position was just above the Tropic of Cancer, as we were
having breakfast, seated on the eleventh deck, which rose 110 or more feet
above the waterline. The morning was bright and cloudless, and we both
happened to be looking down along the starboard side as it cut rapidly
through the sea, when into our line of sight swam an exceptionally large
fish, as much unusual for its great size as its vivid color.

The animal was a remarkably bright, brilliant green from snout to
tail tip, as though electrically illuminated. Although it resembled a typical shark in its lazy side-to-side movement and body configuration from

midsection to tail fin, its head and foreparts were unusually broad. Our Dutch cruise ship was then steaming all ahead full at twenty-two knots (twenty-five miles per hour), churning up a powerfully turbulent wake, but the creature swam into it, skimming beneath the surface (its dorsal fin cut just above the water), a few feet from the *Ryndam*. It swam with an easy motion for perhaps five seconds before slowly swimming away.

Judging from the creature's proximity to passenger quarters below decks, we conservatively estimated that it stretched the breadth of at least two staterooms, about forty feet. Due to our lofty perspective, however, we may have guessed far short of the beast's actual overall length.

Returning home a week later, I found reference on the Internet to the specimen we saw December 10. *Scyliorhinus retifer,* known as the chain dogfish or chain catshark, is unusually bright green because it is bioluminescent. In other words, the surface of its skin produces light when *fluorophores*—fluorescent chemical compounds that absorb light energy of a specific wavelength and reemit it at a longer wavelength— are stimulated by an external light source to produce a fluorescent effect.

Humans cannot visually detect the process, but we can see the photons' changed energy state, which appears as a different color of the visible light spectrum than the color of the external light source.

Just how certain fish evolved biofluorescence and what purpose it serves them are questions not easily answered. The second such shark recorded was fluorescent and filmed for the first time during August 2005; it glowed a brilliant green.

But the chain dogfish grows less than two feet in length, is covered with spots, and possesses a body shape mostly unlike the massive, forty-or-more-foot-long monster we observed in the Caribbean. What we saw appears to have been similarly biofluorescent, but entirely so, and therefore could not have been *Scyliorhinus retifer.* Continuing my Internet investigation, I was surprised to find images of the whale shark (plate 1), because it more closely resembled our sighting. Whale sharks are the ocean's largest fishes, reaching lengths in excess of fifty feet, and their head and foreparts are identical to the configuration Laura and I observed. Moreover, they feature widely spaced biofluorescent spots, but their surface skin is mostly very dark, not overall vibrant green.

I was interested in learning the opinion of my zoologist friend and experienced mariner, Jay Wakefield, who agreed that the sea beast we saw must have been a common whaleshark that only seemed thoroughly green to us because the play of light on the blue water over the animal's fluorophores made it appear to be one solid color. Marine biologists do not admit the existence of thoroughly bioluminescent whale sharks.

But Jay's theory did not sit well with either of us. We distinctly remember the uniformly luminous green of the immense creature. Twenty years before, I was in clear, shallow water with large sharks off the Bahamian island of Bimini, where they were most distinctly gray and dark brown. We are inclined to conclude, expert scientific opinion aside, that Laura and I witnessed an unknown creature, an entirely bioluminescent whale shark.

Such an accidental discovery, while thrilling, is not all that unusual. The catastrophic tsunami that rampaged throughout Indonesia in 2004 washed ashore dozens of specimens new to science. So did northern Japan's tsunami, just seven years later. Public markets at the mouth of South America's Amazon River collect numbers of unknown fish, crustacean, and squid species every week. The sea's potential for mystery is as deep as the ocean itself and deeper, it would appear, than current understanding of life beneath the surface. As the British geneticist and evolutionary biologist J. B. S. Haldane (1892–1964) states, "the world is not only stranger than we imagine; it is far stranger than we can imagine."[1]

Of the two methods by which we learn—from others and from personal experience—the latter is by far the more convincing, and our lunchtime sighting of the glowing green giant made a profound impression that pointed me in the direction of some of the previously unthinkable possibilities addressed in the following chapters. While still at sea, I took advantage of the *Ryndam* library to read up on whale sharks, but strayed into a book about dolphins. Among the anticipated highlights of our cruise was an opportunity to experience them up close in neither the wild nor an amusement park, but at a research facility, the Roatán Institute for Marine Sciences.

In this scientifically controlled environment, the creatures are closely studied, but devotedly cared for in a large outdoor setting, where tourist dollars help fund the international establishment. It is located at an otherwise uninhabited islet just off Roatán, where a shallow barrier corrals more than thirty dolphins within some six square acres. The top of the fence stands so low above the water that all but the most arthritic dolphin can easily hop over it. In fact, several have made good their escape in this manner, I was told, only to jump back inside a few days later.

As part of their daily routine, all the resident dolphins are herded together and taken out to sea, where they often frolic with their friends and relations in the wild for an hour or so—much like walking one's pet dogs—before returning to the fenced-in islet. Perhaps they regard it as a sanctuary from sharks, enjoy its largesse of flattering attention from scientists and tourists, are bribed by free squid and herring—among their favorite delicacies—or appreciate all these amenities and more that no human can understand.

After the close of our visit, when the marine biologists went ashore and the dolphins were left alone, I lingered nearby to watch one of their number suddenly dive and moments later emerge holding a large stick in its mouth. This it flaunted enticingly at three or four other dolphins, which chased after him or her, trying to snatch the object away. That they engaged in this spontaneous game suggested sincere merrymaking, because no one was around to give them commands, applause, or food; they were apparently playing for the sheer fun of it. Earlier, I had been in the water with one of them for the first time. Many people have reported memorable encounters with such creatures, and the Roatán islet provided me with a similar opportunity.

Together with fellow tourists, guided by a local handler, we waded into shallow depths and were immediately met by a female dolphin, which allowed us to come quite close, even touch her. Expecting to feel a hard or at least a tough, scaly exterior, I was surprised by her supple, smooth, warm skin, so humanlike. "No one who has ever touched the skin of a dolphin," writes famed oceanographer Jacques Cousteau, "is likely to forget the silken, elastic, soft feel of it."[2] But a deeper impression was made by her light brown eyes. Behind the anticipated high intelligence and complex awareness, there was something even more compelling lurking deeper inside. If, as the old French saying has it, "the eyes are the mirror of the soul," then her gaze betrayed a core mystery comparable only to a kindred connection.[3]

The feeling is not uncommon. Cetacean researcher Ann Spurgeon speaks for many when she observes, "We looked often into the dolphins' eyes, and the quality of the look they returned was unlike that of any animal we have known."[4]

According to no less an authority on the sea than Cousteau himself, "it is obvious that dolphins are often motivated by curiosity, and especially by curiosity about man. One literally can see it in their eyes. This is a fact that can be doubted only by someone who has never really looked a dolphin in the eye. The brilliance of that organ, the spark that is so evident there, seems to come from another world. The look which the dolphin gives—a keen look, slightly melancholy and mischievous, but less insolent and cynical than that of monkeys—seems full of indulgence for the uncertainties of the human condition."[5]

Belgium's pioneering underwater archaeologist and the world's first aquanaut, Robert Sténuit, goes further: "The glimmer of interest which sparkled in their eyes seemed to be a human glimmer."[6] Sténuit's radical suggestion articulated my, as yet, unformulated suspicion—a wordless knowing beyond understanding, much less expression, as though my own mind had been somehow confronted with or partially overtaken by a significant truth too grand or potent for me to really comprehend or to put into words.

Richard Wagner's Hans Sachs articulates my perplexity in *The Mastersingers of Nuremberg*: "I feel it, but cannot understand it; cannot completely recall it, but can never forget it. I can grasp it entirely, though cannot measure it. But how can I grasp that which seems immeasurable? . . . It seemed so old, and yet was so new."*

Cousteau was no less taken by his first personal contact with a wild dolphin. "It was an extraordinary situation," he confesses, "as though the barrier between man and animal no longer existed. There was some sort of strange understanding between us. It would be very difficult for me to say exactly what our feelings were for one another, but there was undoubtedly something."[7]

Such an inexpressibly profound impression is not unknown to others touched by the creature's singular energy field. "Those who have come very close to dolphins feel it inside themselves," states Dr. Horace Dobbs, a leading delphinologist, "yet cannot explain it. Exactly what it is remains a mystery. For want of a better word, let us call it spirit of the dolphin."[8]

From the moment the Roatán dolphin first approached our gaggle of tourists, I could not escape the strong impression—realization, perhaps—that it was very rapidly probing us with the powerful energy of some unseen and inconceivable instrument; scanning each one of us individually; psychically scoping us out down to the absolute bottom of our souls; reading everything in our conscious and subconscious minds; assessing the totality of our identity; determining our threat or friend potential; yes, judging us—completely and thoroughly within the matter of a few seconds.

---

*"Ich fühl's und kann's nicht verstehn, kann's nicht behalten, doch auch nicht vergessen: und fass ich es ganz, kann ich's nicht messen! Doch wie soll ich auch fassen, was unermesslich mir schien. . . . Es klang so alt, und war doch so neu." From Richard Wagner's *Die Meistersinger von Nürnberg* [The Mastersingers of Nuremberg] in Full Score. NY: Dover Publications, 2009.

Back aboard the *Ryndam*, still full of this unexpected experience, I gravitated toward the ship's swimming pool. I was drawn into the warm water beneath a fifteen-foot-tall set of life-size statues depicting six leaping dolphins (see fig. I.1 on page 8). The massive artwork arching high overhead seemed to connect with something beyond words or names. A fellow passenger in the pool saw me staring at the sea beasts frozen in space and time and volunteered an account of his own recent meeting in a sea aquarium with "the real thing," as he put it, which, he boasted, had planted a wet kiss on his cheek.

"Maybe they are human or a kind of human," I ruminated aloud, wondering at the same instant what had triggered such an outburst, "or once were human." My pool partner was speechless, while his face momentarily betrayed inner consideration of the bizarre possibility I suggested, as though he was momentarily struggling to remember something that might confirm it. But he soon snapped back to consensus reality, stating emphatically, "No! Never!" All this together in the water, the bronze likenesses of dolphins suspended above us.

The occurrence at Roatán was my first encounter of the kind, but it triggered the writing of this book or, at any rate, precipitated the research that eventually crystallized into its pages. I had been long before intrigued by dolphin mysteries, which were suddenly personalized by my Honduras adventure. I always felt there was something more to the creatures than the usual, if still engaging and unanswered, questions concerning their communication skills, intelligence, behavior, and other lingering enigmas currently under investigation. What particularly fascinated me was the dolphin's unique relationship with humans. In it may hide the long-lost cipher to an unspoken, only vaguely felt, though persistent riddle. Its solution might simultaneously reveal a shocking kinship that could throw new light on our own behavior, how we became what we are, and what we are becoming.

To be sure, the conclusions that seemed to force themselves upon me are the most radical I have thus far offered, exceeding those I made for lost civilizations or human antiquity. When describing these

Figure I.1. The *Ryndam*'s poolside dolphins. Photograph by the author.

archaeological puzzles, I confidently relied on decades of research, world travels, editing *Ancient American* magazine, and publishing as an alternative science writer for *Atlantis Rising, New Dawn, Nexus,* and a number of other, similar periodicals. In writing about marine biology, however, I waded out far beyond my usual depths. I have no background in zoology and tremble to lay my determinations before experienced, university-trained cetologists, scientists who study marine mammals—whales, dolphins, and porpoises.

And yet, only some of the mysteries I wanted to explore lay within the limited purview of delphinology. There were associated spiritual, even paranormal, issues—taboo lines of inquiry shunned by modern science—that were too integrally bound up in the whole enigma for dismissal or avoidance. Mainstream scholars jeopardize their careers by even alluding to such forbidden subjects, which have been part of my investigations for more than thirty years. Accordingly, melding our current physical understanding of dolphins with their metaphysical implications opens a holistic panorama, as unexpected as it is revealing.

In this, I felt encouraged by Dr. John Cunningham Lilly (1915–2001), the American physician, neuroscientist, psychoanalyst, psychonaut, philosopher, author, and inventor best known for his decades-long investigation of interspecies communication. "To properly evaluate whales, dolphins, porpoises," he declares, "we must use everything we have intellectually, all available knowledge, humanistic as well as scientific."[9]

Among the revelations that most shocked me into further pursuing the mystery was a dolphin embryo photographed by Dr. J. G. M. "Hans" Thewissen, Ingalls-Brown Professor of Anatomy at Northeast Ohio Medical University. His imagery of the prenatal dolphin's vestigial hind limbs shows they are strikingly human in appearance, with clearly defined thighs, calves, feet, and toes. As writers Martha Clark and Eleanor Devine observe, as long ago as 1967, "X-rays of dolphin flippers show vestigial hand bones."[10] Indeed, they resemble the four human finger bones, an impression deepened when we learn that dolphin ancestors originally had a thumb, which has gone vestigial in maturity, but is still clearly visible on the embryo.

What does the prebirth emergence of these discernibly human traits mean? Answering that question and others related to our

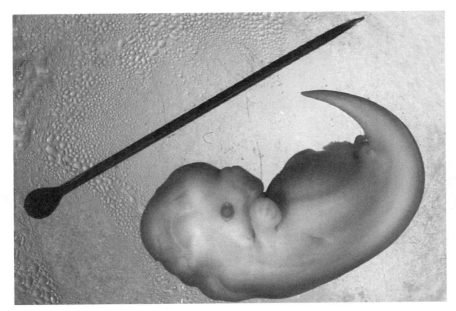

Figure I.2. Dr. Thewissen's remarkable photograph of a dolphin embryo compared with a pin. Thewissen Lab, NEOMED.

peculiar affinity with dolphins is found by the kind of extreme science offered in the following pages. They are accessible only to readers with the courage to think for themselves and consider outrageous possibilities that may lead us into unchartered depths, where the imaginable becomes real, and we meet with our own reflection in a dolphin's eyes.

# 1
# We Are Aquatic Apes

*Science is the belief in the ignorance of experts.*
RICHARD FEYNMAN

We are the result of human evolution stimulated by the sea. This is the fundamental premise of the aquatic ape theory, as presented in my book *Before Atlantis*. It states that some primates, more than three million years ago, were confronted for the first time with the loss of their terrestrial environment by encroaching floods. Faced with a choice between adaptation or extinction, they embraced changes that allowed them to successfully exploit this watery challenge, just as other mammal species succeeded in doing before them.

Among these first innovations was the ability to walk upright on hind legs, as liquid buoyancy shifted the torso's center of gravity toward the chest. In just one of many crucial consequences, the larynx was drawn further down into the throat, where low-pitched sounds necessary for speech could be produced. When the deluge retreated, stranding these hapless creatures back on dry land, they were compelled to readapt, although now endowed with specialized traits acquired during their ocean interlude. Over subsequent millennia, the waters irregularly returned and departed, forcing hominid populations to incorporate within themselves certain characteristics required for survival in either environment.

Alternating bouts with the sea and land were stimuli for change that physically prompted our evolution into modern humans. This, in essence, is the chief point of the aquatic ape theory, namely, that we would have never stepped forth from the ranks of fellow primates had our ancestors not progressed through several aquatic phases, which determined the unique course of our evolution and differentiated us from other hominids. Some fundamental support for this alternative theory of human origins was provided in the opening chapters of my first book on the subject and will not be recapitulated here. But this book must take instead an almost entirely divergent path with additional proofs.

If *Before Atlantis* traced *Homo sapiens'* emergence from water toward civilization, *Our Dolphin Ancestors* projects that development further backward into an even deeper past of shared evolution with other aquatic creatures, then forward to an almost inconceivable future, when humankind may yet again quit the land for a final return to the sea. Envisioning such a radically unconventional panorama grants me the opportunity for the first time to marshal more of the most convincing and fresh evidence pertinent to our ancestral sea interludes, which were only partially presented in *Before Atlantis*.

One month following the April 2013 publication of *Before Atlantis*, David Attenborough publicly voiced his favorable opinion on possibilities for an ancestral aquatic ape at a London conference dedicated to some of the latest advances in evolutionary research.[1] Best known for writing and presenting the British Broadcasting Corporation's (BBC) ten episode Life series, his international prestige as the world's most famous naturalist lends special credibility to a position still too scandalous for most conventional scholars. Attenborough's willingness to reconsider its potential for explaining human evolution shows that it has survived four decades of mainstream criticism and gone on to attract the serious attention of leading scientists.

For some, the very notion of an aquatic ape is too ridiculous for serious consideration. For others, it is a theory that may or may not be correct. Still others believe it more logically explains the course of human evolution than any other proposition. Most conventional scholars continue to dismiss suggestions of an aquatic ape, usually without addressing the evidence upon which the theory is based. They argue that because evolutionary changes occur incrementally over long stretches of time, vestigial traits still allegedly found in our bodies from some hypothetical aquatic phase only a few thousand years ago must have resulted from other, less recent causes. But the usually gradual pace of adaptation is occasionally stimulated by exceptional conditions that challenge a species to either mutate or die out.

A case in point was made in 2014, when animal behaviorists noticed that two different sets of male crickets on separate Hawaiian islands suddenly stopped chirping. Made by scraping one wing across the other, the sound had been emitted to attract females for mating. Beginning in the late 1990s, parasitic flies from North America began arriving on Kauai and Oahu, where they homed in on the chirping crickets and sprayed them with maggots, which burrowed into their hosts and ate them to death. To counter this depredation, the male crickets changed the shape of their wings so they could no longer chirp. This adaptation occurred differently and independently, but almost simultaneously among the crickets of both islands and saved them from certain extinction. More remarkable still, both populations completed the changeover from chirping to silence during the course of just twenty generations, "the blink of an eye in evolutionary time," the lead researcher told the BBC.[2]

Skeptics may contend that such an example is meaningless because humans are not crickets. But this objection misses the point, namely, that the Hawaiian crickets' adaptation to an immediate threat was successfully completed not once, but twice, and at many times their normal evolutionary speed. All species, including humans, evince similar developmental surges when sufficiently stressed, as demonstrated by numerous vestigial characteristics left over from an aquatic phase our ancestors experienced. As Timothy Wyllie, author of several books about his numerous encounters with dolphins, correctly observes, "stress enhances the possibility of mutation in the natural world."[3]

Look at the top of your hand. Notice how the bases of the digits are separated by small membranes of skin, most noticeably between the base of the thumb and forefinger. Although resemblances to a human hand are apparent, chimpanzee, gibbon, and gorilla hands all lack any such membranes between their fingers and thumb. The interphalangeal articulations they have never possessed, but we still do, are the remnants of webbing being gradually phased out because it was no longer needed as a swimming aid after our ancestors forsook sea-mammalhood for life on dry land.

Certainly, one of the most decisive changes that came to distinguish us from our simian cousins is the human ability to walk upright. This unique adaptation came about as our ancestors waded into ever-deeper water, while keeping their heads above the surface. As a surviving indication of that major modification caused by interacting with the sea, "the moment we stand up, our body reacts to the stress by immediately hoarding its inner salt supply," according to Australian biologist Gary Opit.* He explains that quickly assuming an erect position often results in dizziness ameliorated by temporarily curtailing salt supply to the brain. "We have an upright stance essential for wading in deeper water with larger buttocks to support a swiveling hip, so that it is possible for us to bend and twist, as our long, sensitive fingers can grope in the sand."[4]

Precisely the same process may be observed today in Japanese macaques (*Macaca fuscata*), also known as snow monkeys, which spend much of their wintertime in Sapporo's thermal hot springs (plate 2). There, they gingerly walk along the bottom on their hind legs, feeling

---

*Gary Opit was a member of the Royal Zoological Society of New South Wales for forty years and named "Earth Champion" in August 2003 by the International Athena Foundation and Byron Shire Council, which listed him in their interactive Knowledge Pond website. His "Value of Anecdotal Reports," summarizing seventeen years of data collected from about eight hundred listeners, was published by the journal *Australian Zoologist* in 2014.

with the soles of their feet for tasty morsels, their heads above water.

These macaques are also among the most quick-witted monkeys, often observed carrying food in their arms while walking upright to hiding places away from the water's edge. In their forays between dry land and hot springs, we glimpse something of our own aquatic phase. It was preceded long before by another primate that began walking in the direction of *Homo erectus*.

"Known as the 'enigmatic hominoid,' *Oreopithecus* can dramatically rewrite the paleontological map, depending on if it is a descendant from the European ape *Dryopithecus* or some African anthropoid,"[5] according to Dr. Michel Odent, a French obstetrician and childbirth expert. The hominid is "enigmatic," because paleoanthropologists are unsure whether it was one or the other. Still, this ten-million-year-old "hill ape" (from the Greek *oros* and *pithecus*) is usually placed in its own subfamily within Hominidae, if only because its hominidlike hand proportions are typical of the hominid family.

More cogent to our discussion, *Oreopithecus* was at least partially bipedal, because he experienced buoyancy in swamps on a chain of islands running from the Italian peninsula southward into the Mediterranean Sea. Earlier, his primate ancestors had crossed on all fours into these islands when lower sea levels connected scattered territories by slender land bridges to the European continent. Fluctuating sea levels subsequently sank these terrestrial connections and stranded the hill ape in a new insular habitat. Under the local influence of aquatic stimuli, he developed "the elbow of an upright walker," a short pelvis and lumbar curve associated with an erect posture far more hominoid than anything comparable among chimpanzees or gorillas.[6]

The process of standing more and more upright gradually forced the hill ape larynx deeper down its throat, allowing it to breathe through the mouth for the first time, which is necessary for inhaling air before diving into water. As such, the development of erect posture and breath control—with its implications for the production of spoken language—were simultaneous adaptations to aquatic conditions. Indeed, our breath control not only enables us to plan our inhalation in advance of needing to do so, but inhaling quickly and exhaling slowly is itself a breathing pattern akin to speech.*

In fact, fine breath control is preadapted for speaking. *Oreopithecus* evidenced additional hydro influences in other diagnostically hominid traits, such as short jaws and reduced canine teeth, both characteristic of a softer seafood diet, with shellfish chief on the menu. He thus affirms Charles Darwin's observation that "life on islands tends to accelerate the process of evolution."[7]

About 6.5 million years ago, declining sea levels dispelled the hill ape's island isolation, with fatal consequences. Across a newly formed land bridge with the European continent came the infamous saber-toothed cats, or saber-toothed tigers, which quickly hunted *Oreopithecus* to extinction. Had the species survived, we would be more evolved than we are at present by 3.5 million years, because *Oreopithecus* was well on his way to becoming fully upright, the precondition for human evolution. The hill ape demonstrated that the passage of a primate species into an aquatic phase is virtually inevitable, given enough time and changing environmental circumstances, and has undoubtedly occurred more than once—a credible supposition in our forthcoming investigation of mermaids and human-dolphin affinities.

The bonobo is another modern primate undergoing its own watery interlude in the flooded forests of Zaire, where, contrary to the behavior of its hydrophobic relatives on dry land, it wades upright through the water to catch fish.† "Might it not have been in the sea that Man learned to stand up?" wonders Dr. Odent.[8]

Aquatic apes first walked fully upright 3.2 million years ago, just as regional flooding receded throughout East Africa, casting them

---

*Interestingly, marine mammals communicate, not with primate gestures, difficult to see in subsurface environments, but through sound, which travels greater distances under water than through the air.
†Also dissimilar from other chimpanzees, bonobos copulate belly-to-belly, in the fashion of sea mammals.

back upon dry land. It was here that an arched fossilized foot bone was found in early 2011. An arch in the foot provides leverage to push off the ground at the start of a stride and then helps absorb shock when the foot strikes ground again. Ape feet are flatter, more flexible. They use their big toe for grasping tree branches, a talent missing from the East African discovery.

The foot bone belongs to *Australopithecus afarensis,* better known from the partial skeleton of a kindred specimen, unearthed in 1974 by Donald Johanson and his fellow paleoanthropologists, named "Lucy" after the Beatles song "Lucy in the Sky with Diamonds." So too, the human foot is more paddlelike—better for swimming than clenching, grasping, gripping, manipulating, or clasping—and is longer in body proportion than found among other primates.

Ever since Lucy and her cohorts emerged from their aquatic phase to walk fully upright on their legs, our human species has suffered the kinds of back, hip, knee, ankle, and foot ailments addressed by Moshé Pinchas Feldenkrais (1904–1984), an Israeli physicist and doctor of science in engineering at France's Sorbonne, where Marie Curie was one of his teachers, during the 1920s.

About the same time, he worked as a research assistant to nuclear chemist and Nobel Prize laureate Frédéric Joliot-Curie at the Radium Institute in Paris. Feldenkrais went on to originate a methodology for improving human physical functioning by increasing self-awareness through bodily movement. Among his most famous clients was David Ben-Gurion, the first prime minister of Israel. Thousands of practitioners of the Feldenkrais Method are still teaching throughout the world today.

As the leading authority on posture, Dr. Feldenkrais discovered that sensory perception in men and women measurably expands when they become buoyant in water, which relieves gravitational stress on their brains, as well as on their vertebrae. He discovered that their nervous systems are otherwise affected by muscles struggling against gravity, resulting in diminished consciousness of their physical surroundings.

His findings coincide with those made by Dr. Lilly, inventor of the isolation tank for sensory deprivation. The blood pressure and pulse rate of his flotation volunteers dropped substantially when they entered the tank, allowing for increased circulation, which reduced muscular tension and induced a meditative state for improved insight and inspiration. Tensions, worries, or anxieties diminished, replaced by feelings of well-being, tranquillity, inner peace, and a sense of emotional balance.

These experiments eventually led to the application of hydrotherapy as a treatment for arthritis and bursitis, because it reduced physical stress on the entire bodily frame. "From birth," states Jacques Cousteau, "man carries the weight of gravity on his shoulders. He is bolted to earth. But man has only to sink beneath the surface and he is free."[9]

Our body's own painkillers, known as endorphins, are activated by merely entering water, which simultaneously disengages the production of various chemicals associated with illness and stress. "Those with more endorphins released during certain activities," asserts Yale University biochemist Philip Applewhite, "may be happier about any given situation or event in their lives than those with fewer endorphins. That is, doing the same thing may be more pleasurable to one person than another, because for that person, more endorphin molecules are released to the brain. Happiness, then, lies not outside the body, but within it. Joy is not an illusion; it is real and has a molecular basis."[10]

Water immersion reduces adrenalin, the human stress hormone, while simultaneously facilitating oxytocin. This "happiness hormone" promotes trust and empathy, evokes feelings of contentment and security, and reduces anxiety. It inhibits brain regions associated with behavioral control, fear, and anxiety and functions to protect against emotional tensions, with a general enhancing effect on all social relationships.

After having endured trying conditions, we commonly find physical as well as psychological relief in a hot bath. Water-stimulated oxytocin occurs only in primates—such as bonobos, proboscis monkeys, Japanese macaques, and our aquatic ape ancestors—that adapted to a watery lifestyle. Suffering the adverse effects of gravity on their body structure, humans respond to water with expanded consciousness, diminished muscular stress, cure of inflammatory joint illnesses, and improved cardiovascular and emotional health, indications of a prolonged aquatic phase through which our ancestors passed in their evolutionary development.

Unlike apes, we have peripheral vasoconstriction, when blood flowing through the limbs cuts down to save oxygen for important organs while we swim. When we dive, our heart beats less frequently, and as we descend deeper, blood fills our lung vessels and cavities to prevent organs from being crushed by higher pressures. Our bodies excrete salt from seawater with the same kind of multilobed kidneys possessed by sea mammals. Each one of them has a spine that aligns with its legs, enabling the creature to take vertical positions in the water or to swim horizontally, just as our spine does, but unlike the spines of any other four-limbed, terrestrial animals.

Accordingly, humans are the only primates that suffer hernias, because we returned to the land after having spent time enough adapting to life in the sea, where buoyancy relieved body weight on our frame. Although bonobos, proboscis monkeys, and Japanese macaques have likewise adapted to water, they do not suffer hernias, because our weight-to-body-size ratio is much greater than theirs. Also, our shoulders are unsuited to an entirely terrestrial habitat, as demonstrated by the ease with which they are dislocated, sometimes by merely moving our arms too far forward or backward. Apes are far more capable of swinging continuously by their hands, branch by branch, through the forest. We, on the other hand, gave up such jungle mobility for the ability to swim. As a consequence, our shoulders are less useful on land than in water.

Enlarged semicircular canals in our ears, however, allow for improved balance under water—an adaptation to aquatic conditions missing from landlubber chimpanzees. We also have *cerumen,* or "ear wax"—not really a wax, but a sticky substance secreted by glands in the outer portion of the ear canals—for waterproofing. We equalize air pressure in our ear canals as we descend deeper into the water, a talent that would not have developed unless our ancestors had been engaged in diving for enough generations to pass down that ability to us.

Asthma is common among humans and some sea mammals, but not among apes—strangely enough, if they are supposed to be our closest relatives, and not members of an aquatic species. Excessive contraction of the smooth bronchial muscles during an asthma attack reduces lung capacity when diving beneath the surface of the water, thereby avoiding nitrogen intoxication and decompression sickness, because the body is less buoyant than normal. While these anatomical characteristics are utterly different from anything comparable found in all other primates, they typify sea mammals, from which we are descended.

# 2
# Our Sea-Mammal Heritage

*A very great deal more truth can become known than can be proven.*

RICHARD FEYNMAN

In *Before Atlantis,* I briefly touched on the role of a waxy substance triggered by the onset of puberty, because we are unique among primates for the production of sebum, variants of which are used by some sea mammals to make their skin less permeable to water. In fact, sebum keeps human skin supple for swimming. Our adolescence is sometimes troubled, however, by excessive secretions of sebum, resulting in seborrhea, or acne, a condition unknown to apes.

Our ancestors developed specialized strategies for survival in water, changes they brought back with their return to the land, where some of these adaptations to an aquatic environment—like sebum—are still incorporated in our very bodies. The newborns of a few semiaquatic species, such as *pinnipeds*—fin-footed seals—are coated with vernix caseosa. Not found on any other primate, human infants come into the world covered with the same, cheesy varnish.

Like the buoyant mammary glands of manatees, fatty tissues evolved the shape of women's breasts, allowing them to float for better infant suckling while immersed. Cold water prompted the extension of the human vaginal canal away from salty seawater, moving the uterus inward, where the labia and thighs helped conserve heat; in response, men's penises grew longer. The labia major, hymen, and vaginal ridges of human females waterproof the vagina, while a low pH of approximately 4.5 and a colony of *Lactobacillus*—a type of bacteria—in the vaginal canal inhibits waterborne pathogens. Another connection to the sea, human female menstruation is synchronized with the Moon, or tidal, cycles.

Environmental influences determine the forms all creatures take. Cetologists believe a deer- or doglike animal that some thirty million years ago began leaving behind the land of its birth for subsequent adaptation in the sea—as did our species—gradually assumed a sharklike configuration, because, different as they are, both the porpoise and the shark—one a mammal, the other a fish—were challenged by common conditions in the habitat they shared.

Our primate body shape reacted to these same natural forces by evolving away from a hulking, apelike frame toward a straighter, streamlined fusiform body (long and thin with tapering ends), suited less for walking on two hind legs than for swimming with them, while drastically reducing drag in the water. To further reduce drag, we needed less hair.

"There are one hundred ninety-three living species of monkeys and apes," according to naturalist Desmond Morris in his famous book *The Naked Ape*. "One hundred and ninety-two of them are covered with hair. The exception is a naked ape self-named *Homo sapiens*."[1]

All mammals that exchanged terrestrial habitats for life in the water—even those, such as the elephant, that returned to the land after an aquatic phase—doffed most of their now-useless body hair to become naked. Thick body hair alternately cools or warms a primate's skin temperature in open-air conditions, but much finer body hair— a detriment on dry land—allows for streamlined passage through water. Human hair, unlike that of chimpanzees or apes, is greasy for waterproofing. Hair is most suitably located and abundant atop our heads, where it was retained to block excess sunlight in tropical seas.

As a man ages, he often grows partially or completely bald, which further reduces drag in water, resulting in a speed swimming advantage that compensates for his decreasing muscular strength. In sexual selection, modern human adults mostly prefer partners with little or no body hair, especially among females, who often go to extreme lengths on behalf of depilatory countermeasures. Men and women who can afford such a process sometimes have all hair below their heads surgically removed. This preference could have arisen only during an aquatic phase, when hair loss and exposed skin were favored.

Detractors dispute this explanation, but Opit offers a strong argument in favor. "It is believed [by conventional evolutionists] that our ancestors lost their hair covering to become cooler while chasing game across the hot savanna grasslands," he writes, "and that we then developed our subcutaneous and other body fat to keep us warm. This proves not to be the case, because our bare skin actually increases the body temperature when in sunlight, and the fat layers do not keep us warm. . . . Our puny hair covering is an adaptation to regularly swimming in salt water."[2]

As protection against excessive sunlight and wind, ape skin is tougher and more gnarled than a human's smooth, drag-reducing epidermal surfaces, which more closely resemble dolphin skin. Immersed to their necks in water, our aquatic ancestors needed to shield only the tops of their heads from the Sun; hence, the scalp we inherited from them is thicker than that possessed by other primates.

During the break in a January 2014 presentation I was making about this topic at the Minnesota Theosophical Society in Minneapolis, a young man from the audience wondered whether wrinkles on the undersides of human fingers, when submersed in water for more than a few minutes, evolved during an aquatic phase, enabling our ancestors to pick up and grasp small morsels of seafood. I admitted that such an adaptation had never occurred to me, but thought his suggestion seemed worth consideration.

As synchronicity would have it, the following month's issue of *National Geographic* magazine reported that Tom Smulders, an evolutionary biologist, "confirmed that pruney fingers have the advantage in wet conditions," in which they "promote water runoff and aid adhesion, like the treads of a tire. . . . [H]is findings could boost the theory that a million years ago the ancestors of modern humans went through a semi-aquatic state, when skin folds might have helped toes cling to slick rocks and fingers catch wriggling fish."[3]

Originally, scientists assumed that the wrinkles simply resulted from the skin swelling in water. But Smulders goes on to point out that the furrows are caused by constricted blood vessels due to signaling from the sympathetic nervous system in response to water exposure.

Less desirable traits we inherited from our aquatic ancestors are myopia and astigmatism, which originally corrected for light refraction while swimming under water. We also suffer occasionally from monochromacy, another legacy from our beginnings in the water. This congenital vision deficiency, more commonly known as "color blindness," is an adaptation to a marine environment, where the ability to distinguish

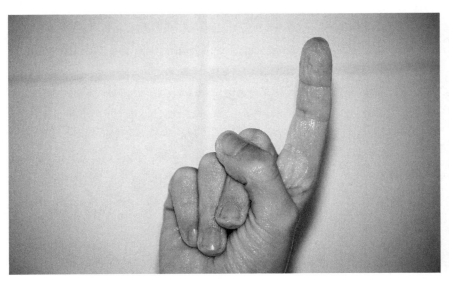

Figure 2.1. Example of finger with wrinkles from the water.
Photograph by Sebastian Wallroth.

colors, rather than shading, is a liability. The overall cream color of Beluga or "white" whales, denizens of the polar seas, camouflages them when they are resting among the ice floes but most effectively against predators unable to visually determine gradations of color.

Neither apes nor chimpanzees are color blind. Indeed, our good subsurface vision is provided by maximally constricting pupils unknown to our closest primate relations. Dolphins and other sea mammals descended from ancestors that lived on dry land have a tapetum lucidum, which aids their vision in dim light. Along with the unique ability among primates to walk on hind legs, this same reflecting membrane was at the back of *Homo erectus*'s eye. Its appearance suggests this feature emerged with him from the sea, if only because his allegedly closest relatives—apes and chimpanzees—never had such a retinal membrane. Neither do we. But all subsequent hominids, through to early *Homo sapiens,* were so endowed, until it vanished with Cro-Magnons, about twelve thousand years ago.

During the previous ice age, with its low levels of light, Cro-Magnon Man found retention of his optical inheritance useful. At the close of the Northern Hemisphere's most recent glacial epoch, however, Cro-Magnons migrated out of continental Europe into Anatolia, today's Turkey, where abundant sunshine rendered the tapetum lucidum useless, and it faded after several generations. But its unique presence among precursors to our species suggests its origins in an aquatic phase.

Nothing more dramatically recalls that stage than our own birth. "When comparing humans and apes," Paula Peterson writes on her Earthcode International Network website, "the mechanics of human births are difficult—and among the apes, it is not. There is no pelvic cavity in apes, and the infant's head is always smaller than the mother's skeleton, which makes birthing easy. In humans, birth is painful and often difficult because the infant's head—from the frontal lobes to the back—is larger than the mother's pelvic floor. The shoulders are larger, too, making it necessary for the baby to advance through the birth canal in a spiral motion in order to come out."[4]

The pain human mothers suffer in delivering children on land is substantially ameliorated when the process occurs in water, where mere contact reduces "adrenalin, the hormone associated with fear and anxiety, and reduces the force of gravity. . . . In labor, this helps the woman to deal with contractions," according to authors and alternative healers Amanda Cochrane and Karena Callen.[5]

A leading proponent of water birthing is among the world's foremost obstetricians, Michel Odent, M.D., "a pioneer who has influenced the history of childbirth," characterized by *The Lancet* as "one of the last real general surgeons."[6] Founder of the Primal Health Research Centre in London and in charge of the surgical and maternity units of the Pithiviers hospital (France) from 1962 to 1985, he introduced the concept of birthing pools after observing "the incredible attraction to water that some [expectant mothers] had while in labor."[7]

A few needed only to see blue water to initiate the birthing process. "When pregnant women dream of water," Odent explains, "it is always a brilliant blue," the color of shallow tropical seas. "In general," he states, "women dream of giving birth in a natural environment. No one dreams of a hospital or even of a bedroom. It is worth remembering that Freud interpreted dreams of water as being about birth."[8]

Odent speculates that "warm water acts directly on the muscular system. Tendons are composed mainly of collagen, and the warmer the temperature, the softer the collagen becomes. So, a warm bath might have a direct, relaxing effect. Thus a bath that is the same temperature as the body protects the mother-to-be against the fight-or-flight response; it achieves the physiological state sometimes called 'relaxation response.' . . . The use of water avoids some obstetric interventions, such as forceps, vacuum extraction, and Caesareans, which bring their own risk of infection." A mother's labor is not only eased in water, but faster than hospital deliveries, according to Dr. Odent. Terrestrial newborns are held upsidedown by their ankles and spanked to make them inhale their first breath, but when they are born into water and rise to the surface, "air is all that is needed to stimulate the baby's first cry."[9]

The newborns of other terrestrial mammals, such as the horse, can stand immediately after birth, unlike the delayed bipedalism of human babies, which are unable to walk for months, but nonetheless swim as soon as they leave the birth canal by vigorously kicking their legs, known as instinctual rhythmic limb action. The Russian godfather of water birthing, midwife Igor Tcharkovsky, demonstrated how "the reflexive motions that babies make with their arms and legs is, in actuality, an example of their natural inclination to swim, and not merely random, arbitrary movements, as has been generally thought. These actions closely resemble an adult's breast stroke."[10]

Human infants crawling about on all fours "is terrestrial dog-paddling never used by other apes," according to Opit.[11] That these newborns instinctively know how to hold their breath, just as marine mammals do—wholly unlike any other primate—is indication enough of our evolutionary passage through an aquatic phase. From their fourth month up to the close of their first year, human infants demonstrate a floating reflex, rolling over on their backs to breathe on the water's surface. Needless to point out, such an adaptation is utterly meaningless in a terrestrial environment.

Human newborns are covered with antibacteriological *squalene*—a natural organic compound for waterproofing the skin—and assisted by *adiposity,* a special fat making them buoyant, common among marine mammals, but missing from our nearest terrestrial cousins, the chimpanzee, which would only be unnecessarily burdened by such weight.

"Humans are unusual amongst land dwelling mammals," writes Opit, "in that we carry large quantities of white adipose fat all year round and this extra weight slows us down and burdens us with heftier infants. Between the thirtieth and fortieth weeks of pregnancy, the amount of fat in the fetal child rises dramatically from thirty grams to four hundred thirty grams, so that it constitutes sixteen percent of the birth weight, which compares with three percent in the newborn baboon."[12]

Dr. Odent holds a similar view, "Compared with the chubby human baby," he observes, "the baby ape is thin and bony."[13] Opit further notes that baby fat does not seem adapted to a terrestrial environment:

> Human adipose tissue is much more mature at birth when compared with the adipose tissue from the newborn of other animals. Its production in such large quantities creates a considerable draw on the energy reserves of the mother during the last weeks of pregnancy that no other primate has to endure. The development of so much fat tissue also disadvantages our babies, in that there are much less available nutrients and energy for the growth of the skeleton, and the growth rate of the fetal body length slows after the twentieth week of pregnancy.
>
> The skeleton is immature at birth when compared with other mammals, and so the infant is less mobile and much heavier to carry because of all the fat. White adipose fat is of no use in keeping the baby warm. That is the role of brown fat that supplies quick increases in temperature as it converts to energy, before the baby is able to shiver. However even this brown fat is converted to white adipose fat at the age of four months. Besides energy storage, there is only one function that white adipose fat performs extremely well, and that is providing buoyancy in water. Only aquatic mammals that need a great deal of buoyancy have large quantities of white adipose fat, and a surface feeding whale has fifty times the amount of blubber it would need to keep warm.[14]

Yet more evidence suggests that human babies are adapted to water birth. Estelle Myers, an Australian researcher experienced in aquatic birthing, concludes that infants born in water mature into less aggressive individuals. Her colleagues add that such children are usually happier, physically stronger, more intelligent, and better adjusted than their playmates born in a hospital.[15]

These observations were repeated in St. Petersburg (formerly Leningrad) at Number 10 Children's Policlinic. Director Igor Smirnov notes that even babies not born in water, but which swam regularly soon thereafter, were able to reproduce monosyllables. They classified objects by shape and color so far ahead of their strictly terrestrial peers that he concludes "the aquatic environment promotes early speech development."[16]

*Before Atlantis* enumerated the unique function of human sweat glands, used to cool the skin through evaporation, because we lost most of our body hair while adapting to life in the sea. "The skin of an adult human can lose huge quantities of sweat," observes Dr. Odent. "His skin is endowed with one hundred and fifty to four hundred sweat glands, called eccrine glands, per square centimeter [0.393701 inch]. The ape's much sparser eccrine glands respond to emotion, but not to heat. Other species that apparently sweat, such as horses, are using their scent signaling glands."[17]

Adaptations to former aquatic phases cited in this chapter are vestigial traces of human evolutionary progress, which was cut short when the seas abruptly retreated, leaving our ancestors stranded once again on dry land. That suspended development appeared when our brain size began to shrink, a downsizing caused by drastically diminished intake of fatty seafood after our transference from marine to terrestrial habitats. We still possess *laryngeal saccules,* or vestigial air sacks long ago used to aid our ancestors in floating in the water. Another vestigial measure of interrupted change is the *philtrum,* or medial cleft, a vertical groove in the middle area of our upper lip—an infranasal depression that would have perfectly fit into the center ridge at the bottom of the nose, as the rest of a longer-grown upper lip covered or uncovered the nostrils, sealing them off from water for improved diving.

"We have a large, hooded nose," Opit writes, "instead of a pair of nostrils like most other monkeys. Imagine what would happen if a monkey or an ape tried to dive or swim under water. The water would, of course, run straight down its nostrils. But if a hooded extension arose to partially cover the nostrils from water, which comes sweeping down across the forehead and face as one dives or swims, the problem would be greatly alleviated. The only other species of monkey that has a hooded nose, the proboscis monkey of Borneo, is also the only other semiaquatic primate."[18]

Our downward-oriented nostrils avoid water splashing into the nose, and paranasal sinuses assist in keeping our head afloat above the surface of the water. "But what is really striking," declares Dr. Odent, "is the great number of characteristics we have in common with sea mammals and that make Man an exception among the apes. The dugong and manatee are descendants of vegetarian hoofed animals; seals, sea-lions and walruses are the descendants of carnivorous animals; beavers are the cousins of purely terrestrial rodents. So why is it impossible that a primate followed the same route? This primate is Man."[19]

Evolution is never static, but a force for change flowing forward through time. We, and all living things around us, continue to evolve, imperceptible to us because of the relatively slow pace of growth. We count our individual lives in far less than ten decades, while human evolution progresses over hundreds of thousands of years. This biological gradualism is occasionally punctuated, however, by surges of change, when powerful events arise to challenge an organism to successfully adapt.

# 3

## *Homo delphinus*

*When we meet dolphins, it is like meeting friends, or relatives.*

JACQUES COUSTEAU

A composite character of all humanity, distilled into a single individual, would resemble a schizophrenic genius, a great thinker in the realms of science and ethics, but with an unparalleled capacity for brutality and self-destruction. In our numerous cultural achievements—from heart transplants to deep-space telescopes, from Da Vinci paintings to Beethoven symphonies—humans approach godhood. But we are also the world's cruelest beast, inflicting needless suffering and senseless death on our fellow creatures far beyond the ravages or needs of the most voracious predators.

The question of Man's uniquely contradictory character was taken up as long ago as 441 BCE by the chorus in Sophocles's *Antigone*: "Numberless wonders, terrible wonders walk the world, but none the match for Man—the oldest of the gods he wears away: the Earth, the immortal, the unchangeable—Man the master, ingenious past all measure, past all dreams, the skills within his grasp—he forges on, now to destruction, now again to greatness."[1]

Above all, we alone consciously subvert and destroy the organic foundations upon which our very existence depends. In this, we are

31

distinguished from every other being on the planet; our species behavior is less characteristic of a mammal than a virus.

"We became the Earth's infection a long and uncertain time ago," concludes the renowned British scientist James Lovelock, "but it was not until about two hundred years ago that the Industrial Revolution began: then the infection of the Earth became irreversible."[2]

For as long as humans have considered these things, they wondered about the meaning of their lives, until, exasperated at failing to arrive at a credible consensus, material scientists began to insist that no such meaning exists, that we are the inevitable, aimless result of time and substance, nothing more. But judging from the behavior of our genus, as observed in the aggregate over the last two million years or so, the well-known Destiny of Man becomes self-evident: namely, to extinguish all life on Earth, including ultimately his own, as each successive culture becomes progressively more adept at exploiting the planet's sustaining resources for short-term benefits.

While the inert human majority may not be directly responsible for fulfilling such an end result, it is nonetheless genetically part of a species' agenda and produces generation after generation of far more dynamic minorities willful enough to carry along the rest of Mankind toward global destruction over the objections of a small minority of impotent protestors. Man is the Great Exploiter, the Great Exterminator.

"He has a history of killing off all of the large mammals on land," writes Dr. Lilly. "The large animals of North America were extinguished by Man. The African species are being decimated by the encroachment of Man upon their territories. In the seas, the pelagic mammals are being critically depleted, as Man invades their territories and hauls their bodies ashore for his purposes."[3]

And not only "pelagic mammals," but everything that swims is imperiled by overfishing and poisoning of the very waters they and their forebears have successfully inhabited for millions of years. All animals, other than humans, behave exclusively within the circumscribed parameters of a specific, given nature and participate in—do not meddle with or upset—the balance of life. Accordingly, they are amoral—as Nietzsche says, "beyond good and evil."[4] The human alone is the moral animal, a novel blend—stew, more likely—of guilt and judgment, of the angelic and the satanic.

Humans are responsible for the Taj Mahal and the atomic bomb, the Hubble Space Telescope and the electric chair, medical care and waterboarding. Our personalities range from the likes of Mahatma Gandhi and Mother Teresa to Charles Manson and Bernie Madoff. As private persons, too, each one of us, during the course of a lifetime, is legitimately proud of our good deeds and haunted by our errors and sins. Few, if really any of us, are either living saints or full-time devils from childhood until death. We are alternately generous and mean-spirited, selfless and selfish, compassionate and indifferent, creative and destructive, loving and hateful.

Faust, Goethe's Everyman, exclaims, "Two souls dwell, alas!, within my breast; one strives to separate itself from the other."[5] This psychotic contradiction, unique in the animal kingdom, is suggested by our mixed origins on the African savanna and in "the cradle of life," as Tennessee Williams describes the sea.[6] If, as the previous chapter argues, we humans were well on our way to joining the formerly terrestrial dolphins and whales as a marine mammal, but ultimately returned to our roots on land—still bearing vestiges of our sea interlude—then our singular hybrid identity as aquatic primates may explain our checkered behavior. This singular dichotomy results, then, from our conflicted pedigree. Accordingly, we bear much in common with our nearest relatives, who are loyal to their own troop, but regard all other chimpanzees as enemies. Group members sort themselves out through a hierarchy of rank, wherein individual status is enforced with physical violence, intimidation, or, to avoid these confrontations, gestures indicating either subservience or dominance.

During her field research in the 1960s, Jane Goodall, the famous primatologist, observed how a loud thunderclap startled an entire "cartload" of chimpanzees—from the lowest-ranking member to the alpha-male leader—into simultaneously making the same skyward gesture, indicating acknowledgment of a higher rank, a superior authority.[7] The chimpanzees' reaction suggests the origin of religion, just as their hierarchical identification and group cohesiveness imply human class consciousness and tribal loyalty, or nationalism, even racism.

Chimpanzees resort to violence among themselves for establishing and maintaining social stratification, but display it especially toward outsiders, as a means of protecting the group. Our religious biases, status climbing, and various forms of chauvinism may ultimately stem from humanity's apish origins on the East African savanna, where we progressed from initially timid scavengers to become the world's dominant predator. If our not-all-that-distant primate past may explain something about our unsavory proclivities, our marine mammal legacy tends more toward social cooperation and empathy.

These and numerous associated parallels quite literally influenced the life of Jacques Mayol (1927–2001) in his career as a university-trained oceanographer and the holder of many world class achievements in free diving. During record-breaking dives to more than three hundred feet beneath the surface of the Mediterranean Sea on a single breath, he observed his heart beat decrease from sixty to twenty-seven beats per minute. This diving reflex was triggered by cold water contacting the face, missing from all other primates, but an instinct in dolphins.

In addition to this, as Opit explains, "Humans and dolphins can control their breathing rate, a feat that allows one to purposely hold the breath before diving. The breathing rate of land dwelling animals, including all other primates is automatically controlled, and only changes as a reaction and not as a conscious plan."[8] These respirtory parallels, unique between ourselves and cetaceans (marine mammals—whales, dolphins, and porpoises), were dramatized by Mayol's deepest free dive in 1983, remarkably, when he was fifty-six years old. At 345 feet, he was met by wild dolphins, which accompanied him back to the surface. Before and after this encounter, he learned by closely studying dolphin techniques to hold his breath longer, plus how to behave and better integrate himself under water. Years of such observations and their application convinced him that our species possesses hidden aquatic potential, which we can access and develop through rigorous physiological and psychological training.

The very configuration of the human body implies as much: ours is aquadynamic, in sharp contrast to that of the wholly terrestrial ape. Based on Mayol's scientific research, he foresaw a time when humans would be able to dive hundreds of feet deeper by holding their breath longer than ten minutes. His prediction came true in 2007, just six years after his death, when Austrian Herbert Nitsch free dove to 702 feet, the current record, followed two years later by the French free diver Stéphane Mifsud, who held his breath for eleven minutes, thirty-five seconds. In this, he began to approach the performance limitations of bottlenose dolphins, which can hold their breath for more than fifteen minutes, but due to their highly superior speed, are capable of diving within that period to 300 or more feet beneath the surface of the sea and returning for their next gasp of air.

Their normal diving range lies between 100 and 150 feet. But during the mid-1960s, Tuffy, a dolphin in the U.S. Navy Marine Mammal Program, regularly delivered supplies to members of Project Sealab, residing 1,000 feet beneath the surface in a self-contained environment module. Professor René Guy Busnel was mid-twentieth-century director of the Laboratory of Acoustical Physiology at INRA, the Institut national de la recherche agronomique, or National Institute of Agronomic Research, and a leading authority on dolphins, which he encountered at 1,500 feet down.

Sonar once tracked a single spotted dolphin to seventeen hundred feet, so the true limits of the animal's diving capabilities are still unknown.*

---

*Lethal air bubbles form in our blood and tissue when we rise back to the surface of the water from depths. This condition, known as "the bends," does not affect the dolphin body because its ribcage completely collapses, forcing air under pressure out of the animal's lungs through the windpipe and into the complex air chambers that lie below the blowhole, thereby achieving the equalization of pressure. Also, dolphins carry more oxygen in their blood than humans or fish.

Figure 3.1. Tuffy, the U.S. Navy's deep-diving dolphin.

Precisely how this particular dolphin was able to reach such depths on a single breath is unknown as cetaceans, humans, seals, and otters conform to bimodal diving patterns—short dives separated by returning to the surface for air at recurring intervals. Such capabilities, Mayol knew, were untypical of and far exceeded the limitations for nonhuman primates.

Accounts of drowning sailors rescued by wild dolphins go back more than two thousand years to ancient Greece and before and are still reported today. On the other hand, weak, isolated, or injured animals outside a chimpanzee troop are typically killed and devoured by chimps. A famous incident involving an ape that went to the rescue of a small child who had fallen into a pit does not apply because the ape had been born and raised in a zoo and was surrounded mostly by nurturing humans—a far cry from survival conditions in the wild. Lilly explains that bottlenose dolphins, on the other hand, establish their own pecking order "by biting, chasing, jaw-clapping, and smacking their tails on the water. Dolphins often show aggression by raking—scratching one another with their teeth, leaving superficial lacerations that soon heal. Traces of light parallel stripes remain on the dolphin's skin. These marks have been seen in virtually all dolphin species. Dolphins also show aggression by emitting bubble clouds from their blowholes."[9] Spotted dolphins are somewhat more sociable than their larger bottle-nose cousins and exhibit less aggressive behavior, in sharp contrast to the violent methods by which chimpanzee hierarchies arise. Cetaceans and primates are very different kinds of animals, but we seem to have incorporated something from both species in ourselves. "If humans had an aquatic ape ancestor," concludes author James William Gibson in *A Reenchanted World: The Quest for a New Kinship with Nature,* "other aquatic mammals were surely some kind of kin."[10]

And no other creature is more naturally kindred to us than the dolphin. Virtually all other wild animals avoid contact with humans, but wild dolphins seek to play and associate with humans, even going so far as to voluntarily rescue them from drowning and other life-threatening situations. But what explains this remarkable natural affinity, an affability closer than that of humankind's supposedly nearest relative, the unpredictably murderous chimpanzee? We do, after all, commonly swim with dolphins in the wild, but cavorting among apes under any circumstances is ill advised. If identity lies in origins, then understanding something about cetacean evolution may provide a clue.

All seventy-eight modern species of whales, dolphins, and porpoises descended from terrestrial creatures, as indicated by their need to breathe air from the surface, the vertical movement of their spines—characteristic more of a running mammal than of the horizontal movement of fish—and the bones in their fins, which resemble the limb bones of land mammals. Whales clearly evolved from Archaeoceti, primitive deerlike creatures during the Eocene Epoch between fifty-six and thirty-four million years before present. *Rodhocetus,* an early, long-extinct whale, swam with four stumpy legs—vestigial traces of which still appear in modern whales—and had triangular teeth like those characteristic of ancient Archaeoceti. (The hippopotamus, whose closest living relatives are the cetaceans, disposed of those triangular teeth after the close of the Eocene.)

The vestigial hind limbs of the dolphin embryo, however, are utterly unlike the legs of a sheep, cow, antelope, or hippopotamus. They are shockingly human in appearance, with clearly defined anthropomorphic thighs, calves, feet, and toes, as revealed by Dr. Thewissen's photograph of a dolphin embryo, provided in the introduction. Dr. Dobbs, founder of the Oxford Underwater Research Group, in Queensland, Australia, notes that "complex changes which take place from the moment the egg is fertilized until the baby dolphin is born are considered by many scientists to reflect the evolutionary path of the species. . . . The growth of a fetus in the womb retraced the path of evolution for that species."[11]

He goes on to cite the work of Sterling Bunnell, described in *The Journal of Hand Surgery,* as "the key person in the founding of the specialty of hand surgery in the United States," for his "collection of drawings of the fetuses of a white-sided dolphin [*Lagenorhynchus acutus*] that showed a startling resemblance to that of a growing human embryo."[12]

The bones in the flipper are more than suggestive of the four human finger bones. "The bones in the flippers of a dolphin," Dr. Dobbs observes, "correspond to those of the human hand."[13] Even Jacques Cousteau could not escape a human comparison with dolphins when he said "it is water that turned the hand of their ancestor into a flipper."[14]

The impression deepens when we learn that dolphin ancestors, unlike the Archaeoceti, originally had a thumb, which has also gone vestigial. "It is well known," Dr. Odent points out, "that when a congenital abnormality takes the form of adding a feature, it usually means that this feature had a reason for being there during the evolutionary process."[15]

Underwater archaeologist Robert Sténuit similarly notes, "in an animal's bones and fetus one can see, like the diagram of a family tree, a resume of the whole history of the race."[16] In other words, an unborn mammal infant embodies the evolution of its species. The dolphin's *humerus,* or upper arm bone, together with the *radius* and *ulna,* the lower arm bones, are very similar to ours. The radius and ulna "form about a third of the length of the flipper, which is roughly comparable to humans, in whom these bones form slightly less than half the length of the arm," observes James G. Mead, curator of marine mammals at the National Museum of Natural History (part of the Smithsonian Institution), and Joy P. Gold, technical information specialist at the museum.[17]

The bones of the scapula, or shoulder blades, in dolphins resemble human counterparts; they were not fused over time to accommodate a streamlined body, but became attached by heavy, fibrous tissue. As Jean Charles Genet, director of the National Center for Integrative Medicine and the National Research Center for Chronic Fatigue, points out, "we humans have a dolphin's skeletal and organ structure, and the same cerebral form. A dolphin has the semblance of a thumb and fingers in each of its pectoral fins that allows it to move left or right in the water. The dolphin has vestiges of hipbones, when it walked upright on land, much like a human."[18]

The famous biologist and nature writer Ivan Sanderson (1911–1973) saw dolphins at flood time in Brazil "lolloping through the trees with their modified mammalian gallop, as if some trick of time had brought them out of the Miocene epoch before my own eyes."[19]

Humans are born with a soft spot on the top of their head that corresponds to the blowhole the dolphin breathes through. This blowhole is an evolved nose that has moved upward from the front-center on its ancestral face to the top of the head. A dolphin can expel air from its blowhole at speeds greater than one hundred miles per hour.

Although both whales and dolphins are cetaceans, they do not seem to share a common evolutionary ancestor. For example, whales are utterly toothless and must sift masses of tiny shrimplike, planktonic crustaceans, known as *krill,* through plates of *baleen*—a horny, keratinous substance found in two rows of transverse plates hanging down from their upper jaws. Atlantic spotted dolphins boast a wholly different mechanism of thirty to forty-two pairs of small conical teeth in each jaw for grasping squid, herring, cod, or mackerel weighing three pounds or more.

Orcas devour seals and sea lions, even hard-shelled turtles. (Although orcas are also known as killer whales, they technically belong to the dolphin family, and their closest relatives are the snub-fin dolphins.) Consequently, whales and dolphins seem descended from very different ancestors. While land-roaming ungulates (hoofed mammals) forced by flooding into a watery environment eventually became *Rodhocetus* and its kind, an altogether different kind of terrestrial mammal faced with the same aquatic challenge increasingly developed dolphin characteristics.

As a lingering remnant of that gradual transition, some modern dolphins are relatively hairy, like the pink-skinned Amazon River dolphin, with hair on its beak. Other dolphins, humanlike, still have hair on their heads. Every dolphin, whatever its species, has hair follicles, remnants from its terrestrial past. Comparisons between ourselves and dolphins are more than skin deep. Physical parallels are apparent, related extentions of underlying genetic and even spiritual commonalities both species share in hitherto unknown ways, as described in the following chapters.

# 4
## The Mind in the Sea

*Can it be that the dolphin is not a new friend in the sea, but a very old friend whom chance or destiny has once more led us to recognize?*

JACQUES COUSTEAU

Could the dolphin be something more than "a very old friend"? Might we possibly share with this singular creature a relationship closer than all but the most unconventional researchers suspect? Contrary to current, general acceptance of human evolution, less obvious, physical parallels between two outwardly dissimilar species nonetheless suggest that their natural, special affinity for each other may spring from a shared background after all.

As described in *Before Atlantis, lanugo* is fine blondish hairs growing in patterns suggestive of water as it moves over the skin of a human fetus, beginning with its sixth month. Lanugo appears the same on the unborn of some sea mammals, but very differently—coarse and dark—in other primates. Author Timothy Wyllie writes that "when a dolphin is born, it's covered all over with the finest layer of hair," and refers to one female in particular: "This one was golden, and she shone like metal in the morning light."[1]

The human body's production of sebum, the waxy matter that makes the skin less permeable to water and more supple for swimming,

41

was mentioned in chapter 2 as one of our lingering aquatic traits. So too, dolphins "continuously secrete an oily substance which slides off the skin and is carried away by water," Dr. Dobbs explains, "reducing friction in the boundary layers between the water and their skin."[2]

Like the human "water babies" described in that same chapter, dolphin newborns are able to swim from the moment they leave the womb, a talent both species share, but unknown to any other primate.

Yet more decisive is "a comparison of dolphin and human chromosomes shows that the genetic make-up of dolphins is amazingly similar to humans," according to Discovery Channel Online News science writer Seema Kumar, reporting in January 1998 on findings announced in *Cytogenetics and Cell Genetics*. "Researchers at Texas A&M University applied 'paints,' or fluorescently labeled human chromosomes, to dolphin chromosomes, and found that thirteen of twenty-two dolphin chromosomes were exactly the same as human chromosomes," Kumar explains. "Of the remaining nine dolphin chromosomes, many were combinations or rearrangements of their human counterparts. Researchers also identified three dolphin genes that were similar to human genes."[3]

Kumar quotes Texas A&M team member David Busbee, who says: "The extent of the genetic similarity came as a real surprise to us." "Until now," Kumar continues, "researchers have never been able to do genetic studies of dolphins, because they are a protected species, making it difficult to get tissues from them. However, Busbee was able to grow colonies of cells from fetal tissues when a female dolphin miscarried."[4]

Commenting on the *Cytogenetics and Cell Genetics* report, Horst Hameister, then professor of human genetics at Germany's University of Ulm, states: "Dolphins are marine mammals that swim in the ocean, and it was astonishing to learn that we had more in common with the dolphin than with land mammals."[5]

His conclusions were foreshadowed as long ago as the early 1970s, when Dr. Lilly and his colleagues examined "three dolphin brains that were totally preserved, so that every cell was still present." He explains, "When we looked at these sections, I suddenly realized that these resembled the human brain to the point where the unpracticed eye could not tell the difference between the cortical layers of the human and those of the dolphin. The only significant difference was that the dolphin had a thicker layer number on the outside of the cortex." Further studies showed that "the dolphin's cell count is just as high per cubic millimeter as is that of the human. The material also shows that the connectivity— i.e., the number of cells connected to one another—is the same as that of the human brain. They have also shown that there are the same number of layers in the cortex of a dolphin as there are in that of the human."[6]

At London's Institute of Brain Chemistry, Professor Michael Crawford revealed that docosahexaenoic acid—an omega-3 fatty acid and primary structural component of the human cerebral cortex—is "found in its highest quantities only in sea-based food chains," Opit notes. "It is no coincidence that the only other mammals with brains large and complex enough to rival human brains are the Cetaceans, whales and dolphins, that also exist on the acid-rich sea foods," he adds.[7]

Described as "one of the world's most eminent researchers into brain function and nutrition, with over three hundred publications," Professor Crawford concludes that "the land-based food chain would simply not have sustained the evolution of *Homo sapiens*. So, *Homo sapiens* had to have evolved in the estuaries and the coastlines, actually swimming and diving and catching fish, collecting mussels and oysters and crabs in the rocky pools; that had to be the eco-system in which humans evolved."[8]

An example of dolphin-human commonality is a shared swimming technique. "The land animals [that exchanged their terrestrial habitat for an aquatic one] evolved to have a far greater strength and flexibility [than fishes]," Dr. Dobbs explains, "by a bending movement of the spine in the line of the body. Thus, although the fish-shape was adopted, it was accompanied by a unique up-and-down movement of the tail, which is characteristic of all dolphins today."[9]

Sharing the water with wild dolphins, physicist and swimmer Volney Wilson patterned a new swimming style after close study of their behavior. Imitating the creatures, he synchronized his legs with each other in a smooth undulation, fusing them together into an up-and-down fashion, a wavelike movement that transferred muscular power into a fluid kick. His feet, pressed together to avoid loss of water pressure, naturally pointed downward, giving added downward thrust. Like seals, but totally dissimilar from other primates, human leg muscles exert maximum force on the first and last toes of our feet, which are paddlelike, yet more trace evidence of our aquatic phase and lingering commonality with fellow sea mammals. Results of imitating the dolphins' swimming style included substantial increases in speed over previous methods, as Wilson demonstrated when he used it to win the 1938 U.S. Olympic Trials. Since then, the "dolphin kick" has become a key technique of professional swimmers.

Foremost among them is Matthew Nicholas Biondi, who won five gold medals, setting world records in the fifty-meter freestyle and three relay events at the 1988 Summer Olympics in Seoul. "Perhaps, in some way, I owe my gold medals to the dolphins," he confesses. "In their trusting and playful way, they taught me the subtleties of swimming technique."[10]

While we are adept at swimming like dolphins, our nearest primate relatives—the great apes—are anatomically unequipped to do the same because their spines lack the flexibility of human backbones. Such revelations amount to a suggestion more radical even than the aquatic ape theory, but, as Gibson writes, "The quest for connection with wild animals can lead searchers into uncharted territory."[11]

Perhaps some, but not all, hominids were compelled to either adapt to encroaching hydrous surroundings or face extinction. Others confronting less threatening conditions did not undergo a marine interlude, only to find themselves in an evolutionary cul-de-sac from which they never emerged. Their evolutionary destiny continued in a different direction. Those who adapted to the watery challenges took on a growing number of seaworthy traits, sharing ever more in common with other swimming mammals, until the tide retreated, casting them back onto the land, where they renewed their march toward becoming modern humans.

Yet, some of those aquatic hominids may not have been stranded on dry territory after all, but continued to pursue their evolutionary development in the ocean. Sufficient time enabled their full adaptation to a subsurface existence, and they grew into the creatures we know as dolphins, without ever suspecting that they are us. Or, at any rate, they are fellow hominids, but adapted to a radically different environment. Human and dolphin normal body temperatures are, after all, equivalent, averaging 98.6 degrees Fahrenheit. This body temperature is typical of cetaceans but lower than that of all other primates.

Furthermore, both humans and dolphins prefer belly-to-belly copulation; male apes and chimps, allegedly our closest relatives, mount females only from behind during copulation. Dolphin infants also spiral out through the birth canal, as do human newborns, although tail first to avoid drowning in the event of complications during delivery. Dolphins do not have a sense of smell—useless under water—but are no less gustatory than ourselves, able to distinguish between sweet, sour, bitter, and salty tastes.

Although most dolphins travel in tight-knit family and social groups, a few leave delphine society to actively seek out human relationships, preferring personal contacts with men, women, or children over fellow members of their own species. What is it in us that would so attract these individuals? Could they possibly recognize a commonality or background we share with them, but no longer remember? Our Classical Era ancestors understood and venerated that connection, as articulated by the second-century Greek poet Oppian, who declares that "it is an offence to the gods to hunt dolphins, and he can no longer approach the gods to offer a sacrifice, nor touch their altars with pure hands, who of his own will has been the cause of the destruction of dolphins. He makes impure even those living under his roof, because the gods hold the massacre of the monarchs of the deep to be as execrable as the murder of a human."[12]

As early as 600 BCE, Athenian law defined the deliberate killing of dolphins as "murder," worthy of capital punishment. Although we have forgotten, the implications of our hybrid aquatic-primate heritage may account, after all, for our conflicted character, a troubled combination of killer chimp and friendly Flipper. Eccentric as such a conclusion may seem, it is suggested by a growing collection of physical evidence that continues to convince some important scholars, such as Dr. Odent, that "dolphins, humans and apes are likely to have evolved from a common ancestor."[13]

Dr. Thomas White, professor of ethics at California's Loyola Marymount University in Redondo Beach and fellow at the Oxford Centre for Animal Ethics, argues that dolphins are not merely like people—they may actually *be* people, or at least, as he describes them, "non-human persons."[14] Olivia de Bergerac, an independent researcher of dolphins, refers to them as "the People of the Sea," just as humans are "the People of the Earth."[15] Watching the dolphins' mating process at the Miami Seaquarium made the director of public relations, Roger Conklin, think that "their embraced figures playing out the drama of creation do look almost human."[16]

Cochrane and Callen wonder, "Is it possible that at some period in the distant past, our evolutionary paths once crossed, and dolphins lived in close contact with people?"[17] Marine biologists believe that dolphins appeared after the close of the Eocene Epoch, some thirty million years ago—about twenty-eight million years before the first hominid was born. Dolphins, however—like any other species—have not been frozen in stasis since then, but continue to evolve over time. Some modern dolphins began to evolve about ten to three million years ago, just when the earliest primate aquatic phase was experienced by *Oreopithecus,* as described in chapter 1. Early hominids were well on their way to becoming sea mammals when fluctuating sea levels forced them back to dry land, where they walked upright toward becoming *Homo sapiens.* But perhaps at least one other group of protohumans may have already evolved too far to return to a terrestrial existence and continued their evolutionary destiny in the water.

As described in the introduction, dolphins at the Roatán Institute for Marine Sciences preferred to remain inside the low wall of their three-square-mile perimeter—not because they had been trained to do so, nor for the free food, which is no less abundant throughout Honduran waters. Instead, do they choose to remain close to their human friends for protection from predators? Some dolphins have been observed carrying terrible wounds and scars made by sharks, and their bigger cousins, the orcas, occasionally eat dolphin calves. "All the older animals [dolphins] in our experience have at least one shark bite on them," Dr. Lilly states.[18] Australian wildlife photographer Hugh Edwards "found dolphin remains in the stomachs of tiger sharks on several occasions when fishing for sharks in the North."[19]

The chief defense against such aggression is close social cooperation, but the pressures of vigilance and organized resistance are constant and onerous. Letting one's guard down for a moment, separation from the pod, distraction, illness, or old age could welcome a successful attack. The sea has always been a dangerous place. Perhaps our aquatic ancestors, after spending several generations there, were not thrown back upon the land by receding water levels or other natural forces, as assumed, but decided themselves that terrestrial life was a preferable, less hazardous environment.

Modern dolphins have among themselves as many species variations as does Mankind. Like ours, they present a diversity of physical appearance, temperament, and intelligences—from the oceanic *Delphinus capensis* to the riverine *Pontoporia blainvillei,* varying in size from Maui's placid dolphin at four feet long and ninety pounds to the thirty-foot-long, ten-ton *Orcinus orca,* which, as its name—the killer whale—indicates, is the most aggressive. In view of this wide diversity of physical, mental, and behavioral types, not all of the forty-two different species in family Delphinidae appear to have descended from the same terrestrial mammal.

Cetologists believe that the evolutionary parents of dolphins were hoofed animals that began to leave the land for a marine habitat about thirty million years ago. But these Artiodactyla embrace a wide variety of creatures, including pigs, hippopotamuses, camels, deer, giraffes, ante-lopes, sheep, goats, and cattle. Such vegetarians may have been proper ancestors for complacent plant- and fish-eating porpoises, but not bel-licose, carnivorous orca hunters. Killer whales are more likely descended from the Artiodactyla's sistergroup: the Mesonychids, wolflike predators. So, too, the exceptionally intelligent and sociable dolphins—particularly regarding their natural, even intimate, kinship with humans—seem to have derived from neither deer nor wolves, but something much closer to ourselves, perhaps a *Homo erectus* that pursued its destiny in an aquatic environment, instead of returning to the land like the rest of us.

*Stenella frontalis,* the spotted dolphin (plate 4), is historically renowned for rescuing sailors drowning at sea, a virtue less common among most of its fellows, and it probably has a slight edge in brain power and friendliness over its nearest cousin, the bottlenose *Tursiops*; both are, in any case, closely related, as they have been observed mat-ing in the Bahamas. At seven and one-half feet, either sex of full-grown *Stenella frontalis* is of an equivalent overall length, although mature females are generally one inch longer, but weigh twenty pounds less than 310-pound adult males.

"Pods," or groups of ten to more than one thousand individu-als, roam the Gulf Stream of the North Atlantic Ocean, where they are endemic to its temperate and tropical areas between Florida and Bermuda, as well as in the Gulf of Mexico. Spotted dolphins are less seen in the colder waters of the Eastern Atlantic, around Madeira and the Azores and Canary Islands to the southwestern tip of Spain, as far north as Cape Cod, as far south as Brazil's Rio Grande do Sul across to West Africa. While a definitive census is lacking, at least one hun-dred thousand spotted dolphins inhabit the Atlantic Ocean. Bottlenose dolphins are more common and divided into three species: the com-mon *Tursiops truncates* (plate 5), the Indo-Pacific *Tursiops aduncus,* and *Tursiops australis,* or the Burrunan dolphin.

The bottlenose dolphins, unlike their spotted brethren, swim the warm and temperate seas of the world. Together, genus *Tursiops* and

*Stenella frontalis* stand out in family Delphinidae for their quick-witted affability. Not all cetaceans descended from the same land animal, at the same time. Whales, porpoises, and dolphins trace their terrestrial lineage back to different, perhaps even distantly related ancestors, who entered upon their own aquatic transformations during separate intervals.

Porpoises, for example, have no beaks and are differentiated by their spade-shaped teeth and blunt, rounded faces, compared to delphinid teeth, which are shaped like rounded cones set in jaws that extend through a beak known as the rostrum. The term *porpoise* derives from *porpais,* Old French for "pork fish," due to the animal's snout, which bears some superficial resemblance to that of a pig. There are additional physical dissimilarities in size, shape, and weight separating porpoises from dolphins, but, more decisively, the latter are an entirely different and significantly higher order of intelligent life. The size of the brain, relative to body size, is smaller in porpoises than it is in dolphins. If dolphins represent the intelligentsia of cetacean society, porpoises are its country bumpkins.

The whale's earliest ancestor was an extinct order of hippopotamus, while the common forerunners of porpoises were artiodactyls. These are the same small deerlike creatures from which dolphins are believed to have evolved. Perhaps some did, but whales and porpoises have two or more stomachs, like cows and other ungulates—the cetaceans' hoofed predecessors—but *Stenella frontalis* and genus *Tursiops* have only one, as found in humans. While the dolphin's stomach is more complexly multichambered, it developed additional features to meet the different challenges of life under water. Delphinidae's diversity of type and intelligence spread far broader than the six porpoise species, however, allowing for additional possibilities. One of them appears to have been human or, at any rate, protohuman.

An early scientific hint of the dolphin's hominid ancestry came to light during the mid-1980s, when Peter Morgane, from the Worchester Foundation of Experimental Biology located in Shrewsbury, Massachusetts, and Ilya Glezer, a City of New York Medical School anatomy professor, joined Russian colleagues to map the dolphin's brain for the first time. The researchers found that the animal's neocortex had grown in size over the course of evolutionary time, "but it still has an ancient organization, as the dolphin has kept this brain structure since it first went into the sea. This raises the question of how intellectually advanced the dolphin's ancestor was when it took to the water."[20]

Made up of six layers, the neocortex comprises the outer layer of the cerebral hemispheres. This structure was already well developed and approximated the modern dolphin's neocortex at the time its terrestrial forbear left the land approximately three million years ago, about the same time *Australopithecus*—an early African hominid that evolved into the *Homo* genus around two million years ago—underwent an aquatic phase. The dolphin's brain is not only larger, more complex, and quite different from that of its alleged deerlike or doglike ancestor, but far more similar to our own.

The spotted and bottlenose dolphins' mutual attraction and physiological resemblance to our species suggests their early dry-land progenitor was our own hominid forefather, compelled by rising floods to adapt to a semiaquatic lifestyle between three and nine million years ago. With the gradual return of terrestrial conditions, some of his descendants went back to full-time existence on land, where they trod their evolutionary path toward *Homo sapiens*. Others continued to evolve in the sea, becoming *Stenella frontalis* and genus *Tursiops*. We may have forgotten that very ancient connection, but perhaps the dolphins still remember.

As Oppian believed nineteen centuries ago, "even now, the righteous spirit of men in them preserves human thought and human deeds."[21] Therein lies the mysterious relationship between the Earth's two most intelligent species, both the children of aquatic phases, separated by radically different environments, but united by a shared heritage closer than we might consciously suspect, but intuitively have always recognized.

# 5

# The Other Humans

*And they experienced all the pleasures of the depths, when, men transformed into fish, they plunged into the waves, and tried their fins for the first time. But dolphins have not forgotten that they were once men, and deep in their souls they retain the memory.*

OPPIAN

Could it be that today's dolphins are our fellow hominids in fish suits? Vague memories of these long-ago transitions swim like archetypical dreams through some of the world's oldest myths and their reenactments. "The natives of Groote Eylandt," according to Cochrane and Callen, "an island in the Gulf of Carpentaria, in northern Australia, regard themselves as the direct descendants of dolphins [a local native cave painting depicts a human figure rising out of the blowhole of a dolphin]. At their traditional ceremonies to celebrate the mythical past, the tribal elders decorate themselves with painted dolphin images."[1]

These colorful rituals are reenactments of a seminal myth conducted by the Wanungamulangwa people, who commemorate their earliest ancestors, the Indjebena, or dolphins. They dwelt in the waters surrounding Groote Island, where their leader, Dinginjabana, was the husband of Ganagja. She alone survived a massive shark attack that otherwise exterminated the Indjebena, whose souls were transformed many

51

years later into the first humans, as they walked out of the sea onto the beach at Groote Eylandt. Meanwhile, Ganagja, still an Indjebena, gave birth to a son, named after her husband.

Dinginjabana Jr. was bigger and stronger than any previous Indjebena, and from him descended all subsequent generations of dolphins. One moonlit night, Ganagja was swimming on the surface, near the coast of Groote Eylandt, when she saw and recognized her husband, now a man. In her excitement, she stranded herself on the shore, but he recognized her, and the happiness created between them was so great, she transformed into a woman. The couple went on to produce a great many more children, the forebearers of today's Wanungamulangwa.

"They are the only ones who remember that dolphins are the ancestors of the entire human race," explains Dr. Diana Reiss, professor in the psychology department at New York's Hunter College. "However, the dolphins in all the oceans, the offspring and descendants of the great mother Ganagja, have never forgotten that the people of Groote are their two-legged cousins. That is why, they say, dolphins are so eager to approach and play with their human kin. . . . This special connection between humans and dolphins among Australian Aborigines may well be the oldest one of all human societies," Reiss remarks, because the roots of Australoid myth go back forty thousand years.[2]

Polynesian myth tells of Ruru, the suitor of a young woman, whose rival threw him off a high cliff. As Ruru plunged into the sea, he uttered so powerful a curse on his attacker, it accidentally killed a nearby dolphin, a capital offense against the gods. A *tohunga,* or tribal priest, magically transferred Ruru's soul into the body of the dead dolphin, which was at once reanimated with a human spirit, but condemned for all eternity to swim up and down the coast, guiding each canoe safely to landfall. Native New Zealanders venerate dolphins as *taniwhas,* believed to have guided the canoe fleets of Maori ancestors across the vast reaches of the Pacific from one island to the next. The same belief belonged to a people far removed from New Zealand—the Picts, who left their original homeland in the Eastern Mediterranean Sea aboard ships guided by dolphins to Scotland, about two thousand years ago. Accordingly, the most common Picitsh symbol was the dolphin, which may have been the royal crest of this Celtic tribal folk.

Similar to Australia's Wanungamulangwa, the Maori of New Zealand trace their descent from the taniwhas' ancestors. "Dolphins," writes Dr. Reiss, "in these people's world, are known as humans of the sea."[3]

The same beliefs have been upheld for time out of mind by another indigenous people on the other side of the world, as described by Brazilian folklorist Béder Chávez:

> The Amazonian river people believe that pink dolphins (the botos) used to be humans many, many years ago, and that they can turn back into humans whenever they want. When they turn back into humans, they kidnap young boys and girls and take them to live with them in their underwater villages and cities. . . . When a person is taken into the dolphins' world of the dark Amazon waters, he or she is immediately transformed into a dolphin. If this happens, this person will never come back to be a human again. . . .
>
> Dolphins are at the top of the food chain in the Amazon River Basin, along with the jaguars, harpy eagles, anacondas, and caimans. All of these animals—except dolphins—are hunted for food or for their skins. Even though there are laws protecting all these animals, dolphins probably aren't hunted because the myths and superstitions help protect them. People don't kill dolphins because they think it's very bad luck to kill them. They don't eat them because they believe dolphins used to be people.[4]

Rarotonga's Ngatangiia natives in the South Pacific Cook Islands relate that when Te Tahi died, dolphins bore the young sorcerer's corpse away to their sunken kingdom, where they transfigured him into one of their own kind. His evolutionary epiphany explains dolphin predisposition for assisting humans at sea. Folk traditions from Classical Era

Greeks, widely separated Cook Islanders and unrelated Australoids all affirm a commonly perceived kinship between humans and dolphins. The earliest known European variant of this theme occurs in southern Spain, between the wild foothills of the Sierra de Almijara mountains and the shores of the Mediterranean Sea.

Discovered by schoolboys hunting for bats in 1959, the Caves of Nerja are more than two and a half miles long, comprising perhaps the Old World's greatest subterranean system, once its full extent has been explored. For now, the dolphins depicted on its walls make the site unique among prehistoric cave art. They appear on a flat, six-foot-square space divided into panels by a fish motif. Executed entirely in red pigment, the realistic images of one male and two female dolphins contrast with the nearby stick figures of men. Their compositional and technical coherence suggest all were executed by a single artist. They are located in the so-called Magdalenian chapel, named after an Old Stone Age culture originally identified at La Madeleine, a French rock shelter, dated from seventeen thousand to twelve thousand years ago.

The Magdalenians were the most materially advanced of Paleolithic peoples, famous for their underground paintings at Lascaux in France and Altamira in Spain. A similar discovery was made on the other side of the world, more than 490 miles west of New Guinea, at the 1,264-square-mile Indonesian island of Misool. In well-preserved red pigment on the sheer face of a cave wall appears the skillfully rendered depiction of a dolphin characteristically standing on its flukes. Six human hand prints in white appear on either side of the figure, which is nineteen inches long from the end of its tail to the tip of its snout and eleven inches wide across both pectoral fins.

Misool's Biga- and Matbat-speaking natives make no ancestral claims on the rock art, speculating it must have been created by foreign giants a long time ago. Their supposition is suggested by the position of the paintings high above ocean water entering the cave. Even at high tide, they are eight to nine feet above the surface, proving that the artists must have labored on their project before the cave was inundated.

Given the current average of three feet of water in the cave, its floor was dry until twelve thousand years ago, when sea level was just beginning to rise, caused by melting glaciers, making ancient Indonesia's rock art contemporaneous with the latest date for Sicily's Grotta del Genovese.

In fact, "new research suggests that humans were painting murals on the ceilings and walls of their caves in Indonesia at the same time as people in Europe," according to Jeanna Bryner, managing editor at *Live Science* magazine, writing in late 2014.[5] Their temporal comparison is highlighted by the highly skilled degree of similar execution shared by both sites, implying a closer relationship, despite the miles separating them, than conventional anthropologists are willing to consider.

If cultural diffusion between East and West did occur, it appears to have traveled to Europe from the Pacific because "the oldest date given to an animal cave painting is now 'a pig that has a minimum age of 35,400 years old' at Maros in Sulawesi, an Indonesian island."[6] Sulawesi is also the home of an ancient lost civilization—perhaps the oldest—whose creators left behind anthropomorphic colossi reminiscent of *moai,* the towering lava statues of Easter Island, 8,600 miles away. In any case, that the earliest verified example of rock art should emerge from the same region as Misool's dolphin figure suggests Mankind's cultural origins in the Pacific realm (plate 8).

Why the artists at Misool and Isola di Levanzo portrayed dolphins on cave walls is not known. But a human relationship of some kind with the animals seems obvious enough, and in the light of world folk traditions dramatizing the delphine origins of humans, the inclusion of anthropomorphic figures in close proximity to dolphins of opposite sexes must give us pause.

If these symbolic implications were, in fact, deliberately represented on the cave walls of Nerja, then the notion that dolphins and ourselves share some kind of ancestral association may be as old as Man himself. Sténuit memorialized the same notion in the title of his book, *The Dolphin, Cousin to Man.*"[7] But how did this concept originate and come to perpetuate itself in world myth?

Joseph Campbell's mentor, the pioneering parapsychologist Carl Jung, might offer that such interspecies relationships are familiar to so many diverse peoples around the world because the merman or mermaid is an archetype of our collective unconsciousness, imprinted there by an experience Mankind (or pre-Mankind) shared in common long ago. These universal memories might refer to fellow primates who did not return to dry land, as did our own ancestors, but chose to pursue their evolutionary path in the water. Perennial accounts of this kind could celebrate that transition some hominids made during the very remote past.

In *De natura animalium*, the third-century CE Roman naturalist Claudius Aelian refers to dolphins as "semi-human whales."[8] He was preceded eight hundred years earlier by the Greek lyric poet Bacchylides, who describes dolphins as "sea people."[9]

Although human evolution was stimulated and its course determined by various floods imposed by Nature on our primate ancestors, some of them may not have gone back to the land, but chose to undertake a complete transformation into sea mammals. Given that possibility, when we gaze into the eyes of a dolphin, perhaps looking back at us is an aquatic version of ourselves. Man's own aquatic phase was not a freak accident, some anomalous singularity occurring once in the very remote past, but a repetitive event that punctuated and determined the course of our evolution, not only millions and hundreds of thousands of years ago, but continuously shaping it into the present time.

Trace evidence of our developmental pelagic stage still lingers in sea-mammal traits—particularly webbing between fingers and toes, or syndactyly—recurring throughout human populations everywhere, but especially among certain groups isolated by often harsh environmental conditions in remote pockets of the world.

A race of Papua New Guinea pygmies inhabiting the swamps of Agaiumba, from which they derived their name, lived almost entirely in the water, where they gave birth, fished, and ate sago—an edible starch prepared from the pith of aqueous plants. Dwarfish in stature, but broadly built, the diminutive marsh dwellers were remarkable for the shortness of their legs and featured "huge nostrils that appeared to dilate and contract," like those of a seal, according to Dr. Odent. More remarkably, "they had an epidermal growth between the toes, and were commonly described as 'duck-footed.'"[10]

The Agaiumba populated Oro Province lagoons in large numbers until around the turn of the twentieth century, when they were steadily reduced through raids undertaken by neighboring cannibals. In his annual report for 1904, the acting administrator of British New Guinea stated that on a visit he paid to the Agaiumba district, he found just six males and four females. These were the last survivors of the now-extinct marsh dwellers. In features, color, and hair, they closely resembled true Melanesians. Nor were the Agaiumba the only human population group characterized by syndactyly in modern times.

Doctors David Stewart and Ray Knox relate that as recently as the midnineteenth century, a southeastern area of the "Show Me State" "had been named 'swamp-east' Missouri. People living there were accused of having webbed feet."[11]

Shortly after publication of my first book about the aquatic ape theory, I received the following correspondence from Douglas G. Nuelle, a prominent orthopedic surgeon from Blue Ridge, Georgia:

While reading about the aquatic phase of man in *Before Atlantis,* I noticed that you are missing another important piece of evidence. In the hand and the foot, there exist structures that you should know about. In the hand, it is the *palmar fascia* and the *palmaris longus* muscle tendon unit. The tendon of the palmaris longus is the most superficial tendon in the palm side of the forearm.

It comes down to the wrist and then spreads across the palm to the fingers, becoming the palmar fascia. It lies just underneath the skin of the palm and firmly fixed to it. It serves no function in humans today, but the muscle is still there, and if you have an injury you can cut it and transfer it to an injured tendon. We have brain

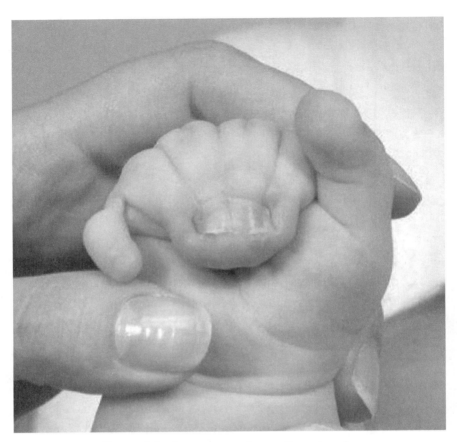

Figure 5.2. An extreme form of syndactyly.

control of it, and a patient can be taught to operate the new muscle, driving the injured finger or wrist tendons. If we were ducks, it is this tendon that, when active, withdraws the webbing from between the ducks' toes, when the animals are walking on land.

In the foot, the *plantar fascia* is firmly developed to hold up your arch, and there is a smaller muscle tendon unit called the *plantaris* that is active also. These structures are not wispy, thin things. The palmar fascia can tie itself into knots, and it will draw the fingers down into the palm (Dupuytren's contracture). The band doing this to one or more fingers must be surgically removed to correct this problem.

I have been telling patients about the ducks for thirty years, and then read in *Before Atlantis* that early man may have had several episodes of water and land existence, thus needing the ability to retract webbing as ducks do today. Your book got me excited, so I thought I would share this very real anatomical fact with you.[12]

*Before Atlantis* discussed *syndactyly* (from the Greek for "together" and "finger"), a medical term for webs of skin growing between the toes, as found in approximately 7 percent of humans, or about one in every two thousand to three thousand live human births. Syndactyly never occurs in chimpanzees or the great apes. All humans have much less prominent webbing between their fingers and toes, most apparently in the triangle of skin connecting thumb and forefinger at their base—features not found among any other primate. Syndactyly is remnant evidence for adaptation to a watery environment, as reflected in its popular name, *mer feet*.

# 6

# From Extinction to Rebirth

*What does not destroy me makes me stronger.*
FRIEDRICH NIETZSCHE

For nearly one million years, the once upward curve of hominid progress had flattened out into a lackluster variety of evolutionary nondescripts incapable of achieving little more than knapping out the same kind of flint points their predecessors continuously produced for the previous half-million years. The eruption of Mount Toba in what is now Indonesia, however, wiped out numerous plant and animal species, including, almost, our own. Immediately prior to that supreme geological incident, our world population stood at around two million. That figure was reduced within ten years to a mere three thousand to four thousand individuals. They not only pulled us back from the brink of extinction, but made us what we are today, not least because we inherited their vastly strengthened immune system.

They escaped the majority's annihilation, because they comprised a tiny minority of the healthiest, most quick-witted and adaptive survivors. These traits passed on to successive generations, which made the difference between static *Homo sapiens* and inventive *Homo sapiens sapiens*. That crucial transition had also isolated survivors and their following generations in the aquatic environments of Indonesia's island archipelagoes. But they were not the last humans to experience an aquatic phase, as demonstrated by Papua New Guinea's duck-footed Agaiumba, mentioned earlier.

Nor were these marsh-dwelling pygmies the final examples of such a transition. Even today, various populations spending most or much of their lives in water evince the kind of physical changes associated with marine mammal adaptation. Indigenous peoples of Tahiti, Hawaii, and other Pacific Ocean islands are more prone to put on excess weight than other ethnic groups, even though native caloric intake is relatively average, not excessive, and, in fact, more nutritious for its relatively higher representation of fish, coconuts, and fruits.

The cause of weight gain among many modern Polynesians is not overindulgence, but something known as "swimmers' fat." This is the excess fat athletic swimmers put on, "despite normal or low caloric in-take of non-fatty nutrition, even though they engage in prolonged, stressful exercise," according to Louise Burke of the Australian Institute of Sport.[1]

Although professional swimmers ordinarily burn thousands of calories per day, "the typical body fat levels of these athletes are significantly higher than runners or cyclists, who expend similar or even smaller amounts of energy in their training," Burke says. While scientists are at a loss to satisfactorily explain this phenomenon, it is comprehensible as a consequence that mammals experience as a result of their transition to a marine environment, where the accumulation of extra fat, or blubber, is necessary for buoyancy and insulation against colder temperatures in the water. In other words, swimmers' fat is one indication that some of today's Polynesian peoples are presently undergoing their own aquatic phase. Taken to its logical extent in the far future, they must inevitably leave the rest of us behind, on land, as they complete their metamorphosis as sea mammals—dolphinlike or seal-like, or perhaps a creature beyond imagining. Such a transformation may be not only the fate, but the solution required of our schizophrenic species, which is half compassionate, quick-witted cetacean, half greedy killer chimp.

"Redemption will come only when we return to the water, as sea mammals did in the past," states Jacques Cousteau; he adds, "gravity is the original sin."[2] He was seconded by another famous Frenchman, Jacques Mayol, cited in chapter 3. The record-breaking free diver joined "those who wonder whether Man is destined to return to the sea," and researched possibilities for reawakening our dormant mental and spiritual faculties, while investigating their physiological mechanisms and genetic makeup.[3] He thus strove to develop the human aquatic potential as a precondition for becoming *l'homo delphinus*—ameliorating our primate savagery with cetacean civility—and, for support, often quoted the insightful Romanian philosopher Mircea Eliade: "returning to our origins gives us hope of rebirth."[4]

Tcharkovsky, who inaugurated the water birthing movement in Russia in the early 1960s, echoes that sentiment. Since then, the many hundreds of infants he introduced into the world through the medium of water have, in the main, grown up to attain degrees of physical, intellectual, and emotional well-being more advanced than those reached by average children born on land. Those water babies who continued a close association with water throughout their juvenile and adult years were, as might be expected, superior swimmers, but also noted for their general fearlessness, compassionate character, and reverence toward Nature.

If our species' innate aquatic inheritance was so easily triggered in these individuals, then relatively few generations, continuously guided by specific criteria in a hydrous environment, might be all that would be necessary to redirect the thrust of human evolution toward sea mammalhood. In fact, such an experiment may have been conducted behind the Iron Curtain at the height of popular interest in Tcharkovsky's controversial work, beginning in the mid-1960s, when two human babies— a male and female—were raised from water birth entirely in aquatic surroundings.

While not discouraged from crawling on dry land, neither were they encouraged to do so. Both developed speech skills earlier than normally raised peers, but were far behind in learning how to walk, which they eventually mastered with a clumsy kind of rolling gait, similar to that of deck hands on nineteenth-century schooners. From infancy on, they preferred living in water, with only infrequent visits to shore. Social interaction with same-age playmates was normal and positive, although both demonstrated unease when prevailed upon to leave the water and were plainly happier in the company of dolphins.

The experiment was allegedly terminated after some of the cetaceans showed increasingly aggressive sexual interest in the children, when the girl began menstruating and the boy entered puberty. An extended debriefing period lasting throughout their adolescence allegedly rendered the children psychologically well-adjusted, although nothing further is known about this dubious exercise in Soviet-era science. Observers at the time supposedly deduced from its results that a relationship between modern humans and marine mammals was not only affirmed, but closer than previously suspected.

This may not have been particularly shocking or even unexpected. More surprising were the physiological changes the test children experienced. Close examination at their birth showed they were normal and healthy in all respects, save only that both were born with webbed fingers and toes. As pointed out in *Before Atlantis,* one in every two thousand to three thousand live births shows some level of syndactyly, or 7 percent of females and 9 percent of males, so the condition is not all that rare. In the Soviet case of experimental children, however, just six months after their births, the natural bridges of skin between fingers and toes indicated incremental growth, gradually progressing over the next eleven or twelve years, until both subjects developed more fully webbed hands and feet.

No less remarkably, their legs, ankles, and feet showed faint signs of fusing together, conjoined by a growing membrane of new skin. A fish-like tail never fully formed in either subject, but its contours were somewhat more evident in the girl; the boy, to a less well-defined degree, evinced morphological hints of a similarly piscine fluke. Impossible as these changes may seem, they are lent some parallel credibility by Wyllie's observation, likewise made by others involved in water birthing, that "most of the water babies have rather unusually shaped heads: large craniums and slight bumps on their foreheads," suggesting the bulge at the front of a dolphin's head known as the "melon," an organ used for transmitting clicks and whistles to other dolphins.[5]

The Russian children developed a game to determine who could stay or swim under water longer. Again, the girl demonstrated a slight superiority in this sport, when she, on several occasions, swam under water for nearly twenty minutes, almost as long as spotted and bottlenose dolphins hold their breath while swimming beneath the surface.

While her accomplishment may seem remarkable to outside observers, experts in the field of water birthing have known about this ability for quite some time. "With appropriate training," Tcharkovsky states, "water babies have been able to hold their breath for up to eight minutes."[6]

The girl was bested by the boy in speed, but, again, just marginally. Their breath performances were among the most credible claims for the experiment, when late twentieth and early twenty-first century examples of children—especially girls—swimming twice the length of an Olympic-size swimming pool became common achievements. Soviet scientists theorized that female superiority was inherited from motherhood during our aquatic phase, when women were more active in the water, attending to the constant needs of their newborns. Known for its often bizarre science, attempts undertaken by the Soviet Union to raise children with dolphins and their strange consequences may or may not have actually occurred. The mere suggestion of such an undertaking, however, reveals something about the modern fascination with our inherent aquatic connections.

Possibilities for the metamorphizing Russian boy and girl were, in fact, lent credence by generally comparable and certainly more verified studies carried out in the United States about the same time the USSR's alleged experiment was terminated by 1978. Given their contemporaneity and fundamental similarity, word of the Soviet dolphin children was perhaps leaked to American scientists, who felt obliged to pursue parallel research. In any case, eight subjects between the ages of ten and seventeen from the South Florida Society for Autistic Children were "volunteered" for half a dozen encounter sessions—each one lasting four to six hours—with dolphins.

Dr. Betty Smith hoped her Project In-reach could establish at least some basis for therapeutic communication between the animals and young humans. Key Biscayne's Wometco Miami Seaquarium provided three Atlantic bottlenose dolphins used to being with people, and Dr. Smith measured signals between both groups with a spectrograph, an instrument that separates incoming sound waves into a frequency spectrum. She also audio recorded and videotaped all sessions. The children were never able to speak and were limited to restricted communication with some hand gestures and facial expressions. After about thirty hours in the water, the subjects seemed more at ease and even joyful about their experience, but showed no interspecies communication skills, except for one teenager.

Unable to produce human sounds since his sixth year, Michael Williams was unchanged by his initial encounter with the dolphins. During his following session, however, something remarkable, even extraordinary, happened: he began speaking the dolphins' language. The clicking noises he produced were so virtually identical to those generated by dolphins, Dr. Smith and her colleagues were at pains to distinguish between them.

Closer and repeated auditing of recordings made of Williams's vocalizations revealed that they were finely differentiated from female dolphin sounds, more masculine, because he used them to communicate with Sharkey, one of the male bottlenose dolphins. The two were often observed playing ball together, with the boy and the dolphin alternately obeying each other's commands. As such, Williams did not just accurately mimic dolphin sounds—an amazing feat in itself—but mastered them within twelve hours' time and used them to communicate with Sharkey. Years after the conclusion of Project In-reach, Williams invariably reacted to photographs or films of dolphins by emitting the same stream of clicks he shared with Sharkey.

Friedrich Nietzsche, whose words began this chapter, believed that "Man is a rope stretched between the animal and the Superman—a rope stretched over an abyss."[7] Jacques Mayol identified that coming Superman as *l'homo delphinus,* a concept foreshadowed by suggestions of a delphine metamorphosis Russia's juvenile test subjects may have experienced, plus an autistic American teenager's natural grasp of dolphin vocalizations. These unsettling implications hint at a common consciousness, a very basic mutual understanding beyond mere words, into the thought patterns of another creature's brain—larger, at least as complex, and perhaps more quickly perceptive than our own. Accordingly, the global primacy of human intellect, as examined in the following chapter, may be less reality than illusion.

# 7

# Are Dolphins the Most Intelligent Creatures in the World?

*Intelligence is the ability to adapt to change.*

STEPHEN HAWKING

Until the late twentieth century, chimpanzees were regarded as the most intelligent creatures after ourselves. But improved methodologies in measuring mammalian brain power developed over the last few decades suggest dolphins exceed our nearest primate relatives, perhaps even ourselves, according to some researchers. According to *The Aquatic Ape* author, Elaine Morgan, "Man's brain size now deviates from the mammalian norm to an extent that is shared only by the bottle-nosed dolphin," which has evolved over millions of years in a continuously brain-stimulating environment.[1]

"When a mammal is swimming under water," Dr. Odent writes, "the carbon dioxide levels in its blood-stream increase. This might be a way to develop and maintain the expansion of the carotid arteries and to improve the vascularization [the formation of blood vessels] of the brain. Carbon dioxide therapy has been used with brain-damaged children."[2]

Given this ability, certain cetacean species could equal or surpass human mental acuity, according to some animal behaviorists. They argue that even the most recent advances in testing still measure non-human aptitude against human perception. Among the first scientists endeavoring to gauge dolphin intelligence was Canada's leading psychologist, the highly esteemed Donald Olding Hebb (1904–1985), who influenced the development of modern neuropsychology at McGill University, a public research institution in Montreal, Quebec. Throughout the 1960s, he conducted numerous comparative studies of both wild and captive dolphins, finally placing them near the very top of a phylogenic scale—a system for ranking animals by their complexity and ability—for their repeated demonstrations of complex problem solving.

Parts of his high intelligence criteria in which the observed dolphins excelled were mimicry, use of artificial language, object categorization, transmission of cultural knowledge to one another and across generations, understanding and use of numerical values, comprehension of symbols for various body parts, the use of tools, and self-recognition. Even before Hebb's research during the early 1970s, that dolphins knew they were looking at themselves in a mirror was generally accepted by scientists. Only after the turn of the following century, however, did they discover how dolphins not only recognize their own reflection in a mirror, but additionally notice changes in their appearance.

Described in the May issue of the *Proceedings of the National Academy of Sciences*, Osborn Laboratory of Marine Sciences cetologists at the New York Aquarium and Emory University in Atlanta, Georgia, conducted a study involving two bottlenose dolphins from the New York Aquarium. They "first marked the dolphins with 'sham' marks, then exposed them to a mirror. After several repetitions, the scientists put temporary black ink on parts of the dolphins' bodies, which the animals could see only in a mirror. In each of the trials, the dolphins went to the mirror to examine the areas the scientists had marked."[3]

These test results show that dolphins have an acute sense of themselves, an important indication of their high intelligence revealed by detailed self-awareness. It is further evidenced in their invention and use of tools. In behavior known as *sponging*, free bottlenose dolphins in Shark Bay, a World Heritage Site five hundred miles north of Perth, on the westernmost point of Australia, routinely fasten a marine sponge on their rostrum to protect the dolphin's snout when probing for food in the sandy sea bottom.

Dr. David Brown of California's Marineland Aquarium and Dr. Kenneth Norris (1924–1998) from Hawaii's Oceanic Foundation reported in the *Journal of Mammalogy* how they observed a wild dolphin intent on playing with a moray eel hiding between a pair of rocks. The dolphin "killed a poison-spined scorpion fish with a blow of his beak in the belly [the only undefended area of the fish's body]; took the fish in its mouth, holding it gingerly by the belly; stung the eel's tail with the scorpion fish's spines; dropped the fish and rushed to seize the eel, which was making a bolt for open water; [then] played with the eel."[4]

Such examples of deliberate tool use are expressions of a calculating mind. Another category of intelligence Dr. Hebb defined is "teaching and learning," handily demonstrated at the University of California, Irvine, where a male bottlenose dolphin, Buzz, was taught how to use a lever that dispensed food when a light was flashing in two different sequences. He was physically separated in the same tank from Doris, a female bottlenose, who could not observe the relationship between food, the lever, and the flashing lights. In a quick series of audible clicks, Buzz conveyed what he learned to Doris, who properly operated the lever during the proper light sequence. Since then, numerous similar and far more complex tests have consistently revealed dolphin receptivity to new information and their ability to pass on such knowledge to other dolphins. Nor is information forgotten.

Dolphins are able to remember identifying whistles made by their old tank mates after an absence of more than twenty years, in the longest social memory ever recorded for a nonhuman species, and far better than anything demonstrated by apes or chimpanzees. "This shows us an animal operating cognitively at a level that's very consistent with human social memory," says delphinologist Jason Bruck.[5] The dolphins' "use of numerical values" were confirmed by later studies conducted at the Dolphin Research Center in Florida, where the animals demonstrated an aptitude for grasping various mathematical concepts, such as recognizing the progressive magnitude of numbers in a logical, ordered relationship to each other.

Even these computative skills were outstripped by discoveries made in 2012 by Tim Leighton, a British professor of ultrasonics and underwater acoustics at the University of Southampton. He told the *Proceedings of the Royal Society* that "dolphins may use complex nonlinear math when hunting" by transmitting pulses of varying amplitude.[6] The first may have a value of one while the second is one-third that amplitude. The dolphin then measures the second echo in relation to the first, enabling a fish target to be picked up by echolocation. Both sending and receiving signals may be scrambled by bubble interference, so the dolphin must subtract "the echoes from one another," writes Jennifer Viegas in *Discovery News,* "ensuring the echo of the second pulse is first multiplied by three. The process, in short, therefore first entails making the fish visible to sonar by addition. The fish is then made invisible by subtraction to confirm it is a true target. . . . The math involved is complex."[7]

Professor Leighton remarks that dolphin echolocation, based on deductive computation, is superior to human sonar technology, which is unable to sort out various solid objects of relative sizes.[8] Sténuit characterizes dolphin echolocation as "a marvel of precision, definition and miniaturization. By comparison, Man's sonar looks like a rough prototype."[9] Roberta Goodman, a former trainer of captive dolphins, tells how "they can send pictures into each other's brain just by sending the echo that they've received from the picture itself. Their hearing is a visual sense."[10]

Author Lana Miller asks, "using sonar, are they seeing something and transmitting what they see through the sound of it? Is that what you are saying?"[11]

"The sonar waves they put out are bounced back to them," Goodman explains, "and then they hear them, and through that hearing, they form a picture. Their hearing is actually in pictures of the object. . . . If they turned around, and instead of sonar, did clicks that exactly matched the echo they heard from something, then they can send that picture to the other dolphin exactly."[12]

The "transmission of cultural knowledge to one another and across generations" was among the criteria for high intelligence cited by Dr. Hebb and subsequently established by cetologists such as Dr. Susan Shane, who, after more than fifteen years of observing dolphins, determined that "local groups develop feeding traditions that are handed down from generation to generation."[13]

While Dr. Hebb's rating system clearly established the animals' high mental acuity in a general, overall view, it lacked detailed analysis sufficient to establish their precise position in relation to other mammals. He did, however, personally conclude that dolphins closely approximate, and may marginally surpass, chimpanzees.

Dr. Hebb is seconded by marine conservationist Frank Donald Robson (1912–1993). He was an early investigator of whale strandings on the shores of his country, New Zealand, where they are most common, and initiated the first, systematic investigation of pollutant levels in marine mammals. His volunteer group, Project Jonah, saved thousands of them, beginning in 1974, leading four years later to the Marine Mammals Protection Act, which made the Department of Conservation responsible for the well-being of endangered wildlife in open water. "I had to conclude that here in the sea," Robson states, "were living creatures superior in intelligence to the finest creatures on land."[14]

A similar conclusion was reached by Aldo Aulicino, a researcher in charge of an international, multidisciplinary project, known as *Kyklos* (Greek for "cycles"), for the study of wild dolphins. "He believes their intelligence factor exceeds that of humans by at least one hundred to one."[15] Dr. Odent wonders if dolphins may "have a type of intelligence that is impossible for us to measure by our own criteria. Because we cannot imagine forms of intelligence other than our own, we concentrate all our curiosity on the neo-cortex as a cybernetic machine, a computer."[16]

For example, some theorists who speculate that mammalian intelligence correlates to the number of nerve cells or neurons in the brain's cortex, claim dolphins, with their 5.8 billion cortical neurons, must be less intelligent than chimpanzees, which have 6.2 billion. But this argument is rendered invalid by the elephant, which has substantially more nerve cells than a human's 11.5 billion; elephant intelligence ranks below that of gorillas, which have 4.3 billion cortical neurons. Clearly, the number of neurons doesn't tell the whole story when it comes to intelligence.

An important criterion for superior intelligence Dr. Hebb overlooked is an active sense of humor. Dolphins often mimic the performance of human divers, commonly exaggerating their awkward movements. Less ambiguous was a man aboard a research vessel, clowning around with a large wad of sargassum seaweed on his head. Shortly thereafter, a dolphin popped up out of the water nearby wearing a makeshift hat of sargassum seaweed.

Dolphins particularly enjoy pranks. They have been observed stealthily surfacing behind an unsuspecting pelican afloat on the water to snatch some of the bird's tail feathers. Dolphins sometimes grab a fish by the tail, pulling it backward a few feet before releasing it to swim forward again. They also enjoy harassing slow turtles by rolling them over and over. Once a dolphin was seen placing a piece of squid near a grouper's rock cranny. When the fish came out, the dolphin promptly snatched the bait away, leaving the puzzled grouper behind.

A college student and former programmer at a dolphin research project, who also participated in dolphin training, recounts the following anecdote:

I played with the dolphins all day, intermixed with calculus lessons. One afternoon, my pen fell out of my pocket into the tank. A dolphin snatched it and swam out into the middle of the tank. . . . I reached out over the water as far as I could, hoping to coax the dolphin to bring my pen back. He approached close enough to where I just barely couldn't reach it, and sat there a while. When I tried to reach out for it, the dolphin tossed it back out toward the middle of the tank, then swam out to the middle of the tank, and got it. Repeat. Repeat again. After that, I managed to snag it, finally. On another afternoon, a trainer taught one of the dolphins to twirl a Frisbee on the end of its snout. Apparently, the dolphin thought this was a big kick because he spent the rest of the afternoon, and all night and most of the rest of the week, swimming around the tank, twirling a Frisbee on his snout.

By the next day, the other dolphin had picked it up too, and both of them spent all their free time twirling Frisbees. Then they got into the habit of putting the smaller Frisbee inside the larger Frisbee, and twirling both of them at once. We had to drill holes in all the Frisbees, because the dolphins were fond of putting a Frisbee over the drain, so that the tank would overflow. Then they would swim around the outer edge of the tank at top speed, causing tsunami waves in the tank and flooding the surrounding deck. Now, do you think dolphins have a sense of humor?[17]

These observations aside, skeptics continue to assert that because dolphins do not build slot machines or atomic bombs, they are necessarily inferior to us. "It is as though our species has become so conditioned by the tools we make," observes Timothy Wyllie, "that we tend to occlude any form of higher intelligence that does not construct an environment for itself. We set the standards of intelligence, and then make the error of trying to assess another species by whether it fulfills the same criteria."[18]

Dr. Dobbs reaches a like conclusion: "If intelligence is related to an ability to devise, manufacture and manipulate tools, then Man is undoubtedly superior to dolphins. If though, the dolphin has deployed its mental capabilities in a completely different direction, then a man, who thinks in mechanical terms, may not be able to understand the working of the dolphin's mind. . . . Dolphins have not created possessions, and they do not need houses to live in. There is no money in the dolphin's world, and no basis for greed or envy. The pressures of keeping up with the Joneses therefore do not exist."[19]

Dr. Lilly suggests:

> that we are severely handicapped in our efforts to measure the intelligence of individuals of other species than our own. . . . We suffer from a lack of secure knowledge of how to measure intelligence in those with whom we cannot communicate. . . . We use inappropriate yardsticks derived from our own history as primates with hands and legs. . . . The chimpanzee and the gorilla have the hands, but they do not have the brains to back up the use of the hands. Man has both the hands and the brain. Thus, we can quite simply and concretely contrast the performance of the large brains of man with his hands to the smaller brains of the primates with their hands.
>
> When we consider the whales, we seem obsessed, as it were, with the necessity of our own nature to look for an analog of the hand and the manipulative ability. May it not be better to find a more general principle than just handedness and its use? . . . Man thinks of himself as the most intelligent species on Earth, and, as proof of this, points to the accomplishments of his hands, his aspirations, his traditions, and his social organizations. In other words, Man is said to be the most intelligent species, because of what he does with his huge brain. May there not be other paths for large brains to take, especially if they live immersed in some other element than air?[20]

More recently, science writer Keith Cooper explains in *Astrobiology Magazine* how

Intelligence wasn't just the acquisition of technology, but the ability to develop and improve it, integrating it into society. By that definition, a dolphin, lacking limbs to create and manipulate complex tools, cannot possibly be described as intelligent. . . . Technology is certainly linked to intelligence—you need to be smart to build a computer or an aircraft or a radio telescope—but technology does not define intelligence. It is just *a manifestation of it* [author's italics]. The dictionary defines intelligence as the ability to learn, while others see it as the capacity to reason, to empathize, to solve problems and consider complex ideas, and to interact socially. . . . To be social, you must be communicative. Personal interactions require communication of some form, and the more complex the interaction, the more complex the communication.[21]

If true, then dolphins, for all their lack of material technology, demonstrate an intellectual superiority through their complex and manifold communication networks, which outstrip today's most sophisticated sonar systems. "Man has always assumed that he was more intelligent than dolphins," writes Douglas Adams, author of *The Hitchhiker's Guide to the Galaxy*, "because he had achieved so much—the wheel, New York, wars, and so on—while all the dolphins had ever done was muck about in the water, having a good time. But conversely, the dolphins had always believed that they were far more intelligent than man for precisely the same reason."[22]

# 8

# The Holographic Dolphin

*And it is an interesting biological fact that all of us have, in our veins, the exact same percentage of salt in our blood that exists in the ocean, and, therefore, we have salt in our blood, in our sweat, in our tears. We are tied to the ocean. And when we go back to the sea, whether it is to sail or to watch it, we are going back from whence we came.*

PRESIDENT JOHN F. KENNEDY

If, as mentioned in our previous chapter, the possession of material technology is not the sole standard by which a species demonstrates its intelligence, here we consider some of the more subtle attributes suggesting the dolphin's multifaceted consciousness.

Technology, far from elevating us head and shoulders above all other forms of life on Earth, is the hallmark of our clumsy artificiality and the mechanism of our potential undoing. We assume it can solve every problem and get us out of any fix into which we get ourselves. Because technology can do many things, we take for granted that it can do everything. The more technology provides for us, the greater we rely on it, until its original purpose—improving the standard of living—is replaced by our presumption that no matter what atrocities we commit against our fellow creatures or the Earth itself, regardless of the magnitude, all can be made well by the bleeding edge of applied science.

The supreme, if indifferent immorality of this assumption has been acted out over and over again for the last five thousand years through dozens of known civilizations that have come and gone from the first high culture built by Sumerians in what is ironically today the failed nation of Iraq, to early twenty-first-century Americans of the United States. There were obviously more civilizations during the past than there are today. Each and every one of them rode the same Ferris wheel of social development from innovative growth, rising to early achievement, higher through economic expansion to increased population, reaching the top in general prosperity, before beginning inevitable descent through over-indulgence, apathy, paralysis of will, dependence on outside help—technology, government, mercenaries or allies—and self-delusion, until bottoming out in destruction and oblivion. Their dead ruins are visited by the modern tourist, who fails to see in them anything more than earlier versions of his or her own society and the reflection of its fate.

Civilization is supposed to be the meaning of Man's life, but it is a history of repetitive failure, because, to function properly, it requires selfless idealism and social cohesion. He may start out with high intentions and succeed for a while, but inevitably the greedy primate in his nature prevails, setting in motion a series of compromises, the accelerating inertia of which eventually unravels the entire fabric of society. For these numerous downfalls scholars attribute different causes, more like excuses for the same simian behavior endemic to our species. The oceanic floor of human history is littered with the broken wrecks of more high cultures than an archaeologist can count, and today's so-called global civilization is no less exempt from sinking than were they.

During our endless loop of cultural grandeur and annihilation over the past millennia, the dolphin world flourished in unpolluted seas because it was not subject to the same cycles predetermined by human nature. If the supreme goal of civilization is "to form a more perfect union, establish justice, insure domestic tranquility, provide for the common defense, promote the general welfare, and secure the blessings of liberty to ourselves and our posterity," as the Preamble to the U.S. Constitution puts forth, then the socially active dolphins have consistently succeeded where our species has failed.[1]

How very few civilizations, even the best of them, have lived up to those sentiments articulated by the Constitution! Human world primacy is based on our mastery of technology and building of civilization, achievements that grew out of our ancestors' urge to survive, thereafter developing into an exponential multiplication of needs, real or imagined. Dolphins were not similarly stimulated and therefore not compelled to invent applied science or a material culture. As author Lana Miller writes, "they no longer had a need to construct or build."[2]

Instead, they flourished on a brain-enhancing diet and adapted to an entirely different set of challenges with greater success, minus recourse to artificial means. Simply put, complex behavior and intense curiosity are the hallmarks of higher intelligence. Given their extraordinarily nuanced lifestyle and persistent inquisitiveness, dolphins unquestionably possess an advanced order of mind.

In the science-fiction classic *Forbidden Planet,* the Krell, an extinct race of advanced beings that inhabited a distant world, Altair IV, two hundred thousand years ago had reached a stage of technological and scientific development so advanced that they operated their supercivilization through sheer thought, because they no longer needed any "instrumentalities"; in other words, they went beyond material technology. Prior to that breakthrough, the Krell used a device able to create a three-dimensional visualization of its operator's thoughts while acting directly on the brain to measure intelligence and impart knowledge.

In fact, as mentioned in the previous chapter, spotted and bottlenose dolphins are able to visualize objects they target with echolocation in three-dimensional pictures of sound. These visions are formed by an advanced kind of side-scan sonar, as the animal emits bursts of broadband pulses—clicking sounds—focused in a beam shooting directly ahead. Returning echoes enter the inner ear through the lower jaw and are forwarded to the brain, which processes the sounds into moving imagery. As de Bergerac puts it, dolphins "share information with each other holographically, transferring images from brain to brain, using sound."[3]

"Their visual system is one-tenth the speed of ours," Dr. Lilly explains. "However, they make up for this in that their sonic and acoustic systems are ten times the speed of ours. This means that the dolphins can absorb through their ears the same amount of information—and at the same speed—that we do with our eyes."[4]

Although the dolphin's brain and ours are anatomically similar, the human brain—averaging twelve hundred grams—weighs less than the bottlenose dolphin's eighteen-hundred-gram brain. Dolphin brains are 20 to 40 percent larger than ours. Ape and chimpanzee brains have much smaller ratios to their body mass than do humans and dolphins. The size of the mature dolphin's body relative to that of its brain is slightly greater than that of an adult man. Yet more decisive than relative weight, or even body-ratio mass, the dolphin brain has more folds, fissures, and convolutions than ours and possesses a higher number of cells.

"What makes the human brain unique?" asks Dr. Odent. "Its most characteristic feature is probably the hugely developed anterior part, or pre-frontal cortex; it is recognized that this plays a role in relating past, present and future, and making anticipation possible."[5] This large brain of ours and expanded neocortex are common traits shared not with apes and chimps, but with dolphins. Their brains, however, may be less equivalent than superior to ours.

"Dolphins have a higher neo-cortical-limbic ratio than even healthy, intelligent humans," states Myron Jacobs, director of the New York Aquarium's Cetacean Brain Laboratory, "and orcas have often shown humor, empathy and self-control that few of us could match under comparable circumstances [i.e., restrictive captivity]. . . . We humans depend on highly adaptive cultures in which most of the mental capacity lies outside the individual and in the traditional knowledge of the culture. As regards our brain and our capacities as individual, conscious beings, we may actually be inferior to some other kinds of large-brained animals."[6]

Writing for the *Earthcode International Network,* Paula Peterson observes: "Dolphins and humans both have huge cerebral (neocortical) development, which is apparently on the same scale. On the other hand, the brain of the ape is small, with very little neocortex development. . . . Special kinds of lipids, known as the essential fatty acids, are the building blocks for brain tissue. These acids—the omega-6 fatty acids from leafy green and seed-bearing plants and the omega-3 fatty acids from marine phylo-plankton and algae—are used in the human brain in a balance of 1:1 and is shared only with the dolphins, which have the same ratio."[7]

Humans have a larger encephalization quotient than other animals, with a cranial capacity and brain-size to body-weight ratio higher than all other species. Encephalization quotient is a measure of relative brain size defined as the ratio between actual brain mass and predicted brain mass for an animal of a given size, which is hypothesized to be a rough estimate of the intelligence or cognition of the animal. Those possessing similar encephalization quotients are aquatic, such as dolphins, whales, otters, sea lions, and penguins—all of them outstanding for their high intelligence. Such a large quotient could have only been obtained through a diet rich in iodine ions and omega-3 fatty acids. In fact, the human brain absolutely requires these nutrients, which are most easily found and absorbed in seafood. They do not occur on the African savanna, where mainstream paleoanthropologists teach that certain primates took the crucial step toward humanhood, but occur in fish and most other seafood. Indeed, the human oral cavity and its teeth—suitable for masticating soft shellfish and snails, not for tearing the tough flesh of land animals—have been modified over generations for a seafood diet.

Dr. Odent elaborates on the value of nutrition with regard to dolphin intelligence: "The sea contains a large amount of vitamins, minerals and other nutrients that facilitate brain development. Dolphin intelligence has evolved in a continuously brain-stimulating environment. Cetologists have uncovered some scientific basis supporting such a belief. They found, for the sake of comparison, that 95.9 percent of the human brain is covered by the neo-cortex, which is involved in higher mental functions, such as sensory perception, generation of motor commands, spatial reasoning, conscious thought and vocal communication. The dolphin's neo-cortex covers 97.8 percent of its brain."[8]

The dolphin brain involves a vast web of complex wiring, some of which is centered on the inner area. This complexity has led some experts to consider the potential for a sophisticated sentience. According to British reviewer A. Stuckey:

> While a dolphin's ear contains only a few more of the same inner-ear cells that humans use to pick up sound vibrations, the cetacean has five times the number of nerve cells running between these hairs and the auditory portion of the brain. The sound-processing center of a dolphin's brain, in turn, is connected to the neo-cortex by a nerve similar to ours, but capable of handling vast amounts of data. Compared to our bicycle path, the nerves connecting a dolphin's brain to its hearing centre are a superhighway. They are twice the size of human nerves and much more numerous. This high-speed connection to the well-developed, outer brain, which we know is associated with higher thought, makes it clear that dolphins may have information-processing capabilities beyond our wildest imagination. It also means that they have the hardware for self-awareness.[9]

In fact, dolphins are capable of hearing frequencies ten times above our level of hearing and, consequently, potentially (if not actually) process ten times the volume of information our brains can process. As another indication of their superior intelligence, the spotted and bottlenose dolphins are able to look in opposite directions with both eyes at the same time, while simultaneously understanding two (and possibly more) diverse sets of data input. In other words, they can see and think in two directions at once. At least. A dolphin's brain is capable of sorting out information received from echolocating many different objects at once, while simultaneously sending, receiving, and comprehending communication via whistling with other dolphins.

Not only the multiplicity and complexity of such information, but the rapid rate at which it is processed defines an order of intelligence unmatched by any other living creature on Earth. Dolphins can produce whistles for communication and clicks for sonar at the same time, a feat analogous to a human speaking simultaneously in two voices, with two different pitches, and holding two different conversations, at several times the speed of human speech. No wonder we are still unable to communicate with dolphins! Their brain's visual and auditory regions are so highly integrated they allow it to form accurately detailed images fashioned from mere echoes. Accordingly, dolphins can differentiate between objects less than 10 percent different in size, down to a few millimeters, and in a noisy environment at that, even while they are vocalizing.

Sténuit writes of the dolphin:

Every signal he sends is returned by numerous obstacles. . . . It strikes both the bottom and the surface, rebounds from one to the other several times, bouncing off other dolphins or the fish in the area on the way. Thus where each echo finally returns, it is mixed with dozens of signals from the same dolphin, reflected directly or indirectly, and a thousand other noises in the sea, including the echoes made by all the other dolphins. To isolate a particular signal from this mass of sonar reverberations, and to deduce from it the distance, the direction, the speed, the size, shape and texture of the reverberating object, takes a computing system, that is to say, a brain, of fantastic complexity.

Dolphins can isolate, interpret and analyze simultaneously several signals of various frequencies; deduce from them geographical information and the respective positions of the other dolphins of the group, in order to work out appropriate hunting tactics; discuss plans with the other hunters, and to select the choicest fish, all while avoiding nets. To do all this, and dolphins do it as the most natural thing in the world, takes a brain which surpasses the most complicated electronic computers, and which, in this regard, surpasses the human brain. It even surpasses our capacity to conceive it.[10]

Dolphins literally hear distance, as well as the shape, density, rigidity, movement, and texture of an object. They can distinguish between a two and one-half inch steel ball and another one inch smaller. When these indices were reduced—to two and one-quarter and two and one-half inches—beyond the ability of the human researchers to determine with the naked eye and without the aid of slide calipers, a test dolphin made the correct distinction nine out of ten times. Going further still, Florida State University's Dr. Winthrop N. Kellogg has demonstrated that dolphins, even while blindfolded, are still capable of distinguishing between fish of different species. Miller points out that "dolphins are able to find food, communicate and maneuver through murky waters."[11]

Some dolphins have come to rely so heavily on sonar, they discarded vision entirely and today possess only a tiny vestigial eye, minus even a lens. The completely blind *Platanista gangetica* and *Platanista minor* nonetheless navigate India's Ganges and Indus Rivers as though blessed with the most clear-sighted visual perception. "The region of the brain that involves the decoding and analysis of sound is very large in the dolphin," writes Dr. Dobbs. "It has often been stated that dolphins 'see with sound.' . . . Because air has a different density to the rest of the body it gives off a different sound signal. The dolphin will therefore 'see' inside the fish, as well as outside. Thus, the information processed in the dolphin's brain will be more like an X-ray than a photograph taken with light."[12]

Dolphins echolocate various separate targets, near and far, simultaneously, a skill beyond today's most sophisticated human sonar operator. "Even a modern supercomputer using thousands of times more energy could never produce such an accurate visual image based merely on the echoes of pings," writes the author of *Death at SeaWorld,* David Kirby. He tells how "resident orca populations in the Pacific Northwest . . . can distinguish a species of salmon by its size, or by echolocating inside the fish's body to determine the dimensions of its air bladder."[13]

As though these supermammalian faculties were not remarkable enough, marine biologists recently discovered yet another secret power dolphins possess, unlike that of any other creature: electroreception, the ability to "sense electrical signals from other animals in the water, such as those emanating from heartbeats, muscle contractions or gills," according to a report in *Science News.*[14] This unique receptivity is made possible by *crypts,* sensory organs located on the rostrum, or snout, that can detect electric impulses. The dolphins' mastery of sound nuance and modulation enables them to communicate as they think—not in words, but in multidimensional imagery.

As Cochrane and Callen explain, "a dolphin detecting the presence of a shark, for example, does not need to sound a verbal alarm. It simply sends out a series of 'clicks' that correspond to the sonic picture created when its echo-location beam rebounded off the approaching shark. The echo that rebounds may also be picked up, not just by the dolphin that emitted the 'clicks,' but by others in the vicinity, so that they can share the information."[15]

Their sound-based holographic language is, therefore, not only more immediate and comprehensively detailed than human speech, but much faster, something only a more quick-witted and powerfully complex brain than ours could process. According to Dr. Odent, "the dolphin can receive at least ten times more information through its sense organs than we can."[16]

His observation is confirmed by Dr. Lilly, who calculated that the dolphin emission and reception of sounds is twenty times faster—with equivalent complexity—than human acoustic capability. "With sonar," Miller points out, "a dolphin is able to hear a single buckshot dropped into water one hundred feet away and get an accurate range and bearing on it. So acutely developed is their sonar, that they can determine the difference between brass and aluminum, or two kinds of fish equal in size. . . . Their sonar is effective up to a quarter of a mile."[17]

Jacques Cousteau was similarly impressed: "A blindfolded dolphin is able to skirt around a line stretched ten or twelve feet above the surface, simply by relying on his echolocation system." To process and apply such an abundance of information, and with the high rate of speed dolphins are noted for, requires an exceptionally powerful intellect. The dolphin's clicking appears to combine imagery with specific meanings, more than thirty of which have already been identified by researchers, and allow dolphins to "identify one another in less than half a second."[18]

Each dolphin has a uniquely identifying, frequency-modulated narrow-band signature vocalization, or whistle—that is, a "name," if you will—by which it is known to fellow dolphins. But given their prodigious mental capacity, what do they think about? Their observed actions—catching fish, mating, protecting against sharks, performing acrobatic tricks, occasionally saving hapless humans at sea, and so forth—require only a tiny fraction of their enormous brain power. On what is the vast majority of it spent? How do they use such energy? They conceivably carry around within themselves great storehouses of information and knowledge, so much so, we might be someday surprised to learn what they know about us. Is their awareness limited exclusively to beneath the surface of the water? Or does it range beyond to the land and farther still?

# 9
# Telepathic Dolphins

*Dolphins have new understandings that seem to lie just beyond our present knowledge. There may be a common thread of consciousness between man and dolphin.*

JOAN MCINTYRE

While visiting the Roatán Institute for Marine Sciences, as mentioned in the introduction, I suspected that the performing dolphin's independent attitude was a form of cetacean forbearance, even impatience with its bipedal handler, the sea beast's physically slower mammalian cousin. In executing its prodigious acrobatic talents—one after another in rapid succession—the dolphin seemed to anticipate human commands, and not because it had become accustomed to some repetitive routine. "Sometimes they'll perform a trick before you even ask or signal," according to dolphin trainer Ric O'Barry, "it's just as if they are reading your mind."[1]

The Institute's student delphinologist said his commands were randomly selected and never followed the same sequence twice. "The animals are easily bored with mundane activity," he explained. "We have to keep their interest up by engaging them in fresh challenges, or else they become so restless and depressed they won't have anything more to do with us."

"Given your experience so far," I asked him at the close of his demonstration, "do you believe dolphins are telepathic?"

The question caught him off guard. It was a provocative, even peril-ous inquiry for an undergraduate studying to become a certified cetolo-gist under professors hostile to pseudoscientific considerations, and I was a stranger who could have been anybody, even an academic agent provocateur. The young man hesitated, looked around to see if anyone else was within earshot, then responded furtively, "Yes," without further elaboration.

His colleague at Britain's SeaWorld, Christine Bowker, recalled, "I was trying to get two dolphins to jump on either side of me, and was actually thinking, 'How am I going to tell them, or indicate to them, something as complicated as that?' when they both did exactly what I wanted, and then went whizzing around the pool making those funny, chuckling noises they make when they are pleased with themselves."[2]

When visiting SeaWorld in the mid-1960s, Sténuit was standing next to a pool inhabited by a pair of listless, disinterested dolphins. With no apparent cause, their lethargy suddenly transformed into keen anticipation, and they "reared their bodies half way out of the water, quivered and squealed, their eyes fixed on the corner of a wall. For a good twenty seconds, they stayed like that, all excited. They were wait-ing. But for what? Then [Adolf] Frohn [their trainer] appeared around the corner of the wall. They could not have seen him coming; they did not smell him, for they have no sense of smell; they did not detect him by sonar, which works only in water; and yet, long before we knew, they knew that the man they had learnt to love was on his way."[3]

Robson claims to have often used mental telepathy for training purposes:

I visualize what I want the dolphins to do, and they do it. . . . I don't know what takes place in their heads, but I think of their minds as something like a video screen onto which images are formed. . . . All former external features [in dolphin anatomy] were eliminated or withdrawn into the body to provide a streamlined shape for swift passage through the sea. It is possible that a parallel development may have taken place in the dolphin's brain; it may have developed into a sophisticated instrument capable of direct transfer of information. . . . If an image were thrown at him—"hitting" him with it was my term—he would usually oblige by doing what was being requested of him.

It was quite clear that the dolphins were able to read my thoughts and were well on their way to responding to them before I had time to utter a word. . . . For a time, I believed they were responding to the sound of my voice when I hailed them from a distance or spoke to them or even swore at them when they got in the way of the nets, but then I observed something that surprised me. However short a sentence I spoke to them, they started to act upon it before the words were uttered. When I raced the boat against them, even the short word, 'Go!,' was anticipated. They were shooting away before my mind had passed the word to my tongue and my tongue had acted upon the impulse. They appeared to be short-circuiting my thought processes, and taking the word directly from my mind.[4]

Robson was convinced that his telepathic rapport arose from genuine concern for their welfare and respect for their right to be themselves:

These sentiments are present in all animal lovers, and are much more important than scientific training, which is often actually a hindrance. People who live close to nature and close to animals are open to fresh leads into new knowledge and less afraid of criticism. . . . I would sit day after day in my boat, alone with the dolphins. It was the best research laboratory, better than anything all the government grants in the world could set up.[5]

While conventional scientists in every field generally dismiss alternative views, a few mainstream cetologists have at least broached the question of interspecies thought transference. Among the most qualified of them is Dr. Denise Herzing, research director of the Wild Dolphin

Project. She tells what happened while swimming with a group of fellow divers investigating a shipwreck in the Bahamas:

> Dolphins greeted us, but they acted very unusual, coming within fifty feet of the boat, but not closer. Captain Dan kept inviting them to bow ride by starting up the motor, but each time the dolphins kept their distance. . . . It was then that we discovered our passenger [on board the dive boat] had expired in his bunk and [we] began consoling his wife and daughter. Could the dolphins have sensed something strange on board? . . . Whether it was coincidence or circumstance, we headed back toward port to deal with the new priority of sad family matters. As we turned to head back south, the dolphins came to the side of our boat, not riding the bow, as usual, but instead flanking us fifty feet away in an aquatic escort. They always rode the bow, or just left, but now they paralleled us in an organized fashion."[6]

These dolphins accompanied the boat in the formation of a funeral cortege.

A telepathic relationship between dolphins and death is nothing new, however, and has been recognized for thousands of years. The late third-century BCE Greek historical writer Phylarchus told of a young man, Koranos, who saved the lives of several dolphins caught near Byzantium in the nets of fishermen about to slaughter them. After Korianos disentangled the creatures and they struggled free, each one lingered long enough to stare at him for a prolonged moment before swimming away. Some years later, a ship in which he was traveling sank during a powerful storm, killing the captain, crew, and all his fellow passengers. Struggling in the turbulent waters, Korianos was suddenly buoyed up by a dolphin, which carried him safely to Naxos, an island in the Aegean Sea, landing him at the grotto of Sycinus, thereafter known as "the grotto of Korianos." After he died at the end of a long, compassionate life, "as the smoke from his funeral pyre rose along the seashore, a silent group of dolphins assembled, heads above water, to join the mourners. When the smoke had almost faded away, they all disappeared, and none of them ever returned."[7]

The story of Korianos is not baseless legend, but reflected in numerous, similar accounts from antiquity to modern times. The first-century CE Roman naturalist Pliny the Elder was certainly not given to myth making when he stated in his magnum opus, *Naturalis Historia* (IX, 8), "I should be truly ashamed to relate this account, if the thing had not been attested to in writing in the works of Maecenas [minister of culture for Emperor Augustus], Fabian [a naturalist colleague], Flavius Alfius [a famed grammarian of the previous century], and many others." Pliny was referring to a boy who daily summoned a dolphin residing in southern Italy's mile-wide Lake Lucrine, across which the animal invariably carried him on its back to school, reappearing in the afternoon to give the student a ride home.

"And this continued for several years," according to Pliny. "Then the child died of illness, but the dolphin kept coming to wait for him, always in the same place, with an air of great sadness, and showing all the signs of the deepest affliction, until he finally died of grief and regret."[8]

Pliny cites the somewhat similar case of young Hermias, who often rode a favorite dolphin across the sea near the Greek city of Iasos, in southwestern coastal Turkey. During one such outing, they were overtaken by a violent squall, the boy fell off into the water and drowned before the dolphin could rescue him. It carried Hermias back to shore, stranded itself on the beach, and lay down to die beside the lifeless body of his beloved companion. As a memorial, the Iasos government struck a coin engraved with the image of a boy riding a dolphin.

The earliest surviving account of this kind was preserved by Hesiod, history's first economist and a major source on Greek mythology and farming techniques, in the early seventh century BCE. He reports that the remains of a missing man thrown into the Mediterranean by his murderers had been borne on the back of a dolphin to the scene of the crime.

Diving dolphins accompanied by flying birds—universal symbols of the soul—illustrate the walls of the sixth-century BCE Etruscan Tomb of the Lioness, at Tarquinia in western Italy. Following the Etruscans, deceased Romans were commonly buried with the small likenesses of dolphins in their hands. Jacques Cousteau writes, "we sense a funeral meaning in these images," referring to a mosaic at the Museum of Antioch, an ancient Greek city on the southernmost shore of Turkey: "This mosaic shows dolphins carrying the souls of the departed to the Isle of the Blessed. The concept may have been art of Aegean heritage, for the people of Crete assigned that same role to dolphins."[9]

Ancient delphine symbolism for the human soul's resurrection after death was not limited to the Mediterranean World. Throughout the pre-Christian Near East, dolphins were avatars of Atargatis, a Syrian mermaid goddess and receiver of the dead, who would be born again through initiation into her mysteries. Among the oldest-worshipped deities of pharaonic Egypt was Hat-mehit, the wife of Banebjed, the very soul of Osiris, the god of rebirth. The divine patroness of life and protection, whose name translates to Foremost of Fish, she was depicted in temple art as a queen with a dolphin over her head.

Associations between human mortality and mourning dolphins are not merely expressions of pre-Christian belief. Symeon Metaphrastes writes in his tenth-century hagiography of a Church elder that the body of martyred Lucian (also of Antioch) was brought to Nicodemia, on the northwestern shores of Turkey in 312 CE by a wild dolphin: "It was a very great wonder to see how the corpse rested on such a round and slippery body."[10]

Such reports are not confined to ancient history. In 2011, Shaun McBride was killed when scaffolding for a construction project on which he was working off the coast of Dampier, Western Australia, collapsed into the sea. He had only arrived in the country six weeks earlier from County Donegal, Ireland, where he "had a huge attachment to dolphins as a young child," according to his mother, Sylvia. First responders arrived too late to rescue him, but were surprised by what they found.

"We've learnt that a few hours after the accident, when divers went to retrieve his body," Perth-based priest Father Joe Walsh said before McBride's funeral, "they saw a big pod of dolphins swimming around him. And there was one dolphin that was using its nose to try to lift the body up to the surface. But it wasn't able to do so because the body was caught up in the scaffolding." He added that "the family had found comfort when he told them about the dolphins' remarkable vigil."[11]

These accounts from across the last several millennia suggest some kind of extrasensory perception of death and sympathy for humans the dolphins possess, an awareness extending beyond their submarine realm into our terrestrial world. Such telepathic powers are evident in the animals' physical actions following or even sometimes paralleling human thought, especially when we register emotion.

My sister, Christine, tells how her friend visiting a wild dolphin up close in the water for the first time was initially taken aback by the sight of its twin rows of large, sharp teeth, capable of severing his arm as easily as a man could bite off the end of a bread stick. In fact, dolphins have been known to chomp six-foot-long barracudas in half with less difficulty. This sobering consideration had no sooner occurred to the man than the dolphin opened its huge jaws, then closed them over and down on his right arm, which it slowly, harmlessly, and tenderly mouthed from bicep to wrist, as though indicating, "I will not hurt you." Similar instances of interspecies telepathy suggest less that dolphins understand human words, even as unspoken thoughts, and that they are then able to conceptualize or perhaps even visualize our emotions. Herzing cites Alexandra Morton, a pioneering expert in cetacean echolocation, who was "thinking of a behavior right before a killer whale (*Orcinus orca*) mimicked the exact behavior. Could the dolphins have a keen sense that we are unable to tap into ourselves?"[12]

Among the few scientific investigations into possibilities for cetacean telepathy is this description by writer Kevin Costa, who describes how Aldo Aulicino separated two bottlenose dolphins twenty miles apart, well beyond the range of their ability to hear each other: "After one was put into an artificial distress mode, at that exact moment, its mate reacted in a rescuing manner."[13]

Although mainstream scholars are allergic to any suggestion of the paranormal, many if not most persons—professional or not—who associate with dolphins are hard-pressed to deny their telepathic bond. Its origins are not difficult to imagine. When the animal's terrestrial ancestor left the land to pursue its evolutionary destiny in the sea, it entered an extremely hazardous environment requiring highly sensitized awareness. An important upgrade to that superior cognizance was development of a sixth sense as a survival mechanism. Extrasensory perception or clairvoyance was not a mysterious by-product of the creature's huge brain, but a necessary means to perceive mortal danger and communicate its threat to fellow dolphins, because the best defense lay, as it still does, in cooperative action.

Sound production is all very well, but nothing is faster than thought. Just as fast is emotion, in which the dolphins appear more interested. For example, an ordinary American tourist wading off Paradise Island, in the Bahamas, impulsively jumped onto the back of a passing dolphin, which she rode at high speed parallel to the shore for about one hundred yards, before veering out into the open sea. The experience was exhilarating, until it took her further and further away from Paradise Island, and the thought suddenly crossed Cathleen Civale's mind that her free ride might end in disaster if the dolphin suddenly decided to dive, leaving her to drown in deep water far from shore. At that precise moment, the creature executed a sharp turn, making a beeline toward the beach, where it gently deposited her.

"Throughout this journey," Cathleen says, "the oddest thing is that I don't recall feeling any physical sensations. I didn't feel wet or dry, cold or warm. My hands didn't feel tired in any way, just secure and safe. Nor did I feel surprised at this; it was almost expected, and all in the greatest of fun."[14] Judging from her strange reaction to the encounter, Cathleen's "journey" was as much a thrilling jaunt across the sea, as it appears to have been an altered state of consciousness generated by her telepathic bond with the dolphin.

Another woman relaxing on the beach at a Florida research center was reading *Dolphins, ETs and Angels,* in which the author, Timothy Wyllie, wonders if a species of extremely flattened, burrowing sea urchins belonging to the order Clypeasteroida might be used by dolphins as communication devices. Commonly known as "sand dollars," they are often found on beaches, the textured skin missing and skeleton bleached white by sunlight, an appearance that suggests a large, silver coin, such as an old Spanish or American dollar (about an inch and a half across). Just as she turned a page in Wyllie's book to see its illustration of a sand dollar, "there was a slight commotion in the water beside her, and she saw that a dolphin had found, and then flicked at her feet, the brownish disc of a living sand dollar."[15]

Wyllie cites another example concerning an Australian couple walking together by a river, in which dolphins were cavorting some six hundred feet away. The women bet her skeptical companion that she could successfully summon the creatures. "Immediately, one of the dolphins detached itself from the pod, swam very rapidly over to them, and executed a perfect tail stand—with a fish balanced on the end of its beak!"[16]

Another case as unique as it is illuminating involves a blind woman, who "saw colors just before Mike [her husband] squeezed my hand," his signal that Fungie the dolphin was approaching. "There were lots of them [colors]," she reports. "They were unearthly." In other words, the colors appeared before the dolphin showed up. "It meant that sound signals could be interpreted as visual images in the human brain," observes Dr. Dobbs. He goes on to state that the colors perceived by the blind woman in advance of the dolphin's approach "may now be explained by the high-frequency sounds emitted by Fungie interacting indirectly or directly with her brain, and causing a shift in brain-wave emissions."[17]

If so, then these high-frequency sounds may be the means by which mental telepathy occurs. Having nonetheless been left in the lurch by conventional scientists, for whom thought transference is academic anathema, the argument for dolphin telepathy is mostly made by such anecdotal evidence. But the profusion of eyewitness accounts over not centuries, but millennia, represents powerfully persuasive proof. After years of firsthand observations, Tcharkovsky, Australian swimming instructor Cookie Harkin, and other researchers concluded by the late twentieth century that "both the fetus and the newborn baby have brain waves that are attuned to those of whales and dolphins, thereby facilitating telepathic contact. Subsequent research by psychotherapist Dr. Olivia de Bergerac and her partner, William MacDougal, of Australia, revealed that dolphin interactions caused shifts in brain-wave patterns."[18]

Scientific basis for telepathy was suggested by Harald Saxton Burr (1889–1973), a researcher in bioelectrics and professor of anatomy at Yale University Medical School in New Haven, Connecticut. The author of ninety-three scientific papers, Burr found that a voltmeter could detect electromagnetic frequencies emitted by all living creatures, which prompted him to propose the term "L-Field" for bioelectric fields associated with organic life in every form. His discovery contributed to the electrical detection of cancer cells, experimental embryology, neuroanatomy, and the regeneration and development of nervous systems. In *Blueprint for Immortality,* published near the close of his career after decades of research, Burr concludes that electrodynamic fields common to all living things mold and control each organism's development, health, and mood.[19]

As such, he prefigured the work of a biochemist and cell biologist at Cambridge University, Rupert Sheldrake, whose theory of morphic resonance posits that "memory is inherent in nature," and "natural systems, such as termite colonies, or pigeons, or orchid plants, or insulin molecules, inherit a collective memory from all previous things of their kind." Sheldrake proposes that this morphic resonance is also responsible for "telepathy-type interconnections between organisms."[20] Everything being learned about dolphin consciousness suggests its capacity for the animal's "telepathy-type interconnections."

Even so, we cannot ask intellectually sophisticated animals to come down to our level of understanding, but must rise to theirs. That, however, may not be as easy as it might seem. If, as they appear, dolphins do indeed communicate via a form of telepathic imagery, true dialogue with them will not be possible, until we ourselves have attained a relative sensitivity. As recently as the late twentieth century, Anindilyakwa oral tradition spoke of shamans inhabiting the shores near Groote Eylandt, the Gulf of Carpentaria's largest island off northeastern Australia, where these "dreamers" allegedly used thought commands to summon wild dolphins. In any case, the rest of us are very far from attaining such a high wavelength. Mainstream scientists do not even recognize the existence of telepathy. Nor are they helped by self-styled psychics claiming to "channel" airy-fairy messages from dolphins. Hopefully, the creatures have something more to tell us than "We bring you peace and love!"

Just what the dolphins might be able to tell us could be startling and in advance of anything we can imagine—from an understanding of marine biology and oceanography that dwarfs our sciences, to finding Malaysian Airlines Flight 370, even sunken civilizations like Atlantis, beyond to the evolutionary history of life on Earth and communication with other intelligences outside our world. In fact, California scientist Laurence Doyle believes dolphin communication skills could help earthlings liaison with civilizations on other planets. Beginning in 1987, he served as principal investigator and astrophysicist at the SETI (Search for Extraterrestrial Intelligence) Institute. Its mission is to "explore, understand and explain the origin, nature and prevalence of life in the universe" by using both radio and optical telescopes for finding deliberate signals from intelligent beings beyond our solar system.[21] Dolphins may indeed possess secrets to mysteries we have not even considered. Sharing these revelations with us, if they have a mind to, would potentially boost our modern culture with an influx of fresh knowledge, if not real wisdom, that might prompt Mankind to take a major step forward.

But we are not likely to benefit from such an intellectual epiphany, so long as we fail to approach cetacean consciousness on its own terms. Only after we have abandoned exclusive reliance on word symbols, and gone on to attain at least some degree of telepathic imagery, may an organic bridge of some kind be established between humans and dolphins.

These possibilities are not as extravagant as skeptics may presume and have already been prefigured by some disclosures, as recent as they are remarkable. In March 2013, an original archaeological find was made off the coast of San Diego during mine training exercises conducted by the U.S. Navy, when a bottlenose dolphin, on its own initiative, without instruction or any human input, discovered a rare, nineteenth-century torpedo. Of the original fifty examples produced in 1890, only two other Howell Mark 1 torpedoes are known to exist and are at museums in Rhode Island and Washington. Since the 1960s, the Navy has been programming dolphins at its Point Loma facility,

Figure 9.1. A Howell torpedo at Keyport, Washington's Naval Undersea Museum, identical to its late nineteenth-century counterpart discovered by a dolphin more than one hundred years later.

where eighty of them are currently being trained for mine detection, mine clearing, and rescue.

In an ariticle on the find, veteran journalist David Strege quotes Mike Rothe, head of the biosciences division at the Navy's Space and Naval Warfare Systems Center Pacific in San Diego, "We've never found anything like this. . . . Never."[22]

Events such as these demonstrate that, so far, interspecies communication has been one-sided. Dolphins seem to understand us to some degree—perhaps far more than we recognize, certainly to a greater extent than we comprehend their thought processes. Until a mind-to-mind correspondence of some kind is established with them, however, researchers continue to explore more down-to-earth possibilities in cracking the code of dolphin language.

# 10

# The Order
# of the Dolphin

*Dolphins may well be carrying information as well as functions critical to the regeneration of life upon our planet.*
BUCKMINSTER FULLER

"It is of interest to note," observes the TV astronomer, Carl Sagan, "that while some dolphins are reported to have learned English—up to fifty words used in correct context—no human being has been reported to have learned dolphinese."[1] Since Sagan's death in 1996, dolphins have learned an additional ten words (at least), with which they formed more than two thousand complete sentences. While these numbers may seem unimpressively few to skeptics of interspecies communication, humans, by comparison, have not learned a single world of dolphinese, even after so many years of extensive research into the subject.

More recently, in summer 2013, a dolphin used a particular whistle it had been taught meant "sargassum," when playing with strands of the brown seaweed. This "sargassum whistle" was invented by Herzing, who introduced it to a pod of dolphins under investigation for more than twenty years, in the hope they might incorporate the sargassum whistle into their own vocabulary. "The dolphins had been playing with sargassum and with each other," she said. "However, it should be made clear that the mimic of a sound does not mean that the function of that sound is understood. That comes over time with exposure to how a word is used, and this is a challenge in the wild."[2] In view of the dolphin's predetermined audible association with a specific object, however, it seems clear that the creature did indeed properly connect the sargassum whistle with its correct meaning.

The production of certain sounds is just one of several methods, including touch, taste, posturing, telepathy, and mental image transference, dolphins use to communicate with each other. Moreover, they produce an unknown variety of different sets of sounds in a complex frequency far beyond human hearing, let alone spoken reproduction. Prevailing upon them to comprehend and elucidate human language is no less unrealistic than encouraging a toddler to thoroughly understand and capably spit out Morse code. It does not necessarily follow that because dolphins and humans have anatomically similar brains that they think alike, if only because the demands of their underwater realm are vastly different from the imperatives of our life on dry land. Even if they became fluent in English or humans mastered Dolphinese, neither mammal would necessarily understand each other. All our references are terrestrial; most of theirs, subaquatic. Although our evolutionary paths appear to have crossed sometime in the deep past and we share some mysterious commonalities with dolphins, we are not the same species.

Learning Dolphinese is not like learning Hungarian: if only we study hard and long enough, we'll eventually get it. Instead, decades of scientific attempts at transcribing dolphin squeals and clicks into word-for-word English seem as simplistic as they are futile. The only person known to have at least temporarily communicated audibly with dolphins was Michael Williams, the nonverbal autistic child whose story was told in chapter 4, and his condition points to the incomprehensibly different state of mind wherein such discourse may take place. If interspecies dialogue with dolphins is at all possible, it can never come by forcing them to grasp our language, but through our understanding of theirs. Early explorers of the African interior did not begin by teaching European languages to the tribal peoples there, but themselves learned the native tongue. Trying to intellectually converse with dolphins on our level seems like an anthropocentric presumption and is at present and for some time yet to come a virtual impossibility, given the current level of science. Captive dolphins have advanced beyond vocabulary to demonstrate their understanding of syntax—the difference between a statement and a question, or past and future tense.

The fourth-century BCE Greek philosopher Aristotle notes how "the voices of dolphins in air are like those of a human, in that they can pronounce vowels and combinations of vowels, but have difficulties with consonants."[3] Surprisingly, he was investigating possibilities for interspecies communications more than 2,300 years ago and seems to have gone further in his research than twenty-first-century delphinologists, given his statement regarding dolphin pronunciation. Tragically, whatever else he knew about such matters was lost with the late fifth-century collapse of Roman civilization and subsequent Dark Ages that descended on Europe for the next eight hundred years.

Most mainstream biologists today believe there is no such thing as a dolphin language. Their assumption has been contradicted often enough by real-life experience, such as an incident that took place during 1957, when several thousand killer whales assembled to spoil the operations of a Norwegian fishing fleet off Antarctica by eating up all the catch.

Within half an hour after one of several boats carrying a harpoon gun fired a single shot, mortally wounding an orca, every dolphin had vanished from the entire region. They eventually returned to plague the fishing boats as before, but came nowhere near the few, otherwise identical craft mounting a harpoon gun on their foredeck. A few dolphins had immediately grasped what the weapon had done and communicated its lethal capacity to far greater numbers of their fellow pod members, every one of which thereafter distinguished between armed and unarmed vessels. While the alert they sounded may have been conveyed via a language of sounds—dolphins can pick up each other's signals over six miles—that it was transmitted over more than fifty square miles inside a few minutes from a handful of individuals to thousands more suggests telepathic possibilities.

That the orcas clearly distinguished between armed and unarmed whalers was no revelation, however, because they were known long prior to 1957 for their ability to recognize different types of vessels. They prefer the company of fishing boats, ferries, and passenger liners, while avoiding warships, which explains why there are only very few reports of servicemen adrift at sea during military conflicts having been rescued by dolphins.

The only such incident documented by the U.S. Navy during World War II concerned survivors of an American destroyer sunk in the South Pacific, where their life raft was pushed by several dolphins toward a Japanese-occupied island. Vigorously fending off their would-be rescuers with oars, the sailors wondered if the animals were sincerely trying to save them or were deliberately delivering them into the hands of their enemies.[4] No dolphins, for example, came to the aid of some five hundred American men killed by sharks—the most shark attacks during a single incident in recorded history—after the sinking of the heavy cruiser, USS *Indianapolis* on July 30, 1945.

Although numerous examples of human-to-dolphin thought transference have been and continue to be credibly demonstrated by the animals' appropriate responses, whatever they may have to tell us, if anything, is not heard. Perhaps because we have not been listening properly.

Early in his research of captive dolphins, Dr. Lilly tape-recorded hundreds of hours of every sound they produced above and beneath the surface of the water, but was unable to determine the slightest significance in any of them. On a frustrated whim, after weeks of listening to meaningless noise, he played back the audio at one-sixteenth its original speed and was shocked to hear the dolphins speaking clear English. On a tape in which he had been recorded as saying, "Here, three hundred and twenty-three feet," a dolphin's voice, when drastically slowed down, repeated distinctly, "three hundred and twenty-three feet."

Earlier, Lilly had said, "The T.R.R. [ for "Train Repetition Rate"] is now ten per second," repeated in reduced speed, but unmistakably, by a dolphin, "T.R.R." Elsewhere in the audio, the laughter of Lilly's wife was almost identically mimicked by another dolphin.[5] That these revelations became audible only after their frequency had been sufficiently lowered within human range demonstrates how the dolphins were thinking and "speaking," if you will, at a rate and level far beyond our cognition.

The development of spoken language is a uniquely human achievement. Forcing chimpanzees or even dolphins to approximate a syllable or two is no more than a circus trick, as unnatural as it is pointless, if only because the animals use sounds as verbal cues to elicit specific actions, not words to be understood. Neither creature is anatomically equipped to form words, the former because the larynx is too high up in the throat passage to allow for the utterance of speech, the latter because it lacks vocal cords altogether. Instead, dolphins are masterful whistlers, and therein may lie a key to not only unlocking the enigma of their language (or one of the ways they communicate), but to a similarity we share with them.

During the conquistadors' early occupation of southern Mexico in the early sixteenth century, for example, the Spanish conquistadors found that they were sometimes outmaneuvered by warriors of the indigenous Mazatec people, who rapidly issued and answered often lengthy, complex orders using whistling commands. One hundred years earlier, on the opposite side of the Atlantic Ocean, the Spanish encountered a fully developed whistling language employed by the original inhabitants of the Canary Islands, off the northwest coast of Morocco. Known as the Silbo Gomero, or "Gomeran whistle," the language allowed the native Guanche to exchange surprisingly detailed information across the deep ravines and narrow valleys radiating throughout Gomera.

Today's Canary Island *silbadores* (whistlers) can still communicate such complicated messages as "Don't forget to buy a loaf of bread on your way home tonight," or "Take your sheep to the meadow up there" over distances of six to eight miles.[6]

A similar whistling discourse is used by another mountain folk in the French Pyrenees, the Aas. Like the Silbo Gomero, it is a remnant of a prehistoric culture, but the Aas villagers are the only practitioners of the fifty-five or so known language-whistling folk in Europe, Africa, the Near East, Oceania, and the Americas who have been scientifically studied, most notably, by Dr. René Guy Busnel, mentioned in chapter 3. His remarkable *Animal Sonar Systems: Biology and Bionics* tells how X-raying the people of Aas showed that they produce the articulated whistle through bypassing the larynx, which remains motionless. They "do not use their vocal chords, but an apparatus quite similar to that of dolphins," by forming "a pocket of air in the back of the throat. . . . Oscillograms of this human whistled language are extraordinarily similar to those of the whistling of the Odontoceti ["toothed whales," or cetaceans with teeth, rather than baleen, such as sperm whales, beaked whales, orcas, dolphins, and porpoises], each being characterized by typical modulation in frequency and amplitude. The scales of frequency are sometimes different, but there are also examples of whistling on the same wave lengths."[7]

Jacques Cousteau goes further: "There is a remarkable analogy between the 'sonograms' of the whistled languages and those of the underwater whistles of the dolphins. The dolphins' sounds represent the same kinds of modulation, though their modalities are much more limited, and are produced at a much higher frequency. An analogy between physical structures, therefore, allows one to hypothesize that the whistling sounds produced by dolphins could, in theory, be used as the phonetic elements of a true language."[8] Native inhabitants of Australia's northern coasts summon and even allegedly communicate with wild dolphins through a system of whistles. "It may seem an idle dream to think of communication between dolphins and human whistlers," Cousteau continues, "but it may also be the beginning of a communication between the two species. For whistled languages represent a 'language skeleton,' which is adequate to express what one wishes to say. The mode of expression may be the vehicle of human communication with dolphins."[9]

That such a unique form of communication should have arisen independently among culturally and racially unrelated peoples unconnected and separated by thousands of miles and as many years demonstrates something basic in Mankind that connects us with dolphins. Unaware of that fundamental tie-in and mostly of each other's existence, the Aas villagers and their fellow language-whistlers around the world create their communicating sounds in the same manner as their cetacean cousins, a common denominator that highlights Sténuit's statement that "both Dolphin and Man, since the far distant epoch . . . began to diverge from a common ancestor."[10]

Our primate cousins relate to one another with physical displays, touching, and cries. Dolphins also employ these basic methods, which are elements of a much larger, far more complex communication system that nevertheless does not include speech. One need only try talking under water, where dolphins live, to appreciate the absurdity of such attempts.

But any effort aimed at compelling members of a different species to intellectually interface with us through verbal cues—which developed through millennia of terrestrial experience specific to our own immediate ancestors—is misdirected. "We still don't understand the natural language system of dolphins and whales," admits Lori Marino, a biopsychologist from Emory University in Atlanta, Georgia. "We know a little bit more now, and there have been investigators working on this for decades, but we haven't really cracked the code."[11]

Because cetaceans do not have "a language system," but exchange information through mentally projected images combined with appropriate sounds—like communicating with each other through instantly produced 3-D movies—mainstream attempts are aiming in the wrong direction and caught in an endless loop of repetitive failure. Instead, a statistical analysis technique used in telecommunications to determine the complexity of languages showed that dolphin communication shares a surprisingly high degree of similarity with human speech. This so-called information theory operates on the legitimate premise that all knowledge can be broken down into "bits" of data, which can then be rearranged into innumerable permutations. Analyzing dolphin whistles with this information theory demonstrates how the development of dolphin communication in the young almost exactly parallels human speech, as it is learned by babies, a progress referred to as a –1 slope.

"Much of their [dolphins'] learning is similar to what we see with young children," says Diana Reiss, a cognitive psychologist from Hunter College at the City University of New York.[12] In view of this close association between two different yet intelligent species, astrophysicist Dr. Laurance R. Doyle believes that SETI should search for signals with information content that has a –1 slope. In this, he was preceded by Dr. Lilly. "Convinced that dolphins had a sophisticated language of their own, he suggested that the species might provide the key to unlocking humanity's potential to commune with extraterrestrials," writes Marino. "He became part of the initial SETI group of radio-astronomy pioneers, who were so impressed with his tales of dolphin intelligence, that they voted to call themselves 'The Order of the Dolphin.'"[13]

Marine biologists already know that enough commonalties exist to give us reason to hope that a link may be established someday. For example, dolphins, like ourselves, average eight hours of sleep per night. They float at or near the surface of the water, swimming slowly and automatically in a condition referred to as "logging," occasionally closing one eye. During their sleep cycle, they are really half awake because the dolphin brain is able to shut down one hemisphere into unconsciousness, while the other remains active and alert. A dolphin can be in deep REM (rapid eye movement) sleep—the dream state—in one hemisphere, while simultaneously in a state of quiet wakefulness with the other half of its brain. While qualities such as these clearly define a sophisticated intellect with abilities beyond our own limitations, the seat of yet higher powers lies in the dolphin's thalamus.

**Plate 1.** Whale shark, captured near Taiwan, at Atlanta's Georgia Aquarium. Photograph by Zac Wolf.

**Plate 2.** A troop of Japanese macaques at the Jigokudani hot springs near Nagano, Japan (another location where they can be spotted).

**Plate 3.** A baby "wolphin," an extremely rare hybrid born from mating a female bottlenose dolphin with a *Pseudorca rassidens,* or "false killer whale." Its eye is, nonetheless, typically delphine. Photograph by Mark Interrante.

**Plate 4.** An Atlantic spotted dolphin, *Stenella frontalis*.

**Plate 5.** A bottlenose dolphin (*Tursiops truncates*) passing a research motorboat running at top speed on the Banana River, near the Kennedy Space Center, in 2004.

**Plate 6.** Spirit photography? Dolphinlike forms appear in the bottom, right of this snap-shot of the author and his wife, Laura, at Colorado's Stanley Hotel, in the Rocky Mountains, at the time he was completing *Our Dolphin Ancestors*. The Stanley is famous for its paranormal activity.

**Plate 7.** Some of the oldest known paintings of dolphins survive after about twelve thousand years at the Grotta del Genovese, located on the small island Isola di Levanzo, off the Sicilian west coast. Photograph by the author.

**Plate 8.** Misool's dolphin rock art, discovered in 2008 by Jean-Michel Chazine. Photograph © Ducourneaux-Chazine, Maison Asie-Pacifique/CNRS-AMU.

**Plate 9.** Sixteenth-century BCE Minoan fresco at Akrotiri, Cyprus.
Photograph by the author.

**Plate 10.** Vase depicting humans riding
dolphins while an aulos player guides them.

**Plate 11.** Vase painting of young aulos player riding a dolphin, depicted on a red-figure stamnos (a type of Greek pottery used to store liquids), circa 360–340 BCE, found in Etruria, western Italy. Red-figure pottery employs the technique of painting red figures on a black background. Pottery is in National Archeological Museum, Madrid.

**Plate 12.** A makara is the *vahana* (vehicle) of the goddess Ganga in this painting, reproduced during the nineteenth century for Hindu pilgrims visiting Calcutta's Temple of Kali.

**Plate 13.** Fishtailed humanoids painted on the walls of a South African cave may be the oldest examples of rock art yet found.

**Plate 14.** The Sumerian Ea, later known in Babylon as Oannes, was regarded as a merman and the bringer of civilization to Mesopotamia. Image from *Gods and Goddesses of Ancient Babylon* by Stuart Wallingsford.

**Plate 15.** As though to celebrate its arrival at Point Dume, this dolphin creates a special effect with rings of water beginning to spiral from behind its head, growing wider and more pronounced as they encircle its torso, then rising up over the dorsal fin to form larger hoops that pass away from the animal's body, above its tail, onto the surface of the sea. Precisely how the creature pulls off such a bizarre stunt is a cetacean secret.

**Plate 16.** An adult bottlenose dolphin and two young.
Photograph by Peter Asprey.

**Plate 17.** Dolphin worship in Atlantis, illustrated by Kenneth Caroli.

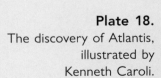

**Plate 18.**
The discovery of Atlantis, illustrated by Kenneth Caroli.

This "chamber" containing both hemispheres of the brain assimilates all sensory functions, except the olfactory, before passing them on to the cortex. It also contains intrinsic nuclei, groups of cells receiving no outside stimuli, and projects what are known as "associative" or "silent" zones on the neocortex. Scientists are not sure just what the function of these projections might be, although some suspect they could be related to abstract thought, instinct, intuition, and subtle perception—depending on a particular animal's intellectual standing—possibly even some form of spirituality and/or supersensory receptivity.

According to Peterson, "Recent studies imply that this mysterious area of the brain may serve in achieving meditative states, contemplation or abstract thought. A favorite theory is that this chamber is not only responsible for all these activities, but that it additionally serves in telepathic communication and in visualizing in holographic fashion."[14] More cogent to our discussion, "the nuclei of the [dolphin] thalamus are identical and of the same dimensions as those of humans." In other words, Sténuit points out, "if all the nuclei of the thalamus, called the 'nuclei of association,' are present, it could indicate that the dolphin also possesses the same zones of association in his cerebral cortex as we do, in relation to the nuclei . . . comparable cortex = comparable intellectual superiority."[15]

Intrinsic nuclei occur in all mammals. The only information a rabbit's brain analyzes is that which it receives directly from sensory organs, leaving no apparent room for intrinsic nuclei, but, in fact, 10 percent of the animal's neocortex is nevertheless "silent." Half of a cat's neocortex is "associative," compared to three-quarters in apes and barely 90 percent in humans. In 1988, neurobiologists Myron Jacobs, Peter Morgane, and Ilya Glezer showed that "much more than ninety percent of the dolphin's neocortex can be considered as 'silent' or 'associative,'" a discovery echoed by Miller's observation that "the foldings in the dolphin cortex are more highly developed" than in humans.[16]

The brains of most mammals are smoothly surfaced, unlike those of humans, which are extremely convoluted. The dolphin brain is even more "folded" than ours, an indication of its superiority, because the number of "folds" is often used by scientists as a measure of intelligence potential. So too, the larger "silent" area covering the dolphin's neocortex implies a progressive index of intelligence—from the "dumb bunny," with his 10 percent "associative" zones, up through the ape's 75 percent, and our own 90 percent, which is surpassed by 90-plus percent in dolphins.

If we had as many intrinsic nuclei, we might enjoy conscious application of those paranormal talents so often observed among dolphins by human eyewitnesses. Perhaps therein lies our aquatic destiny as a newly evolving species with inherent capacities presently unrecognized by conventional science. Among those latent energies could be the dolphin's sometimes miraculous power to heal not only themselves, but human sufferers, as described in the following chapter.

# 11
## Healing Dolphins

*"Will you walk a little faster?" said a whiting to a snail.*
*"There's a porpoise close behind us, and he's treading on my tail."*

LEWIS CARROLL,
*ALICE'S ADVENTURES IN WONDERLAND*

"Thank God for this little dolphin, Keppler," exclaimed the resident of Panama City, Florida. Patricia Stoops was referring to an encounter at the British Virgin Island of Tortola, where she joined some fifteen other Caribbean cruise tourists in swimming with captive dolphins. One of them paid particular attention to her for no apparent reason, circling close and jumping out of the water, as though trying to call attention to itself. "He kept running into me, and I explained to the trainer that the dolphin had hit me. The dolphin trainer said the dolphin detected something wrong with me," and wondered if she was a beneficiary of the Make-A-Wish Foundation, a nonprofit organization that arranges experiences for people with life-threatening medical conditions. "He asked if I'd ever had cancer. I said, 'no way!'"[1]

Patricia, in fact, had never been healthier in her life. One week after returning home, however, she began feeling a slight but persistent pain in her chest. She was initially inclined to dismiss the sensation as something unimportant and transitory, probably heartburn, but then thought back to Keppler's unusual behavior toward her and his trainer's words. She scheduled an appointment with a doctor, who discovered a spot on her lung, the first indication of lung cancer. Because it was detected in time, treatment was successful, and Stoops has been cancer-free ever since. But she credits the Tortola dolphin with warning her in time: "He saved my life."[2]

Ryan DeMares, the first person to hold a doctorate in interspecies communication, was informed by the trainer of a facility offering public swims with captive dolphins that they "often cluster around a swimmer who has an interesting internal feature, such as a hip implant." He goes on to tell how "a dolphin was seen scanning a man's chest at close range. Then the dolphin swam away, got the attention of another dolphin, and brought the other dolphin back with him to the man. Both dolphins began scanning the man's chest," which had been installed with a heart valve implant. "It was as if the first dolphin had told the second dolphin, 'Hey, I've found something really interesting. Come look at this.'"[3]

A more delicate case in the 1980s concerns Joey Hoagland, a toddler whose recovery from a third open-heart surgery caused a stroke that paralyzed his left side, which prevented him from raising his arm or moving his fingers. Nor was he able to sit upright without support. He had been seriously disabled, and as far as his doctors were concerned, the damage was permanent. As a last resort, Joey was carefully immersed in water in the company of Fonzie. The eighteen-year-old, 650-pound bottlenose dolphin immediately gravitated toward the three-year-old boy, treating him with constant, gentle attention. Almost at once, the child began to experience some relief, until, during the following months, he regained the use of his body.

Joey's mother, Deena, went on to become a licensed clinical social worker, a professional therapist, and the founder of Island Dolphin Care in Key Largo, Florida, among the foremost dolphin assisted-therapy facilities in the world. In writing of her work, Scott Taylor, author of *Souls in the Sea*, tells how similar cures are effected at research institutes in Mexico, "where hundreds of children with central nervous system chal-

Figure 11.1. Fonzie with Joey Hoagland.
Photograph by Ronald Lear.

lenges (birth defects, cerebral palsy, muscular dystrophy, stroke victims, injuries, paralysis, etc.) were being taken through a simple process, putting them in water with a facilitator or two for safety, allowing the dolphins to do anything they were inspired to do; positive effects were impressive."[4]

Similar results were additionally borne out by Michael T. Hyson, Ph.D., research director at the Hawaii-based Sirius Institute, which advocates captive dolphins as therapy for people with various disorders. Hyson tells of a woman who was swimming with Dreamer, an amiable spotted dolphin who possessed seemingly miraculous abilities to heal humans. The creature had suddenly and uncharacteristically "rammed" her right side, and she was rushed to a hospital. Examination showed she did, in fact, have a large bruised area. But near its center, under the ribs, X-rays revealed the presence of a small malignant growth of tissue. "It is my feeling," writes Hyson, "that Dreamer likely 'zapped' the tumor with a powerful sound pulse, perhaps to heal it, and the high intensity sound left bruising from hydrostatic shock. At the least, the bruising called medical attention to the tumor."[5]

Numerous similar reports of *sarcomas* detected and sometimes made benign by dolphins have been circulating since the mid-twentieth century, although most mainstream scholars dismiss such individual testimonies as unreliably anecdotal. Their skepticism is meaningless, however, for a growing number of people who are healed by such encounters. Timothy Wyllie, who has been intensely interacting with wild and captured dolphins since 1985, is convinced that "they can 'see' into the body, as if their sonar gave them X-ray vision. . . . Dolphins, with their thirty-million-year history, are able to gauge their companions' welfare with an accuracy that we would find literally supernatural."[6]

Actually, they have been associated with healing for many thousands of years by various cultures around the world. "The ancient Kelts attributed special healing powers to dolphins, as did the Norse," states neuroscientist Lori Marino. To illustrate, the image of a boy riding a dolphin appears on the famous Gundestrup Cauldron—a twenty-pound, seventeen-inch-high, twenty-seven-inch-wide silver ceremonial vessel found in a Danish bog in 1958—used some two thousand years ago by Kelts as part of their reincarnation cult. "Throughout time," Marino continues, "people as far apart as Brazil and Fiji have traded in dolphin and whale body parts for medicinal purposes."[7]

During 1955, the rock crystal likeness of a dolphin emerged from the bottom of a well at the ancient city of Carthage in Tunisia. The 2 1/16-inch-tall, 6 5/16-inch-long, 1 1/4-inch-thick effigy was probably an offering to Coventina, a Keltic goddess of wells and healing commonly represented in sacred stone art accompanied by a pair of dolphins. She became popular with the Roman conquerors of Britain around 300 CE, the period to which the effigy dates, when North Africa was also occupied by Rome. At that time, crystal was commonly valued throughout the Roman world as protection against kidney ailments and other diseases, as defined by first-century naturalist Pliny the Elder. Accordingly,

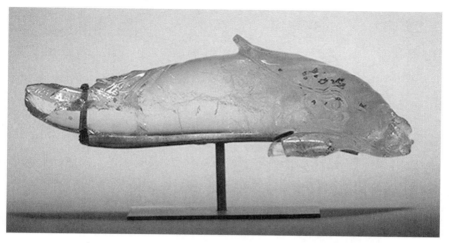

Figure 11.2. Tunisia's crystal dolphin.

the mineral's perceived therapeutic qualities logically combined in the Tunisian figurine with the shape of a dolphin, recognized even that long ago for its healing capabilities.

The chief deity associated with Carthage since its foundation in 814 BCE was Tanit. She was a mother goddess and divine nurse, often portrayed on surviving stone monuments as a simple, if stylized, skirted figure bearing the caduceus symbol of life, or health, in her right hand, and joined by a dolphin (see figure 11.3, page 114). Keltic legionnaires in the Roman occupation of Tunis perpetuated her worship through their version of Tanit: Coventina.

Beyond these venerable folk beliefs, a scientific basis for the dolphin's capacity to heal is beginning to appear. Cochrane and Callen point out that various applications of ultrasound "are now being used as an alternative to invasive therapy, to destroy cataracts, kidney and gall stones, and even some kinds of tumors. Is it possible that the dolphin's ultrasonic frequencies work in a similar way, hence the numerous accounts of tumors shrinking and cancers regressing in patients who have swum with dolphins?"[8]

"They know where that is in your body," answers Athena Neeley, a former registered nurse turned midwife for water-birthing mothers.

Figure 11.3. Tanit stele
at the Louvre, Paris.
Photograph by the author.

"They can sense that, and they send out rays to that part of the body for healing."[9]

Another woman had been suffering from debilitating arthritis for so many years, her life was consumed with anxiety. In desperation, after failing to find any relief from modern medicine, she swam with dolphins, and her condition improved remarkably. "I stopped getting pains," she stated in 1994, "and I was a lot more relaxed, which felt great. I know for sure there was a spiritual bond between them and me."[10]

But their astonishing therapeutic powers only first scientifically came to light during the next century, as recently as 2011, at Washington, D.C.'s Georgetown University Medical Center, a $225 million biomedical research and educational establishment. While working for its Transplant Institute of the Department of Surgery, Dr. Michael A. Zasloff was surprised to learn about the dolphins' extraordinary recovery from serious shark bites—some larger than a basketball healed in weeks, without the animals bleeding to death, becoming disfigured, or having any apparent pain or signs of infection.

"If I saw this in a human being," Zasloff told the *Journal of Investigative Dermatology,* "I wouldn't believe it. The healing ability itself is pretty miraculous."[11] He was referring to antibacterial properties in their skin and blubber that help stop infections in open wounds. The dolphins can completely replace the missing tissue in a few weeks, without leaving so much as a dent in their body shape. This healing ability arises from special proteins—possibly stem cells—that resprout limbs and large epidermal areas. "This is an animal of extreme similarity, structurally, to us," Zasloff says. "It should awe us. You have an animal that has evolved in the ocean without hands or legs, which swims faster than we can, has intelligence that perhaps equals our social and emotional complexity, and its healing is almost alien compared to what we are capable of."[12]

Zasloff is known for his work on antimicrobial peptides (also referred to as host defense peptides), part of our innate immune response, but found among all classes of life. He explains that dolphin regenerative techniques could someday, with further research, be available to humans, especially the appropriation of certain proteins the creatures are known to produce during their remarkable healing process. They also create their own antibacterial, pain-relieving compound, which, if proven applicable to humans, may prove to be not only superior to anything currently available to us, but not addictive, as are many pain relievers on the market today. "This could be the source of information," he remarks, "the place to find some [answers to the] great mysteries that we, as physicians, are trying to solve."[13]

Another great mystery surrounding dolphins is their profound effect on the sufferers from a genetic disorder caused by the presence of all or part of a third copy of chromosome 21, hence, its medical term, trisomy 21. More commonly known as Down syndrome, it is typically associated with physical growth delays, characteristic facial features, and mild to moderate intellectual disability. The average IQ of a young adult with Down syndrome is fifty, equivalent to the mental age of an eight- or nine-year-old child. In his study "Using the Atlantic Bottlenose Dolphin to Increase the Cognition of Mentally Retarded Children," Dr. David Nathanson, a psychologist and professor at Florida International University in Miami, found that "the learning abilities of some of the children involved in the project increased by as much as five hundred percent."[14]

Dr. Nathanson "developed a programme which used dolphins as part of a simple behavioral modification—as a stimulus and reinforcement," involving word-captioned picture boards that children were asked to learn. The boards were pushed toward them by the dolphins. If the children answered correctly, they were rewarded, or "reinforced," by being allowed to feed or touch the dolphins. The children clearly enjoyed kissing, petting, and swimming with them in exchange for providing desired responses, while the dolphins participated in the project with no less obvious enthusiasm.

Dr. Nathanson's colleague, Dr. Betsy Smith, an educational anthropologist and associate professor at Florida International University's School of Public Affairs and Services, documented the case of her adult brother, David, who had suffered neurological impacts from a childhood disease. His condition exerted a notable effect on an aggressive and unruly dolphin named Liberty. "The dolphin became gentle, patient and attentive," she reports, "when David entered the water and initiated contact." Cochrane and Callen write how the man, "who was usually very cautious near water, and slow to adapt to new stimuli, entered the water almost immediately, and began talking to Liberty, reaching out to stroke the animal. The results of the initial studies also showed clearly that dolphins could increase autistics' communication skills, and encourage such people to relate to the real world, whilst improving their learning abilities."[15]

Since Dr. Smith's experiments during the 1970s, the growth of autism has surged; according to the disorder's best-known investigator and researcher, Mary Temple Grandin, author of *The Autistic*

*Brain: Helping Different Kinds of Minds Succeed* and professor of animal science at Colorado State University: "In early April [2014], the CDC [Centers for Disease Control and Prevention] released its latest, shocking report on the disorder, which showed a massive up-tick in the number of diagnoses—according to the numbers, one in eighty-eight children and one in fifty-four boys are now on the autism spectrum. That's an astonishing seventy-eight percent increase since 2002. In the weeks since, pundits and doctors have spent a lot of time debating what these changes actually mean: Are they due to increased detection, loosened definitions of autism, or are we in the middle of a genuine upsurge in autism among American children?"[16]

As Dr. Thomas Frieden, the director of the CDC, told reporters, this change may be "entirely the result of better detection. We don't know whether or not that is the case."[17]

"I think severe autism has really increased," says Grandin, herself diagnosed with autism at age two.[18]

Repeated experience has convinced Dr. Hyson, cited above, that personal contact with dolphins is therapeutic for persons with autism. Likewise, Jean Charles Genet, director of the National Center for Integrative Medicine and the National Research Center for Chronic Fatigue in Joliet, Illinois, and a leading researcher in brain wave therapy, believes that dolphins exert an ameliorating effect on people with the disorder. "The reason a child with autism cannot maintain a presence in [our] reality," according to Genet, is that "the brain of a child with the disorder loses the ability to ground to its physical body. This grounding stabilizes the different frequencies the brain uses to maintain a mental, physical, and emotional connection to our reality." Once the brain loses this grounding, it starts running out of control into what Genet terms as "hyper-drive."

He points out that while conscious, "the human brain vibrates between thirteen and thirty cycles per second of brain wave energy. In hyper-drive, the brain can vibrate at levels well above one hundred thousand cycles per second. The only other mammal that can vibrate at this level of consciousness is the dolphin. . . . [It] can move into hyper-drive and vibrate over two hundred fifty thousand cycles per second of brain wave energy in its conscious state. While in hyper-drive, the dolphin and children with autism communicate in much the same way."[19]

This communication, in itself, is therapeutic and forms the basis for continued healing, as illustrated by Dr. Horace Dobbs's work with autistic children. "They do not show emotional responses," he explains, "apart from frustration. Thus, they appear to be cocooned in their own worlds, where they cannot be reached."[20] He describes the severe case of Eve Hanf-Enos, who had never spoken during the first fourteen years of her life. In 1985, after consistently resisting all forms of conventional medical treatment, Eve was taken, as a last resort, to Sealand, a dolphinarium at Cape Cod, a spit of land jutting out into the Atlantic Ocean from the easternmost portion of Massachusetts.

Initially terrified to enter even shallow water, Eve was gradually prevailed upon to do so by her mother and thereafter taken under the charge of Patricia St. John of the International Marine Trainers' Association. An adult male dolphin known as Scotty stopped in front of the mute child, and they stared fixedly at each other for a prolonged moment. St. John believed both had communicated somehow. The brief encounter noticeably affected Eve, who was untypically calm and serene. A few minutes later, unbidden and unexpectedly, the first word passed from her lips, when she said to her mother: "Good."[21]

Scientists have more specifically pinpointed the source of resonating commonality between dolphins and humans, not only those with autism. Dr. John Lilly was the first investigator to suggest that "the dolphin's brain waves equate with those in the alpha and theta regions."[22] His supposition was later championed by Dr. Stephen Jozef, a biofeedback researcher formerly with the Drake Institute for Behavioral Medicine in Irvine, California. "He hypothesizes that because they [dolphins] live in the alpha state themselves," writes Lana Miller, "they facilitate that state in humans."[23]

But what exactly is the alpha state? Our brain cells, called neurons,

Figure 11.4. A dolphin involved in autism therapy touches the area of a young sufferer's forehead corresponding to the cerebral cortex's frontal lobe, the area of the brain associated with this disorder.

produce electricity, and we are able to determine or measure their different electrical patterns, or waves. An electroencephalograph recording electrical activity along the scalp measures voltage fluctuations of current flowing within the neurons to show that neurons generate certain rhythms, or cycles. These rhythms are: beta, from fourteen to twenty-one cycles per second; alpha, from seven to fourteen cps; theta, from four to seven cps; and delta, from almost zero to four cps. These brain waves each have their own characteristics or properties. Alpha waves predominantly originate from the occipital lobe during wakeful relaxation, and when properly stimulated, they possess great potential to create health, happiness, and spiritual-intellectual growth. If alpha waves are neglected or obstructed, physical illness, emotional depression, and mental paucity ensue.

In 2006, Jason T. Nomura, M.D., director of the Emergency Medicine Ultrasound Fellowship at the Christiana Care Health System in Wilmington, Delaware, designed an experiment to determine if alpha brain wave stimulation could ease the pain of patients undergoing an endoscopy. According to the research, "Forty consecutive patients (twenty-five men and fifteen women) were included in the study. Twenty of the patients received photic 9 Hz alpha stimulation for twenty-five minutes, in addition to the usual premedications."[24] Anything relating to light is "photic," especially an agent of chemical change or physiological response.

An alpha state of consciousness can be induced by subjecting the patient to a regularly interrupted light source. In the second century CE, the Greco-Roman scholar Claudius Ptolemy noticed that observers of flickering sunlight through the spokes of a spinning wheel experienced a sense of euphoria.[25]

Returning to Dr. Nomura's research:

> The other twenty patients in Dr. Nomura's control group received the same treatment, but without photic stimulation. All of the patients used a five-grade scale to evaluate the discomfort/pain they felt during endoscopy, in comparison with what they had experienced in their previous examination. Of the patients who received the alpha stimulation, eighteen out of twenty reported feeling less discomfort/pain than they had experienced before, compared to just three/twenty in the control group. A clear correlation was found in the review of this EEG data: more alpha brain wave activity meant less pain.[26]

In March of that same year, a paper published in *BMC Neuroscience* reported the effects of alpha brain wave stimulation on memory. Subjected to stimulation at 10.2 hertz, the experimental group outperformed the control group by 15 percent. Another study conducted six years earlier among employees at a Dutch addiction care center investigated the possible effects of alpha brain wave stimulation on stress and anxiety. Subjects were given a single stimulation session of five minutes at 30 hertz, then another thirty-five minutes at 10 hertz.

The results were undeniable. "Before and after the session," report

Cochrane and Callen, "all of the subjects completed Spielberger's State-Trait Anxiety Inventory (STAI) test, which is an evaluation tool that is very widely used to determine stress and anxiety levels. Those who received the stimulation showed a significant, immediate decrease in state anxiety after the sessions, and this effect was consistently demonstrated across four tests: the alpha stimulation resulted in lower stress levels every time."[27]

India's outstanding biochemist, Ajit Vadakayil, previously a ship's captain for thirty years, explains:

> After swimming, touching, playing or diving with dolphins, a participant's dominant brainwave frequency slows significantly from a beta frequency [the state of ordinary consciousness] to something resembling an alpha state, the brainwave frequency of light meditation or dreaming. The brain hemispheres synchronize, so that the brainwaves emitted from both the left and right hemispheres are in phase [peaking and troughing at the same time] and of similar frequency [speed] . . . . Dolphins produce low-frequency, electromagnetic and scalar [or standing] healing waves. Production and uptake of the brain's neuro-transmitters are strengthened by dolphin contact. The dolphins, being conscious creatures and friendly to humans, know how to lower or raise their frequencies. Dolphins induce both Alpha brain state and hemispheric synchronization in the brain.[28]

Dr. Lilly concludes that dolphin brains additionally operate on the theta frequency, that transitory realm between alpha and the deep sleep of delta. It is also referred to as the hypnagogic state, where lucid dreaming and visionary experiences occur, including sudden insight, free association, creative ideas, and problem solving. That both these dimensions of altered consciousness should be part of the dolphin mind suggests a basis for the creature's renowned capacity for healing emotional disorders in humans.

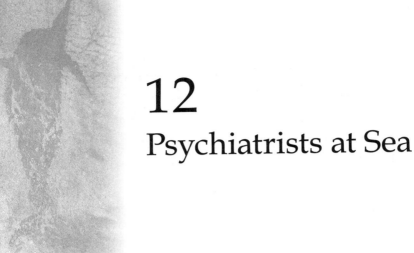

# 12
## Psychiatrists at Sea

*Dolphins have perhaps overtaken us in some respects on the*
*road to evolution, and we might have some catching up to do.*
HORACE DOBBS

Cancer, strokes, nervous system challenges, and autism are among the
many physical ailments our cousins in the sea have helped alleviate, as
we saw in the previous chapter. Yet, they have even more to offer in the
realm of curative talents—emotional healing.

Recent studies on the nature of alpha brain waves demonstrate how
they boost our immune system, remove stress, and increase mental agility.
Alpha frequencies are indicative of a creative state of mind, where free
association is prominent. Psychologists use alpha brain wave stimulation
to help patients overcome phobias, calm down hyperactive children, and
help those with stuttering problems to relax enough to facilitate regular
speech. Clinical examination has also shown how Zen-trained meditation
masters produce noticeably more alpha waves during meditation.

Reporting for *The Philippine Daily Inquirer,* Jaime Licauco explains
the phenomenal skills of these meditation experts:

> At the alpha level, he or she can project his or her consciousness or
> awareness into the future and know what's going to happen before it
> does (technically called *precognition*). He can project his conscious-

ness into the past and know what happened without being there (called retro-cognition). He can project his awareness to another person and know what he is thinking of (through telepathy). He can project his awareness to a distant place he has never been to before and describe it accurately (through remote viewing or traveling clair-voyance). He can also heal himself and others through mental imag-ery or visualization. Why is this possible? Because it is believed that at the alpha level, the brain waves, the left brain hemisphere and those of the right, are synchronized. And when this happens, he is able to consciously tap the tremendous powers and knowledge hid-den in the subconscious mind.[1]

To elaborate, Cochrane and Callen write of Dr. Peter Guy Manners, a British physician with twenty years' experience in the therapeutic use of sound: "When energy in the brain is low, or when the left and right hemispheres of the brain are unbalanced, it cannot function effi-ciently. However, if you can restore this balance, you can go on to treat areas of disease in the rest of the body." Cochrane and Callen tell of "reports back in the 1970s that several people suffering from psycho-logical disturbances, such as acute depression, had made remarkable and apparently permanent recoveries after swimming with friendly, wild dolphins."[2]

Among these accounts is the experience of Geoff Bold, a lifeboat mechanic "who was close to a nervous breakdown," until he swam with a dolphin that paid him close attention. As soon as these encounters took place, Bold's chronic depression began to lift and soon after com-pletely dissipated, never to recur.[3]

In a similar case, fifty-four-year-old Bill Bowell suffered a heart attack, followed by mental collapse and severe despondency, accompa-nied by feelings of hopelessness and inadequacy. In a last-ditch effort, he was taken by Dr. Dobbs, the same physician who worked with Eve Hanf-Enos, to visit Simo, a popular wild dolphin near the Welch coast. Bowell said his dolphin encounter was "more therapeutic than all the anti-depressant drugs he had been taking," and "started to change from being apprehensive, withdrawn and nervous into an altogether more confident and out-going person."[4]

Impressed by the curative effect that close proximity to dolphins had on Bowell, Bold, and others, Dr. Dobbs established Operation Sunflower, a long-term international dolphin watch research project to investigate the healing power of dolphins. He made tape recordings of them interacting with his patients, then issued them as individual audio cassettes to a control group of people suffering from clinical depression.

According to Dobbs, "Each recipient was invited to give brief details of their medical history and their personal response to the tape in complete confidence on an assessment form enclosed with each tape. Evaluation of the first responses by the Applied Psychology Unit of the Medical Research Council was encouraging. A comprehensive analysis at Swansea University of the responses returned from 1987 to 1993 revealed that over seventy-five percent of those suffering from mental stress benefited from listening to *Dolphin Dreamtime*," a series of recorded dolphin vocalizations he used as part of his emotional therapy program.[5] The recordings are "now being used in hospitals, prisons, by stress management consultants, students taking exams, women in labor, hyperactive children, autistic and cerebral palsy victims, as well as those just wishing to relax after a busy day." Dr. Dobbs relates that "a mother of two used *Dolphin Dreamtime* to have pain free birth."[6]

Dr. Manners, mentioned above, found that "people with paraplegia or mental depression tend to feel better when they interact with dolphins."[7] A case in point is Jemima Biggs, a woman in her twenties, unable to enjoy close personal relationships and suffering from anorexia so severe her menstrual periods ceased, due to deep depression. After swimming two years with dolphins, her eating problems improved only marginally, but her emotional condition lifted sufficiently for her to marry and give birth to a pair of healthy children.

Wendy Huntington suffered since her early twenties from myalgic encephalomyelitis (also known as chronic fatigue syndrome), an inflammation of the brain and nervous system that causes pain, muscle weakness, and a general feeling of exhaustion. After a single session in the water with wild dolphins, "Wendy felt really fine again, and was looking towards the future with excitement and enthusiasm," according to Dobbs.[8]

A writer for the website Dolphinspedia reports how "one study into dolphin therapy documented by the BBC demonstrated that volunteers who stopped traditional treatment for depression and swam regularly with dolphins showed much more improved mental health than those who hadn't."[9]

Dr. David Cole of the Aquathought Foundation has proposed a scientific basis for such unconventional healing. He suggests that dolphin ultrasounds produce cavitation, the formation of an empty space within a solid body, which stimulates the production of lymphocyte T-cells. These are any of several closely related lymphocytes—small white blood cells—developed in the thymus that circulate in the blood and lymph and regulate the immune system's response to infected or malignant cells. The T-cells attack and destroy infected cells, including those hosting the AIDS and myalgic encephalomyelitis viruses.[10]

While curative miracles such as those experienced by Jemima Biggs and Wendy Huntington may not be all that uncommon, they are nevertheless irregular. Not every human suffering from various and sundry ailments is instantly made whole by the touch of a dolphin, wild or captured. The animal's mending properties, while real enough, as attested by many eyewitness accounts and despite official skepticism, are still deeply enigmatic and certainly beyond human control. The day may come when improved understanding and at least some level of interspecies rapport might allow for reliable curative procedures. Until then, no less miraculous than the dolphins' own remedial power is their eagerness to unhesitatingly offer it to us for healing.

# 13
## They Owe Their Lives to Dolphins

*The happiness of the bee and the dolphin is to exist. For man it is to know that and to wonder at it.*

JACQUES COUSTEAU

Much of what seems futuristic to us was well known in the past. When rediscovered, the old becomes new. Prior to leaving home in Ithaca for the Trojan War and years of wandering, Odysseus had his shield and signet ring emblazoned with the image of a dolphin in commemoration of his son, Telemachus, who was saved from drowning by the creature when the boy was just an infant. The lad's escape represents the kind of sensitive behavior for which dolphins are most renowned. And although the Bronze Age story of Telemachus is the oldest example of its kind, countless reports of humans similarly carried away from trouble at sea were made throughout antiquity, over subsequent centuries, and into modern times.

The variety of these rescue missions suggest that the dolphins were not automatically stimulated by some blind, instinctive impulse, but consciously evaluated different situations, adapting their actions to a particular set of different circumstances. In other words, they do more than provide free rides to the nearest shore for persons floundering in the water.

Figure 13.1. Rendering of a fifth-century BCE Greek vase painting showing Odysseus carrying his dolphin shield. Voelkerkunde Museum, Vienna. Photograph by the author.

In 1965, a West African fisherman, Zachious Benga, was swept out into the Atlantic Ocean on a disintegrating canoe for some seventy or more hours. During that time, Benga was kept awake day and night by attentive dolphins, who splashed water on him as relief from the merciless equatorial Sun, but especially whenever he began to fall asleep and risked tumbling into the sea, where he would have drowned. Demonstrating their telepathic link with the unfortunate man, they left him only after he gave up all hope of survival and resolved to die. Benga was accidentally sighted shortly thereafter by crewmembers of a passing trawler, rescued, and eventually nursed back to health.

A similarly illustrative account from November 1988 tells of the *Elphina III,* a tanker wrecked off the Indonesian coast. Two sailors tossed into rough water were nudged and guided by wild dolphins all through the night and into the next morning to the nearest island off Ujung Kulon, a national park located at the westernmost tip of Java. These survivors raised the alarm, enabling the rescue of nine of their mates still at sea.

Mass human rescue by dolphins is less well known than their individual life saving, but other examples have been documented.

In 1989, twelve divers were lost in the Red Sea for thirteen and one-half hours. Throughout their ordeal, a group of dolphins constantly encircled them and prevented numerous sharks from attacking. The dolphins even sought out a search and rescue vessel cruising the area, alerting its crew to the hapless divers by leaping high into the air over their precise position.

More recently, on the morning of August 28, 2007, California surfer Todd Endris was repeatedly savaged by a fifteen-foot-long, five-thousand-pound great white shark at Marina State Park, a marine wildlife refuge off Monterey. "That attack shredded his back," reports *Today* magazine, "literally peeling the skin back, he said, 'like a banana peel,'" and mauled his right leg down to the bone. Losing half his blood, he was rescued at the last moment from certain death by a pod of bottlenose dolphins, which formed a protective ring around him, keeping the shark away and allowing a severely injured but eternally grateful Endris to reach the shore. "Truly, a miracle," he stated four months after undergoing physical therapy to repair muscle damage inflicted during the encounter.[1]

Wild dolphins successfully employed the same protective ring tactic on the other side of the world three years earlier, in November 2004, when four New Zealand lifeguards, swimming 330 feet off the coast near Whangarei, were threatened by a great white shark. Just before it could reach them, a pod of bottlenose dolphins appeared out of nowhere, herded the swimmers together, and surrounded them in a tight circle that prevented the shark from attacking for forty minutes, as the creatures slowly swam the men to shore.[2]

Later that month, off the same beach, another lifeguard, British-born Rob Howes, was swimming with his daughter, Niccy, and two of her friends when they were joined by several dolphins, which began closely encircling the humans, forcing them together. When Howes attempted to swim away, the *Daily Mail* reports, the creatures pushed him back with the girls. It was then that he noticed a ten-foot-long great white shark making directly for them. "I just recoiled," he said. "It was only about two meters away from me, the water was crystal clear, and it was as clear as the nose on my face. They had corralled us up to protect us."[3] Over the next forty minutes, the dolphins swam round and round, occasionally smacking their tails on the surface of the water to keep the shark at bay. It eventually moved off, allowing Howes and the girls to reach shore.

Tail whacking was employed again near the Sinai Peninsula, when a British tourist was swimming with dolphins in the Gulf of Aqaba, where he was bitten by a shark, the first of more heading his way. Before they could reach him, three dolphins blocked their approach, then vigorously slapped the water with their tails, frightening the sharks away, while the man was pulled back to safety aboard his tourist boat.

Although fundamentally similar, all these reports feature individual twists of detail. In December 2008, Ronnie Dabal was fishing for tuna amid the turbulent seas of Puerto Princesa Bay, off the Philippine island of Palawan, when a sudden squall capsized and sank his small boat. At that moment, the only thing in the vast Pacific Ocean separating him from eternity was a tiny Styrofoam float, to which he clung with hopeless desperation. Continuously pummeled by the relentless waves for twenty-four hours and near the end of his strength, he was joined by some thirty dolphins in the bizarre company of two whales. The cetaceans formed up on either side of Dabal and took turns gently shoving his puny life raft toward the nearest landfall with their pectoral fins. He passed out in the midst of this surreal scene, only to regain consciousness sometime later on the beach of Barangay, where he was discovered and nursed back to health by local residents.

At least a suggestion of extrasensory perception is common in these accounts. How, after all, do dolphins know when people are in trouble upon the vastness of the deep?

A particular incident hints at just such a telepathic awareness. The crew of the research vessel *Aquanaut* was forced one morning to temporarily suspend underwater life-saving drills off Penzance, on the south coast of Britain, because a dolphin could not be discouraged from playing with the men and their equipment. A team member would simulate distress of some kind, while his colleagues trained with various rescue techniques, but the young bottlenose's whimsical interference rendered further practice impossible. Later that day, diver Keith Monery got into serious trouble, but this time the same dolphin's behavior shifted instantly from playfulness into rescue mode. The creature gently brought the man to the surface and kept him there until assistance arrived and then helped him to the boat's stepladder. Even after Monery was safely aboard, the dolphin swam quietly alongside the *Aquanaut* until he could see that the man had recovered.

A very similar episode, though in reverse, reaffirms the dolphin ability to discern the subtleties of changing situations. Another mock drowning was staged by Dr. Lilly, who wanted to film his captive dolphin, Sissy, coming to the rescue. For the first take, she performed as expected, gently pushing the actor to the side of the pool in shallow water. Unfortunately, Lilly had forgotten to remove his camera's lens cap, so when he tried to reshoot the scene, which Sissy now realized was staged, instead of endeavoring to save the actor a second time, she roughed him up.

Incidents such as these dramatize the broad spectrum of awareness and healing voluntarily provided by dolphins, from their curative influence on mental illness to physically rescuing humans in distress amid the waves. The animal's life-saving virtues alone are sufficient to guarantee its protection and further study. A man, woman, or child attacked by sharks or drowned at sea could have been saved by a dolphin killed for profit or captured for degrading entertainment in some amusement park. In choosing to become either a steward of life on Earth or its exploiter, Man determines his own fate.

# 14
## Musical Dolphins

*Discovery, in my experience, requires disillusionment first,
as well as later. One must be shaken in one's basic beliefs
before the discovery can penetrate one's mind sufficiently
above threshold to be detected. A certain willingness to face
censure, to be a maverick, to question one's beliefs, to revise
them, is absolutely necessary.*

JOHN C. LILLY

Sunny Sicily was the scene of a great musical competition staged by Greek
colonists and an attraction for performers from around the civilized
world. Playing his *kithara*—a professional version of the two-stringed
lyre—and singing the words and melody of his own hymn to the god
Apollo, the handsome young man who had traveled from Methymna,
on the island of Lesbos, on the other side of the Mediterranean Sea,
made a clean sweep of the competition. Arion was showered with popular acclaim and loaded down with costly prizes, then accompanied
by throngs of admirers all the way to the southern Italian port city of
Taras, where he boarded a ship for home.

The return voyage was uneventful enough, until the ship neared the
coast of Greece, when Arion was abruptly confronted by hostile crewmen.
They were determined to confiscate his newfound wealth and murder
him. As a last request, he asked them for permission to sing once more the

song that had won him success back in Sicily. The sailors consented, and he performed under the inspiration of approaching death, then tossed his kithara aside with a contemptuous gesture, and threw himself overboard. As the vessel with its avaricious ship's company sailed away, leaving him alone to drown in the vast sea, Arion was unexpectedly buoyed up on the back of a dolphin that had been attracted by his music. The creature carried him safely all the way to Cape Tainaron, the southernmost point of mainland Greece, but died of exhaustion on the shore for its heroic effort.

Arion eventually made his way to Periander, ruler of Corinth, who ordered an honorable funeral for the dolphin rescuer, together with the construction of its own monument. In time, the same ship that Arion had boarded in Taras docked at the port of Corinth, and its villainous crewmen were brought before Periander. They lied that during the voyage from Italy, their young passenger unfortunately passed away from an illness of some kind, but had been buried with all due respect at sea. "Tomorrow, you will swear to that at the Dolphin Monument," Periander vowed and had them arrested.

The following morning, they were brought to the newly consecrated site on the shore at Cape Tainaron and commanded to swear by the departed spirit of the dolphin that Arion had died of natural causes and that they had lowered his corpse into the sea, just as they reported. At that moment, Arion, who was hiding inside the monument, stepped out and presented himself, to their utter astonishment. Thereafter, the soul of the dolphin that had saved him was set in the sky by the god Apollo as the constellation Delphinus. Its group of ten stars in the northern sky is visible to the naked eye.

The Italian port from which Arion sailed foreshadows his adventure in this tale, because the city had been established by one of Poseidon's sons, Taras, who was himself rescued from drowning by a dolphin. The creature brought him to shore, where Taras built a settlement he named after himself. Today known as Taranto, Roman-era Tarentum did, in fact, issue coins emblazoned with the likeness of its founder riding the back of a dolphin.

Figure 14.1. Tarentum coin, late fifth century BCE.

This coincidence—more likely, an elaboration after generations of retelling—has persuaded skeptics to dismiss the story as merely a fable. But the physical existence of Periander's dolphin monument at Cape Tainaron was affirmed by Classical Era scholars, most notably the Greek geographer Pausanias, who personally visited it as late as the mid-second century CE: "Among other dedications at Tainaron is Arion the musician in bronze on a dolphin."[1]

This tale, moreover, has a modern counterpart at Opononi beach, in New Zealand, where a new monument to a friendly dolphin that died almost sixty years before was erected at Hokianga Harbor in September 2013, after the original statue was vandalized beyond repair (figure 14.2). Both were dedicated to the memory of Opo, a wild dolphin who delighted to play with local children. "Swimming in close to the shore," *Life* magazine reported in 1956, "she would wait for one of them to climb up on her back, then take off on a ride, which usually ended in a friendly dunking."[2] The actions of the dolphins in the New Zealand and Cape Tainaron stories seem poignantly humane.

The same conclusion was arrived at by naturalist Roger Payne, famous for discovering in 1967 that whales actually sing to one another.

Figure 14.2. New monument to the memory
of Opo at New Zealand's Opononi beach.

The low-frequency sounds they emit are not random, meaningless bellows, but finely organized and richly complex patterns of sound, which can be produced only by an order of high intelligence. Payne went on to find that their tonal structures are remarkably similar to human music, and observed the emotional responses of men and women, who often wept "as though something unaccountably ancient was overmastering them," when listening to his best-selling 1970 record, *Songs of Humpback Whales.*[3]

"This commonality of aesthetic," Dr. Payne states, "suggests to me that the traditions of singing may date back so far they were already present in some ancestor common to whales and us."[4]

That common ancestry appears in another Greek myth dramatizing music's mystical association with dolphins, while hinting at their evolutionary kinship with humans. Some twenty-seven centuries ago, the anonymous composer of the Homeric Hymn to Dionysus told how the god of wine and pleasure was traveling disguised as a young man on a ship bound for his Ikarion Sanctuary in northern Athens.

When crewmembers attempted to seize their immortal passenger and sell him into slavery, the masts and rigging of their vessel changed into grape vines, as strangely beautiful music filled the air. Panicked by these portents of divine presence, the sailors jumped overboard into the sea, where they were transformed into the first dolphins. Commenting on this myth, Oppian states that nothing more divine than dolphins has been created, "for they were in past ages men, and lived in cities along with mortals. But by the devising of Dionysus, they exchanged the land for the sea, and put on the form of fishes."[5]

Like the story of Arion, music figures in the Dionysian version of dolphins' singular relationship with humans and gods. Physical evidence for this mystical bond has been found in the small effigies of dolphins still grasped in the well-preserved hands of Romans who were mummified two thousand and more years ago. The gold, bronze, or terra cotta figures ensured safe passage for the deceased in their journey with the afterlife ferryman, because dolphins were believed to carry souls to the Islands of the Blessed. Earlier still, Bronze Age Minoans regarded dolphins as "symbols of music and joy."[6]

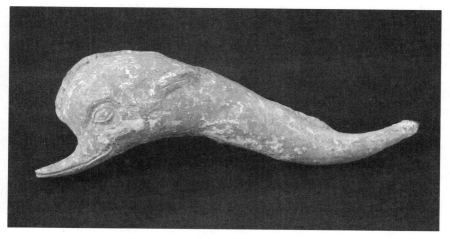

Figure 14.3. Roman-era dolphin figurine placed
in the hands of the deceased. Photograph by the author.

"Greek playwrights, too," write Devine and Clark, "knew the dolphin's fascination with music, and considered it second only to his love of men and ships."[7] In *Electra*, Euripides (480–406 BCE) depicts "dolphins, drunken with the lyre."[8]

Clearly, an intimate relationship between music and dolphins has been observed by various people since very ancient times. "The dolphin is an animal that is not only friendly to mankind," writes the Roman naturalist Pliny the Elder around 70 CE, "but is also a lover of music, and it can be charmed by singing in harmony, but particularly to the sound of the *hydraulis*"—literally, a water-powered pipe instrument.[9] This early type of organ operated by converting the dynamic energy of water blown by manual pumps through an arrangement of pipes, each sounding a different note. The world's first keyboard instrument, it was invented by Ctesibius of Alexandria, a Hellenist scientist and engineer of the third century BCE. Due to its sonorous tones, the hydraulis was most often performed inside temples, where its resonance was empowered by the vast, stony acoustics, just as modern pipe organs are usually associated with the voluminous interior spaces of cathedrals.

Most Classical Era water organs were small enough to be portable and were often played outdoors, especially at seaside festivals or ceremonies, where wild dolphins were attracted often enough for Pliny to have described their appearances. Cochrane and Callen add, "The high notes would have given out ultrasonic vibrations which the dolphins could hear."[10]

"Dolphins are known to follow the sound of the human voice," writes medievalist Richard H. Randall Jr. for the New York Metropolitan Museum of Art, "or even to gather together at the sound of music."[11]

Pliny's statement that dolphins "can be charmed by singing in harmony" was verified two thousand years later on the other side of the world, along the shores of New South Wales, where indigenous Australians achieved the remarkable "by singing the dolphins in. This

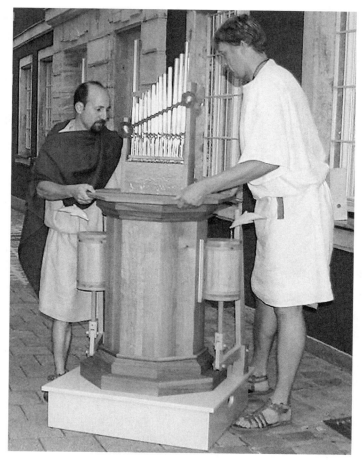

Figure 14.4. This modern recreation of a second-century hydraulis was constructed with close attention to the details depicted in Roman-era paintings and mosaics—including dolphin figurines above both cylinders. Photograph by Manfred E. Fritsche.

was accomplished, in the main, by the women of the tribe, the dolphins reciprocating by herding the fish in toward the waiting spears of the male Aborigines," according to Dobbs.[12]

Jacques Cousteau believed "that dolphins are sensitive to music. Aboard *Calypso,* our two guitar players, Louis Prezelin and Dr. Millet, on several occasions attracted dolphins by music."[13]

De Bergerac writes of a man who "was singing in Latin [a particularly mellifluous language], and as soon as he started, the dolphins moved towards our boat and started playing. It was like they responded."[14]

Dobbs tells of a late twentieth-century Scottish sailor, who "discovered that the sound of his children singing would attract a school of dolphins, when he and his family were cruising off the Riff Bank, in the Moray Firth."[15] Dobbs also cites a skipper able to conjure wild dolphins at will by striking a very large tuning fork on the gunwale of his boat, then holding the vibrating instrument against the hull. The sound transmitted through the water appears to have had an irresistible effect on the animals.

Elsewhere in coastal Australia, indigenous oral tradition along the northern Gulf of Carpentaria tells of the power of local shamans to summon dolphins "using a complex series of whistles," according to Dobbs.[16] The same technique is employed half a world away by another indigenous people, the Amazonian natives of Rio Tapajos in Brazil. The Indians whistle at a special pitch, which summons the river dolphins for cooperative fishing. The consistency of so many reports from wholly unrelated peoples, separated from each other by thousands of miles and by as many years, tends to affirm the dolphins' musical attributes.

Classical Greek accounts likewise tell of dolphins attracted by the playing of flutes, as illustrated by a deep, two-handled, fourth-century BCE wine cup (called a *skyphos*) decorated with the images of helmeted men riding dolphins toward a standing, robed musician playing an *aulos*. This was a twin-reed instrument, its sound somewhat like that of Scottish bagpipes. Both instruments were associated with martial music; hence the depiction of warriors together with the *aulete* (the aulos player) on the Greek skyphos.

The depicted relationship between pipe music and dolphins was put to the test by Dr. Diana Reiss, director of the Dolphin Research Program at the National Aquarium in Baltimore. Performing on her flute attracted the attention of two captive dolphins that were part of her ongoing investigation into their behavior.

"I discovered by simple experimentation that if I picked up the tempo," Reiss observes, "they swam faster. And if I played slowly, they became somewhat languorous."[17] The dolphins were not only attracted by the flute music, but danced to it.

According to de Bergerac, "they can hear the sound of a whistle as much as twenty kilometers [twelve and one-half miles] away."[18]

Cetologists know that the dolphin's tonal whistles are the most melodious sounds it produces, and these are used to maintain close contact with others—particularly used by mothers and their offspring and for coordinating hunting strategies, which require tight cooperation. In other words, dolphins sing to each other. Dr. Lilly "obtained evidence that shows that the dolphins communicate most of their information in the band of frequencies extending from about one kilocycle to one hundred kilocycles by means of whistles and sonic clicks. However, as shown by [William E.] Schevill and [Barbara] Lawrence [delphinologists during the early 1950s], they can hear sounds at least to one hundred twenty kilocycles, and, as shown by [Winthrop N.] Kellogg [author of *Porpoises and Sonar*], can produce sounds at least to one hundred seventy kilocycles. . . . In these bands, we find that they can produce musical tones."[19]

Other scholars argue that dolphins do not actually create music, but are only communicating to each other with sounds humans misinterpret as songs. Notwithstanding such skepticism, a peculiar confirmation of dolphin musical interests was documented as recently as 2011, when researchers from the University of Rennes 1 (in France) for the first time attempted to record the sounds, if any, dolphins might make while sleeping. The half-dozen subjects in question were kept in a large pool at an amusement park, where they performed daily for public audiences.

French audio technicians were shocked to hear that 1 percent of the vocalizations they recorded between midnight and 3 a.m.—the dolphins' deepest level of sleep—were utterly unlike any sounds the animals uttered during daylight hours: all the dolphins were singing the songs of humpback whales. Their performance was all the more amazing because whales were never in residence at the amusement park, and none of the dolphins had ever met or seen any such creatures. When the researchers were informed that a recording of whale songs was played over the loudspeakers after hours, when the park was closed, they concluded that the dolphins had selected to learn those cetacean songs over all the variety of audio input to which they were daily subjected for repetition in dreams.

"It's quite consistent with what's known of memory consolidation in other mammals, like humans," says sleep specialist Matthew Edlund, M.D. "Dolphins only 'sing like whales' at night," he adds. "Their 'whale' songs may be sung during the night and sleep, but never during the day."[20]

But his conclusion is based only on a handful of captive specimens at a single amusement park. Paul Tyack, a dolphin researcher at St. Andrew's University in Scotland, claims to have heard dolphins in the wild making similar forms of song. According to Dobbs, "a dolphin's brain is a slightly different shape, but the cerebral cortex, the highly convoluted part on the top which we associate with higher mental processes, such as the appreciation of music, is more highly evolved in dolphins than it is in humans."[21]

Their better musical appreciation is supported by their superior hearing. Most of the sounds dolphins emit are inaudible to us. As would be said of extraordinary opera singers, their "range" is far greater than anything we can recognize. True music, not merely melodious calls, is the hallmark of high intelligence, and how much higher than ours must be that of the dolphins, with their far broader capacity for sound production?

"I've been in the water when it's filled with dolphin sonar," Dobbs remarks, "and the feeling is that of being a musical instrument; an instrument that's being perfectly played. The vibrations move through our tissue and bone, and palpate us at our deepest levels."[22] Palpation is physical examination by pressure of the hand or fingers to the surface of the body, especially to determine the condition of an underlying organ.

To be sure, a relationship between sound and healing seems clear.

British physician Dr. Peter Guy Manners found after investigating the therapeutic application of sound for more than two decades that every body part in the human anatomy generates a specific vibration. When any organ or gland does not function properly, its tone grows measurably weaker or dissonant. Given so many instances of healing associated with wild dolphin encounters, plus the animals' prodigious potential for audio production, it seems likely that dolphins sonically home in on the deteriorated sound of a stricken body part like a medical distress signal and instantly use their own kindred tone to energize, realign, or reinvigorate the injured or ill organ.

In the late twentieth century, electronics engineer Tony Bassett artificially and partially duplicated dolphin energy when he substantially mitigated withdrawal pains for heroin addicts by subjecting their brain waves to sound vibrations at two thousand hertz. This particular frequency, he determined, triggered the production of endorphins, pleasure-inducing chemicals in the human brain. Two thousand hertz is well within the frequency range of dolphins, which may explain why most people who share the water with them experience a surge of positive emotion. Dolphins are playful creatures, if only because their levels of oxytocin are kept high by the animals' constant immersion in water, which stimulates this "happiness hormone," as described in chapter 1.

The spotted, bottlenose, white, and many other dolphin species have eighty-eight teeth. The sixth-century BCE Greek philosopher and mathematician Pythagoras determined that eighty-eight was synonymous with the Music of the Spheres. This number is expressed in the same amount of keys belonging to a grand piano, the number of constellations in the night sky as defined by the International Astronomical Union, the number of days the planet Mercury requires to complete its orbit of the Sun, and more. If there is anything to these parallels, then they could define dolphins as part of a cosmic harmony broader and deeper than we might suspect and sorely need. In fact, their musical attributes may comprise a direct means of communication.

A 1976 film, *Close Encounters of the Third Kind,* suggested that music might allow a basic dialogue between humans and extraterrestrial beings. Music has been long referred to as an "international language." Perhaps it is an interspecies one as well. Dolphins and humans have already begun to approach each other through the music we make to attract them and the healing sounds they direct at us to stimulate our endorphins. Efforts over the last several decades at decoding the complex audio patterns dolphins emit have largely come to nothing. We are still unable to translate Dolphinese, probably because it is built of an ever-changing stream of nuanced subtleties.

Centuries after Jean-François Champollion first began to translate the language of dynastic Egypt in the 1820s, early twenty-first-century Egyptologists came to realize that many of the translations made by their predecessors over the last 180 years were badly flawed because the inhabitants of the Nile Valley preferred to speak in puns. For example, scholars concluded that ancient Egyptian royals married their siblings based on texts in which kings typically described their queens as "sisters." It is now generally understood that the Egyptian word for "sister"—*senet*—was not meant literally, but as a term of endearment signifying someone personally very close.

Dolphinese is analogous, but infinitely more complex and forever beyond our understanding, save perhaps by the invention of a computer not only powerful enough to process vast streams of data and collate them into a coherent form, but also sufficiently cognizant of every linguistic nuance that dolphins produce. Until the advent of such technology, we might do far better by meeting the dolphins on a more direct common ground: our shared love of music. Once there, we may come to learn that communication with them is not intellectual, but emotional.

A beginning might be made in duplicating the humpback whale songs they apparently enjoy singing at the French amusement park. The songs should not be exactly replicated to avoid disrupting the whales, but played back in human fashion, perhaps scored for standard musical instruments or electronic synthesizers, or sung by children, which dolphins appear to love. If the dolphins repeat the sounds, we might respond by playing the musical selection back with slight variations. Should those variations be repeated by the dolphins, which might add some of their own, then the basis for making music together may become possible. Such harmonizing might open up preconditions for communication we cannot at the present moment imagine.

# 15
## Dolphins and Men

*Oh, my good, kind dolphins,*
*beware the savagery of men!*
AELIAN

The rescue of humans by dolphins has its reciprocal side. On January 11, 2014, a scuba diver was under the waters near Kona, Hawaii, when he was approached by a bottlenose dolphin with a fishing hook caught in its pectoral fin. "The way he came right up and pushed himself into me," recounts Keller Laros in the *Huffington Post,* "there was no question this dolphin was there for help." It rolled over to properly position itself for assistance. "There was a line coming out of his mouth. But the line wrapped around his pectoral fin was so tight, I was worried if I tugged on it, it might hurt him more. I was able to cut the fishing line and unwrap it, and got the fishing hook out of the pectoral fin."[1] Thus liberated, the dolphin momentarily surfaced for air, then returned to Laros, who completed the disentangling, after which the creature swam away.

Another dolphin ensnared in an anchor line was similarly rescued fifty-five years earlier by fishermen in the Black Sea, after they were suddenly surrounded by several other dolphins, which literally pushed the small boat to a buoy, where the helpless creature was trapped. When the baby dolphin was freed, the rest of its pod began loudly whistling in obvious joy, then escorted the Russians for the length of their homeward voyage. *Tursiops truncatus* ssp. *ponticus* is an endangered species of dolphin native to the Black Sea.

Rescue, however, is not the only basis for a relationship. At times, humans and dolphins seek each other out for mutual benefit. In 1856, naturalist William Fairholm witnessed a remarkable event on the northeast coast of Australia. "Near Amity Point, some of the natives may constantly be found during the warmer months of the year fishing for mullet," he told the Zoological Society of Queensland.[2] Continuing, he recounts:

> In this pursuit, they are assisted in the most wonderful manner by the porpoises [sic, dolphins]. It seems that from time immemorial a sort of understanding has existed between the blacks [Aborigines] and the porpoises for their mutual advantage, and the former pretend to know all the porpoises about the spot, and even have names for them. The beach here consists of shelving sand, and near the shore are small hillocks of sand, on which the blacks sit, watching for the appearance of a shoal of mullet. Their nets, which are used by hand, and are stretched on a frame about four feet wide, lie ready on the beach. On seeing a shoal, several of the men run down, and with their spears make a peculiar splashing in the water. . . . The porpoises, being outside the shoal, numbers of fish are secured before they can break away.
>
> In the scene of apparent confusion that takes place, the blacks and porpoises are seen splashing about close to each other. So fearless are the latter, that strangers, who have expressed doubts as to their tameness, have often been shown that they will take a fish from the end of a spear, when held to them. For my part, I cannot doubt that the understanding is real, and that the natives know these porpoises, and that strange porpoises would not allow so little fear of the natives. The oldest men of the tribe say that the same kind of fishing has always been carried on as long as they can remember.

Porpoises abound in the bay, but in no other part do natives fish with their assistance.[3]

A revealing twist on this same interaction was described more than fifty years later by another reporter:

> I remember witnessing a great scene of fun and excitement at Amity Point. A large school of mullet was coming in along the shore, but was too far out in the deep water for the blacks, when a number of porpoises was observed rolling about five hundred yards away, and sunning themselves, in complete unawareness of the feast so near them.
>
> One black fellow went down to the beach with a spear, which he prodded into the sand several times, and then struck the water with it at full length horizontally. Instantly, the porpoises answered with a signal by dashing in, and, of course, driving the poor mullet before them, when there was a rush of about twenty natives into them with their nets, and for the next two minutes, nothing was to be seen, but a confused mass of fish, porpoises and blacks, all mixed up together, out of which the blacks emerged with their nets as full as they could hold, and left the balance of the school to be taken care of by their curious allies.[4]

This incident provides an example of fundamental interspecies communication. All a man need do was strike the surface of the water as a signal for the dolphins, a practice that preceded nineteenth-century accounts by countless generations. New Zealand native folklorist Te Rina Sullivan-Meads recounts an ancestral oral tradition concerning the Maori: "The dolphins were the frequent companions of the people, as they gathered the abundant sea-foods in the lagoon [North Island's Inner Harbour] and along the coast."[5]

The same kind of cooperative fishing occurred on the opposite side of the Atlantic Ocean, along the shores of Mauritania in West Africa. Around 70 CE, when Pliny the Elder was procurator (governor) of Gallia Narbonensis, a Roman province in the region of Nîmes in southern France, he describes Latera, a marsh:

Dolphins catch fish in partnership with human fishermen. At a regular season, a countless shoal of mullet rushes out of the narrow mouth of the marsh into the sea, after watching for the turn of the tide, which makes it impossible for nets to be spread across the channel.

Indeed, the nets would be equally incapable of standing the mass of the weight if even the cunning of the fish did not watch for the opportunity. For a similar reason, they make straight out for the deep water produced by the nearby eddies, and hasten to escape from the only place suitable for setting nets. When this is observed by the fishermen—and crowds of spectators collect at the place, because of their interest in this sport—and when the entire population from the shore shouts as loud as it can, calling for "Snub-nose," the dolphins immediately respond to their wishes, and they rush to the spot to help out.

Their line of battle forms up into view, and at once deploys in the place where they are to join in the fun. They bar the passage on the side of the sea, and drive the frightened mullet into the shallows. Then the fishermen put their nets around them and lift them out of the water with forks. Some frenzied mullets leap over the obstacles, but are caught by the dolphins. . . . But as they are aware that they have had too strenuous a task for only a single day's pay, they wait there until the following day, and are given a feed of bread mash dipped in wine, in addition to fish.[6]

Some years later, Pliny witnessed the same interspecies cooperation take place after dark, in the glare of torchlights, near Iasos, a Greek city located on the Gulf of Güllük in southwestern Turkey: "The dolphins are so beloved there because they drive the fish together from every quarter into the nets of the fishermen."[7]

Oppian records a variation on this nocturnal tactic about one hundred years later during his stay at Euboea, the second-largest Aegean island after Crete:

> When the fishermen hasten to the toil of evening fishing, carrying to the fishes the menace of fire—even the swift gleam of the brazen lantern—the dolphins attend them, speeding the slaughter of their common prey. Then the fishes in terror turn away and seek escape, but the dolphins from the outer sea rush together upon them, and, as they try to break for open water, they drive them towards the unfriendly land, leaping at them ever and again.
>
> And when the fishes flee close to the shore, the fishermen easily spear them with the prongs of their tridents. There is no way of escape for them, but they dance about in the water, driven by fire and dolphins, the kings of the sea. When the work of capture is happily accomplished, then the dolphins draw near and ask reward for their assistance, even their allotted portion of the spoil. The fishermen do not deny them, but gladly give them a share of their successful catch. For if a man sins against them in his greed, no more are the dolphins his helpers in fishing.[8]

Ancient Italian tomb paintings at the Etruscan city of Tarquinii depict fishermen working together with dolphins, vivid proof that such interspecies cooperation was already practiced at least 2,500 years ago. Even today, villages in the remote lowlands of Burma have their own dolphins (*Orcella fluminalis*), which answer to individual names. These creatures importantly assist fishermen with bringing in their catch. In the province of Yunnan, in far southwestern China—an area that is entirely landlocked—Han Dynasty fishermen were so dependent upon members of *Lipotes vexillifer* from 200 BCE to 25 CE that each family or village had its own specimen. Owners were forbidden by law to make their river dolphins drive fish away from the nets of another family or village. Yet more ancient examples of such interspecies cooperation date as far back as India's mid-Vedic age, some three thousand years ago, when captive dolphins served men their entire lives as fellow fishers.

This rather wondrous working relationship between two different kinds of animals almost certainly extends much further into the mists of prehistory, and may have even accompanied early protohuman evolution, during Man's earliest aquatic phase, when, even then, dolphins lent assistance to the clumsy primate just getting his feet wet. Dolphin participation in human fishing diminished after the collapse of Western civilization, but was still known in a few isolated locations.

The nighttime operations Pliny saw at Iasos persisted among Asia Minor's post-Greco-Roman population of local Turks into the sixteenth century, and even today, at a few remote places on Earth, dolphins and fishermen form active partnerships in the ancient style. Since 1847, a pod of bottlenose dolphins has driven fish toward men wading amid the shallow waters near Laguna, a small town in south Brazil. When a single dolphin gives its sign to the fishermen by rolling over, they throw out their nets for a rich harvest. Escaping fish are devoured by the dolphins, which have never trained for such interspecies' collaboration.

"We would not know how to train them for such a thing," confesses one of the fishermen. "No one remembers how it all began. It seems natural. We do not understand why they do not take all the fish themselves. Instead, they eat only left-overs for their payment."[9]

Brazil's border with Peru and Colombia converges in the Upper Amazon Basin, where the *Inia geoffrensis* is revered as the *boutu* or *boto*, meaning "sacred dolphin," by the Rio Tapajos indigenous people because it frequently volunteers rescue missions, pushing drowning people to a nearby riverbank after their canoe capsizes.

Bruce Lamb, a visiting American agriculturist writing for *Natural History* magazine in 1954, reported how the natives were able to swim and cavort in the piranha-infested waters of the Rio Tapajos without fear, thanks to protection provided by watchful boutus. He joined the Indians on one of their tribal fishing expeditions: "As we progressed, the fish scattered ahead of us and went for deep water, but there they were encountered by our friend, the dolphin, who was also fishing, and so they came rushing back to the shallows. Several times, they sped back so fast, they ended up flopping on the beach." Meanwhile, the dolphins literally herded the fish together, pushing great schools toward the waiting Indians, who scooped a bountiful harvest, but never failed to reward their cetacean coworkers with a generous surplus of such Amazon specialties as the pirapitinga, redtail catfish, and jacunda.

"The *boutus* actually accompanied us at fifty to a hundred feet for over an hour," Lamb writes. "This differed greatly from the random feeding movements I have seen dolphins engage in on other occasions."[10]

Not unlike the rescue of humans in distress at sea, there is more than a hint of interspecies extrasensory perception in cooperative fishing with dolphins. A particularly illustrative account concerns an unlucky Australian, who trolled some forty miles without making even one catch. At the end of his unproductive day, the despondent fisherman, wading knee-deep at the stern of the boat, was amazed to see a large snapper continuously swimming around his legs. As he grabbed the big fish, he saw that it had been driven to him by a trio of dolphins watching quietly from just a few feet away.

The man's encounter can only mean that the animals had telepathically picked up on his frustration and, perhaps more remarkably, felt sorry enough for him that they went out of their way to find a handsome snapper (*Chrysophrys*), which they presented as a gift. Such a conclusion is underscored by the fact that *Chrysophrys* is never eaten by dolphins because it is too large for them to swallow. Although not in their diet, they knew that the man wanted a pink snapper and especially selected it for him.

Of course, relations between men and cetaceans are historically far from consistently amiable, but rarely have the latter defended, much less revenged themselves against the former. The most famous exception was Herman Melville's *Moby Dick,* based on *The Narrative of the Most Extraordinary and Distressing Shipwreck of the Whale-Ship Essex,* written by first mate Owen Chase, one of eight survivors from a

Nantucket vessel rammed and sunk in 1820, two thousand miles from the western coast of South America, by a large sperm whale.[11]

Another instance of cetacean vengeance took place during the following century along the northwest coast of Canada. On a summer morning in 1956, two British Columbia loggers were laboring high atop a steep hill that declined precipitously toward the sea, when one of the lumberjacks caught sight of a few orcas peacefully lolling at the surface very near shore. The mean-spirited man deliberately cut loose a particularly large tree trunk, and it skidded rapidly down the slope, striking an orca in the back. Fortunately, the abused animal survived and painfully swam away with the rest of his or her pod. That evening, as both men were rowing back along the coast to the company camp, the orcas suddenly appeared around their small boat and overturned it. The loggers swam for shore, but only one survived. His partner, who had maliciously unloosed the tree trunk, was never found. He had been devoured by creatures that—in this case, at any rate—lived up to their name, "killer whales." The incident demonstrated their ability to recognize cause and effect in the nature of this unprovoked attack, plan a retribution strategy, and carry it out at the proper moment, selectively against the guilty party.

A happier example of cetacean compassion and thought transference involves a wild dolphin that escorted ships between the North and South Islands of New Zealand. Connecting the Tasman Sea in the northwest with the South Pacific Ocean on the southeast, the fourteen-mile-wide channel is among the most dangerous and unpredictable waters on Earth. Named after Captain James Cook, the first European commander to sail through it in 1770, Cook Strait's original Maori name—Raukawa Moana, "bitter leaves"—was not chosen without cause. Its waters are dominated by strong tidal flows, resulting in powerful, erratic currents, while submarine ridges running from the coast contribute to ocean flow and turbulence. These perilous conditions are aggravated by many rocks lurking unseen just beneath the surface of the ocean.

Numerous ships were lost in the strait until 1888, when a strange white dolphin with gray markings and a round, white head began excitedly bobbing up and down directly ahead of an oncoming schooner—the *Brindle*—as though signaling it. Entering Admiralty Bay running from Cape Francis to Collinet Point, between D'Urville Island and the South Island, near the French Pass, the *Brindle* approached Raukawa Moana's most dangerous stretch. A crewman was about to shoot the dolphin for sport, but the captain's wife stopped him in time. Then, to their amazement, the thirteen-foot-long *Grampus griseus,* or Risso's dolphin—rarely seen in these waters—proceeded to guide them safely through the perilous, narrow channel. The animal frequented Pelorus Sound—largest of the Marlborough Sounds north of the South Island—hence, his popular name, "Pelorus Jack."

For the next twenty-four years, he piloted literally hundreds of vessels across the supremely treacherous Cook Strait by swimming alongside them for twenty minutes at a time, skirting all the submerged rocks and overpowering currents. Observers sometimes noticed a white patch in the shape of an anchor on the dolphin's ventral side. The design seemed curiously, even weirdly, appropriate, given the creature's service to ships at sea. The famous Spanish poet, art critic, and mythologist Juan Cirlot (1916–1973) writes that "the anchor always signified salvation and hope," while the archetypical dolphin itself "is associated with that of the anchor . . . twined around an anchor, it comes to signify arrested speed; that is, prudence," necessary qualities for successfully negotiating the hazardous passage of "the bitter leaves."[12] The anchor emblem characterizes *Grampus griseus* and was not unique to Pelorus Jack; he wore it as though it was the insignia of a fraternal organization to which he belonged.

If crewmembers failed to see him when their vessel entered Admiralty Bay, they would wait for the white dolphin to appear. He thus saved an untold number of lives and was seen by thousands of seamen and passengers alike; he was featured in newspaper articles and depicted in postcards. Early film footage of him still survives and shows him leaping in and out of the water close to a ship, leading it through

Figure 15.1. Pelorus Jack riding the bow wave of the SS *Tutanekai,* one of numerous ships the white dolphin guided to safety through New Zealand's perilous Cook Strait.

the Cook Strait.* By 1900, his fame had spread to Europe and America. And during nearly a quarter century of voluntary service, no ship was wrecked along the Cook Strait, save one.

In mid-1904, a rifleman aboard the 220-foot SS *Penguin* took a shot at the white dolphin, narrowly missing the creature. Pelorus Jack nonetheless continued to guide all vessels through Raukawa Moana, with a single exception: the *Penguin,* which he assiduously avoided

---

*A mid-twentieth-century short film from New Zealand, *Two Famous Dolphins,* is the only known footage, however brief, of Pelorus Jack. It was made in the year he disappeared, 1912, not four years later, as stated by the narrator. See it on YouTube at www .youtube.com/watch?v=3R1Ih-QFWxw.

Figure 15.2. The SS *Penguin* before her final voyage.

whenever she approached Admiralty Bay. On February 12, 1909, the 900-ton interisland ferry smashed into Thoms Rock, breaching her hull and allowing cold seawater to flood the red-hot boilers. They burst in a massive explosion that tore apart the entire ship, which sank off Cape Terawhiti, near the entrance to Wellington Harbour, amid "the bitter leaves" of Cook Strait. Most lifeboats, filled with women and children, were dragged under water by rough seas.

Of the 105 passengers and crew aboard the SS *Penguin,* just thirty survived, making her loss New Zealand's worst peacetime disaster at sea. On its one hundredth anniversary, Wellington's mayor unveiled a plaque commemorating the sinking at Tongue Point, near the site of the wreck. The unknown rifleman who fired on Pelorus Jack less than five years before the *Penguin* sank had set in motion a series of events that culminated in human tragedy. His action was a microcosm of the ongoing atrocities commited by twentieth- and twenty-first-century Man against the world's dolphin population and the very foundations of all life on Earth. There are always consequences. What goes around the world, comes around it. If, as some philosophers tell us, karma is the moral law of action and reaction, then its application may not, after all, be restricted to individual men and women, but applied to an entire species, in something Buddhists term "group karma," the implications of which are hellish.

A few weeks after Pelorus Jack's close call with the *Penguin's* rifleman, New Zealanders passed legislation granting him official protection by Order in Council under the Sea Fisheries Act of September 26, 1904. He was the first individual sea creature protected by law in any country. For the next eight years, he continued to fulfill his piloting duties unmolested and undiminished, but mysteriously vanished in early April 1912, within days of the loss of the RMS *Titanic* half a world away.

What connection, other than coincidence, joins the loss of the white dolphin and the sunken liner remains unknown—unless Pelorus Jack, whose concern for the safety of humans at sea was his life's work, left New Zealand for the North Atlantic to warn the *Titanic* or rescue her survivors. If so, he does not appear to have made it. While some cetologists speculate he simply died of old age, his strength and vigor never waned. Nor did he ever look ill or infirm. Risso's dolphins commonly live forty years, although Pelorus Jack's age could not be determined. His alleged demise at the hands of Norwegian whalers is unfounded and unlikely. In any event, he lives on today in a popular Scottish country dance named after him, and his likeness has been used since 1989 as the symbol for regular ferry service crossing the Cook Strait. The Interislander ferry service even incorporated the image of Pelorus Jack in the livery of its ships' staff.

Among his most extraordinary achievements was an ability to tell the difference between the SS *Penguin* and all other ships. Such discernment implies a sensitivity beyond anything we know. Why, after all, would a wild creature even care whether anyone survived the "bitter leaves" of Raukawa Moana? Nor does it seem merely coincidental that he chose to protect against shipwreck in one of the world's most hazardous stretches of water. He appears to have recognized the danger of Cook Strait, understood its threat to humans, and acted to save them on a regular basis, even though their passage and survival were not important for his survival. Indeed, the more benighted among them tried to kill him.

But he was neither unique nor the first of his kind, but rather the latest in a venerable lineage of cetacean pilots. Helpful volunteers like Pelorus Jack go back to deep antiquity. When Hellenistic Greeks ruled Egypt during the Ptolemaic Dynasty, after 323 BCE, two sailors, Dionysius and Soteles, were making for the north coast of Asia Minor, today's Turkey, when violent winds blew their vessel so far off course, they were completely lost at sea. In the midst of their distress, a dolphin surfaced near the ship and guided it safely to the nearest port. Events such as these dramatize the depths of a mystery no one may ever fully comprehend. Yet, we suspect a profoundly ancient, living bond between these unfathomable creatures and ourselves that somehow continues to endure.

# 16
## Dolphins and Women

*They say the sea is cold, but the sea contains the hottest blood of all, and the wildest, the most urgent.*

D. H. LAWRENCE

*The Cape Times,* an English-language morning newspaper published in Cape Town, South Africa, reported a remarkable rescue on September 8, 1972. It described how twenty-year-old student Yvonne Vladislavich was aboard her twenty-three-foot cabin cruiser, the *Scorpio,* when it capsized and sank during a freak storm in the middle of Delagoa Bay, an inlet of the Indian Ocean, on the coast of Mozambique. Today known as Baía de Maputo, or Maputo Bay, it is more than fifty-six miles long from north to south and nearly two hundred miles wide. Her boat had gone down so quickly and unexpectedly that Yvonne was thrown into the angry sea without a life preserver, and none of the *Scorpio*'s floating wreckage was substantial enough to support her.

A strong swimmer, she had received a bronze medal for life saving just a few years earlier, but she was alone now, and far from any shipping lanes; no one even knew she was in trouble. All she could do was swim for what seemed the nearest landfall, out of sight, beyond the horizon. But Yvonne's desperate situation would soon turn abruptly worse. Half a dozen sharks began eyeing her, and their numbers grew as they drew nearer. When they seemed about to close in on the hapless woman, two dolphins miraculously materialized and began aggressively swimming around her to keep the sharks at bay. They continued to stay with Yvonne even when the sharks seemed to lose interest, and nudged her back to consciousness whenever she came close to exhaustion, or came up under her and supported her above the waves to keep her from drowning. She was too disoriented by her plight to realize that the dolphins were guiding her to the only marker buoy left standing; all the others that had been carried out to sea by the storm. With barely enough strength to climb on the anchored float, she passed out for a few minutes, but came to in time to see a tanker coming in the distance.

"I screamed, and somebody on deck waved. But, ironically, my screams chased away the dolphins, and I never saw them again."[1] Yvonne later calculated the distance from the sinking of the *Scorpio* to the marker buoy. The dolphins had escorted her more than forty miles across the Indian Ocean.

While dolphins do not discriminate between the sexes when rescuing members of our species in difficulty, their attitudes toward human females are otherwise quite different from those toward human males. As described in the previous chapter, dolphins and men engage in common work: fishing and piloting. Dolphin interest in women is directed at their reproductive capacities. A completely different, although more representative, incident serves to illustrate.

During the early spring of 2002, a young woman walking with her friends along a pier that extended into shallow water from the western shore of the island of Bimini in the Bahamas, fifty-five miles east of Miami, Florida, noticed a dolphin swimming slowly parallel to them, just beneath the surface of the sea. When she paused to get a better look, the dolphin suddenly dived to the bottom and just as quickly returned to toss a small pebble from its snout at the woman, striking her gently on the stomach. The incident was also observed by her companions, who were amazed and delighted to see the dolphin submerge again and reappear to flip another pebble with the same accuracy at the woman's midsection. The dolphin repeated its mystifying trick a third time, then swam speedily away into the vastness of the Atlantic Ocean.

"Well," the woman told her much-amused friends, "that dolphin knows something you don't. I'm pregnant."[2]

The dolphin probably used its sensitive echolocation ability to "CAT scan" the woman's womb, although dolphins, cetologists tell us, cannot echolocate out of water. In any case, why a wild dolphin would want to establish interspecies communication with the woman by letting her know that it was aware of her condition verged on the paranormal. Similar incidents have been recorded throughout history, and modern experiments tend to confirm their basis in fact.

"According to many delphinologists," write Cochrane and Callen, "dolphins hold a fascination for pregnant human mothers. Bizarre as this may sound, there have been many reports by women, who, during pregnancy, have swum with dolphins, that the animals home in on the unborn fetus, and pay it special attention."[3]

Dolphins know when women nearby are menstruating because they quite literally taste the change in the water around them; hormones associated with human menstruation probably taste similar to dolphin estrous hormones. More mysterious is why they would be so fascinated by a menstruating human female, unless they felt an intimate bond of some kind with her.

"Women, unlike female apes, can have sexual intercourse all through their menstrual cycle," Dr. Odent states. "This is another point in common with female dolphins, who make love several times a day, all the year round, even if they are not in 'heat.'"[4]

Research involving dolphins and pregnant women about to give birth in the same water together was conducted by parapsychologists and animal behaviorists at a former Soviet naval base, now a Ukrainian spa resort, in Sevastopol. As the mother-to-be went into labor, the dolphins swam excitedly around her in circles, as they normally do when protecting swimmers from sharks. This swirling motion engendered a relaxing effect on the woman that seemed to dissipate pain and worry.

"It was magical," recalls Dr. Igor Smirnov. "The minute the dolphins appeared, all of the mother's fears and anxieties were diminished; a very serene and tranquil birth took place."[5]

She and other pregnant women giving birth told how they felt strangely soothed, as though they had been electronically massaged by rippling sonar impulses directed at them by the dolphins. They were not entirely responsible for her easy birth process because warm water itself reduces adrenalin, a hormone associated with apprehensiveness and panic; ameliorates the sense of increasing heaviness by lessening the pull of gravity; and eases her into the so-called relaxation response, a restful psychological frame of mind that minimizes the worst effects of contractions. At the very least, the human female's sympathetic birthing process in temperate water points to our aquatic ancestry.

The bottlenose dolphin, Lilly writes, "likes warm water (75–85 degrees Fahrenheit) water, and so do humans."[6] The renowned British archaeologist Jacquetta Hawkes (1910–1996) describes Man as "a basically tropical primate."[7] Lilly continues, "*Tursiops* seems to like best a temperature somewhere between the high seventies and the middle eighties. Above ninety degrees is too hot for him, and he becomes sluggish. Below seventy degrees, the water is too cold for him, and he spends all of his time keeping warm by rushing around. A comfortable temperature is apparently around eighty degrees to eighty-five degrees."[8]

The Ukrainian facility expanded its dolphin-assisted therapy from water birthing to include a miscellany of medical challenges. During its first seven years of operation, 96 percent of the more than two thousand people admitted for the treatment of hundreds of different ailments reported at least some improvement in their condition. Seventy percent of children under age seven were cured of various neuroses.

While these results are remarkable, the facility remains best known for its water birthing. Pregnant dolphins are themselves aided by midwives, older females and their assistants, who closely wait on them, and gently bring the newborns to the surface of the sea, where they take their first breath. If it is a difficult birth, the midwife pulls out the baby. During this vulnerable procedure, males of the pod protectively encircle the participants against shark attack.

At the Sevastopol spa, where pregnant women were giving birth in the water, "the dolphins sometimes participated in the process by nuzzling the newborn babies to the surface," reports interspecies communication expert Ryan DeMares. "The mothers seemed to gain a sense of protection and safety from the dolphins' presence. . . . Babies born in the presence of dolphins were said to be extraordinary children with IQs over one hundred fifty, extremely stable emotional bodies, and unusually strong physical bodies."[9]

DeMares is seconded by de Bergerac, who claims that "water babies are far less fearful and argumentative. In short, they show the characteristics of human dolphins."[10]

While cetologists have only recently begun exploring the relationship between dolphins and human mothers, inhabitants of the Nile valley appear to have recognized that peculiar intimacy five thousand years ago. Among Egypt's most important and beloved spiritual conceptions was the goddess Eset, better known today as the Greek Isis, the Queen of Heaven and ideal mother. Surviving temple paintings at Busiris, her cult center, depict her attended by dolphins as she gives birth to Horus (originally, Haru), the Sun god.

In Greek myth, the virgin Amphitrite fled the amorous advances of Poseidon by hiding out at the far edge of the known world, in the western realm of Atlas. But a dolphin found her and was so eloquent in describing the sea god's positive qualities that the creature carried her away to his submarine palace, where they were wed. In thanks, Poseidon, the Earth Shaker, placed the constellation Delphinus, the Latin name for dolphin, in the northern hemisphere of the heavens, close to the celestial equator; its ten stars—although dim—are still visible to this day. Among the offspring she bore to Poseidon were dolphins. Her myth is especially intriguing because of the dolphin's ability to persuasively communicate outside its species, prompting us to wonder how much the classical Greeks knew about such things.

After Amphitrite became Queen of the Sea, an oracle established in her name ordered the earliest settlers of the Eastern Mediterranean island of Lesbos to offer up a virgin to ensure the success of their colonial efforts. They accordingly required their unmarried daughters to draw lots for the sacrifice, and Metyma was chosen. Just before her scheduled execution, the girl was embraced by her lover, Enalos, and they plunged together into the waves, but were saved by wild dolphins.

Love is the theme that weaves these myths together between deities, humans, and dolphins. The mythic traditions of other cultures likewise demonstrate ancient awareness of personal connections between human females and dolphins. Aphrodite, the goddess of love herself, was escorted by dolphins to Cyprus after she first emerged from the sea. Ganga is the goddess after whom India's sacred river is named.

In Hindu mythology, her descent to Earth from the heavens (i.e., her birth) was heralded by dolphins; she shape-shifted into the Ganges. Ganga later rode through the Indus Valley on a *Makara* (plate 12), a beast synonymous with the Ganges River dolphin, which once existed in large schools near ceremonial centers, but has since been reduced to the level of an endangered species due to pollution. Just in the last fifteen years, the species has dwindled to a quarter of its former numbers. Perhaps no more than three thousand specimens still survive throughout the entire Ganges River system, which is unfortunate, if only because they represent just one of three freshwater dolphins alive in the world. Even so, Indian priests still speak of Ganga's "nets of gold adorned with the emblems of the dolphin."[11]

China's *baiji* (*Lipotes vexillifer*) of the Yangtze River went extinct around the turn of the twenty-first century, likewise the victim of industrial waste. Asia's remaining, if struggling, cetacean is the Indus River dolphin, in Pakistan. The animal is popularly associated throughout the Sind province with nymphomania because the first *bhulan*—a term meaning both a woman with excessive carnal desire and *Platanista gangetica minor*—was born from a human mother who had sexual intercourse with dolphins. As such, the Indus River dolphin is regarded as half human, a belief so venerable and common that present-day Sind province musicians continue to combine thematic elements of the river, love, dolphins, and *bhulans* in their ribald songs. Similar liaisons between women and dolphins occur in folkish traditions on the other side of the world.

The previous chapter discussed the boutu of the Upper Amazonian Basin's indigenous Brazilians, who are fishing partners with their "sacred dolphins." A Portuguese rendering of the term is *Encantados,* or "enchanted ones," because the Rio Tapajos Indians believe the boutu habitually seduce native women and impregnate them. Accordingly, some tribal members claim they are half-human hybrid descendants—blood relatives—of the Encantados, which are said to flirt with young women, which they occasionally abduct, and are greatly attracted to music. Boutu are also shape-shifters and will take on the good looks of young men to woo a native girl.

"Sometimes, the transformation is incomplete," writes Deena Budd at BellaOnline, "and one will see oddities, such as Encantados with human hands at the end of their flippers."[12] Her description calls to mind Dr. Thewissen's haunting photograph, mentioned in the introduction, of a dolphin embryo, its flipper translucently revealing the bones of a human hand.

Thousands of Brazilians residing along the Atlantic coast engage every February 15 in erotic veneration of Yemanja, originally a dolphin-shaped goddess of water worshiped by numerous West African tribes. Their slavery beginning in the seventeenth century brought the Yemanja cult to Brazil, where practitioners know her as Janaina, light candles in her honor on the beach, dress in blue (her color and that of the sea), "and fall into the water, where they have ecstatic communion with Janaina."[13] As a fertility figure, she assists in achieving pregnancy and sexual potency, especially if her followers, both male and female, can achieve orgasm by coupling with her near shore. Janaina is "their greatest love, their impossible desire," writes Jorge Leal Amado de Faria (1912–2001), Brazil's best-known author. In his poem "All Saints Bay," sailors are "thinking of Janaina of the long, perfumed tresses and ship-wreck eyes."[14]

The boutu's attraction to music and occasional abduction of women are well-attested attributes of dolphins. Nor is their sexual interest in human females entirely legendary. Dean Bernal cautions female visitors to his Marine Wildlife Foundation in California, that floating on their back sexually excites his dolphins.[15] As cited in chapter 6, the alleged Soviet-era attempt at raising human children with dolphins had to be terminated when the animals took too much interest in the girl with the onset of her first menstrual cycle. Although most of their attention was focused on her, two or three of the mature male dolphins allegedly made sexual advances to the boy as well.

"Menstruating women are advised not to swim with dolphins," warns Cochrane and Callen, "as this state can sexually arouse the males. . . . There have also been occasions when dolphins have enticed or towed female swimmers right out to sea, as if attempting to 'kidnap,' which can be unnerving."[16] The animals' sexual attraction to women implies an earlier, closer relationship between humans and dolphins perhaps going back millions of years ago to a common, evolutionary path of some kind.

This behavior explains the symbolism of certain Classical Era coins, such as the Thracian specimen from around 300 BCE, depicting the god of sexual attraction, Eros, riding the back of a dolphin. Throughout Greek myth and vase painting, the supreme love goddess, Aphrodite, was escorted by dolphins, which went on to attend her Roman incarnation, Venus.

Something in the tales of the Hindu bhulan and Brazilian boutu began to materialize during early 1964, at Dr. John Lilly's Communication Research Institute on St. Thomas in the Virgin Islands, where a custom-made delphinarium was the center for the investigation of interspecies communication. Twenty-year-old assistant researcher Margaret Howe Lovatt began living with a six-year-old bottlenose dolphin named Peter for twenty-four hours a day, six days a week, over a twelve-month period, in the hope she could teach him to understand and speak English in much the same way a child learns language from its mother. While Peter could, with difficulty and after many hours of instruction, vocalize a few words, or their approximation, that he actually understood their meaning was never unequivocally established.

Dolphins are skilled at mimicry, but so are parrots and myna birds, and dolphins are less anatomically disposed to the intelligible pronunciation of words. Nevertheless, meaningful exchanges with our seaborne cousins have already taken place through the unspoken medium of mutually sympathetic emotion. But the communicative use of sentiment, or passion, is an unstable, even volatile technique.

During the long, intensive period of Lovatt's persistent efforts at getting Peter to speak English, their relationship grew increasingly close. He eventually expressed persistent interest in her body, so much so, she obliged her cetacean friend by relieving his urges manually. "It wasn't sexual on my part," she later insisted. "Sensuous perhaps."[17]

Dr. Lilly, her boss at the St. Thomas delphinarium, had been chiefly interested in determining the most direct and effective means of dolphin contact. "One such area is a common human communication path," he wrote. "This is the path of the man and woman in love, making love. Their best form of exchange and communication is in their sexual activities. Can sexual activities be used for communication across the interspecies barrier? On the delphinic side, the answer would probably be yes."[18] Peter, at any rate, would have doubtless agreed.

When, after the termination of Lovatt's mostly fruitless experiment, he was transferred to another facility, Peter never saw her again, and missed the woman so terribly, he grew increasingly lethargic, slipped into a deep depression, and stopped breathing, the preferred suicide method among dolphins. They lack our automatic respiratory mechanism, which would cause them to drown, if ever they passed out under water from head trauma or a high fever. Whenever suffering ailments or accidents sufficiently serious to render them unconscious, they stop breathing to keep water out of their lungs and depend of their fellow pod members to push them to the surface, where they may begin to breathe again.

"An animal that was being delivered to an oceanarium," Dr. Lilly writes, "struck his head on the side of the pool, as he was being let into it. He was knocked unconscious and dropped to the bottom. The other dolphins pushed him to the surface, and held him there until he began to breathe again."[19]

Peter was neither ill nor the victim of a blow to the head, but died of a broken heart. Similar accounts from ancient Greece likewise tell of loving relationships between humans and dolphins, which sometimes killed themselves when their interspecies affairs broke up. As women grow older, however, male dolphins are less erotically attracted to them, as the following two examples illustrate.

In 1949, the middle-aged wife of a lawyer was swept off a Florida beach into a series of overwhelming rollers and began to drown. "Someone pushed me violently from behind, and I landed on the beach with my nose in the sand. When I was able to do so, there was no one near me, but in the water, twenty feet from the shore, a dolphin was swimming and jumping in circles," she told *Natural History* magazine. "A man came running over to me. He said, when he arrived, that I looked like a corpse, and that a dolphin had pushed me back to shore."[20]

On February 29, 1960, another Floridian, Yvonne Bliss, fell from a ship into the Old Bahama Channel, a strait off the northern coast of Cuba and south of the Great Bahama Bank, approximately one hundred miles long and fifteen miles wide. Because she fell into this vast abyss late at night, no one aboard noticed that the fifty-year-old woman was missing. All she could do, in her desperation, was swim to stay alive, not an easy task amid high waves that incessantly slapped her face and forced seawater down her throat. Terrified, with no sense of direction, and nearing the end of her strength, Yvonne was doomed, until a dolphin suddenly appeared to act as her escort.

"Later," she said, "he swam behind me and placed himself on my right. I swerved to make room for him. I understood only later that if the dolphin had not helped me, I would have continued to drift in the current toward the deepest, roughest waters. In fact, the dolphin guided me toward the shallowest part. Soon, my feet touched bottom. When I arrived on dry land, my rescuer darted off like an arrow."[21]

These two incidents show that delphine interest in women is not entirely sexual. After women have passed the zenith of their reproductive years, they are increasingly regarded by dolphins less as erotic objects and more as human beings to befriend, or, if need be, save from distress in the water. No other mammal on land or in the sea is as attracted to human females, perhaps because the dolphins recognize their kinship with us and understand that it may be closer than we realize or are prepared to admit. Occasionally that attraction is reciprocal, lending some substance to the closeness of such a relationship, which is still dramatized by mythic accounts of the bhulan, boutu, and Encantado.

But all myths that take root and are carried through many successive generations of a people have at their core some fundamental truth; if they didn't, they would lack the power to endure over time. Accordingly, there might be at least a kernel of biological fact empowering folk fantasies of the enchanted ones, their human lovers, and their hybrid children.

# 17
## Dolphins and Children

*There's a tale that they tell of a dolphin, and a boy made of gold. With the shells and the pearls in the deep, he has lain many years fast asleep. What they tell of the boy on a dolphin, who can say if it's true?*

FROM THE TITLE SONG OF THE 1957 FILM
*BOY ON THE DOLPHIN*

Dolphins relate differently to men and women. Their reaction to children is likewise singular. Several representative incidents from the ancient world have been described in previous chapters, but many more were recorded throughout classical antiquity. Around the turn of the third century CE, a Greek rhetorician, Athenaeus Naucratita, and the Roman writer Claudius Aelianus told of a child named Dionysios, who befriended a wild dolphin so much so that it bore him far across the sea. The pair would often be gone for the better part of a day before returning by sundown. The youth never disclosed where they went or what they experienced together.

At Hippo Diarrhytus, a Roman colony in Tunis, a lad who swam out too far from the north coast of Africa was saved by a dolphin. It thereafter played with the other children, but reserved special affection for the boy who had needed rescue, allowing only him to ride on its back. "What is also remarkable," writes Pliny the Elder, "another dolphin accompanied this one as an onlooker and escort. It did none of the same things and submitted to none of the same familiarities; it merely conducted the other one to and fro, as the other boys did with their companion."[1]

One hundred years later, an orphaned baby dolphin was adopted by an elderly couple and their young son at a harbor near Poroselene, in the Eastern Mediterranean, off the island of Lesbos. As the boy and dolphin grew up together, they increasingly resembled each other in their mannerisms and attitudes, and intimate communication passed effortlessly between them. "I saw the dolphin obeying all his commands," reports Pausanias, "and carrying him wherever he wanted to ride."[2]

The mature dolphin was also friendly toward strangers, whose acts of kindness it repaid by presenting them with gifts of fish. Incidents such as these led Aristotle to observe that "small boys and dolphins develop mutual, passionate attachments."[3]

Despite the proliferation of these accounts, often compiled by some of the most esteemed writers in the Greco-Roman world, they are still discounted as merely legendary by many if not most scholars today, despite parallel encounters in modern times. An enlightening example belongs to Ashley, the thirteen-year-old son of Horace Dobbs. Both were in the water together off the Isle of Man, located in the Irish Sea between Britain and Ireland. A wild dolphin burst from the surface to execute a perfect jump high over the teenager, dove back into the sea, and then came up directly beneath him.

"I saw Ashley rise slowly out of the water with his legs astride the head of the dolphin," his father remembers. "At first, the boy looked slightly scared and incredulous. Then he broke into a grin and held both arms aloft, like a footballer who has just scored a goal. . . . Ashley was perfectly balanced on the dolphin's head. The dolphin, with Ashley riding like a jockey, circled the harbor and came back alongside me, before suddenly diving to leave the boy once again floating on the surface."[4]

His experience was something straight out of the pages of Pliny or Pausanias, and "proved that the Greeks and Romans had not written nonsense," writes Sténuit in describing a similar incident.[5] Nor was it unique. According to the Jakarta newspaper, *Berita Buana,* eleven-year-old Ace Walandau and his two younger brothers were thrown overboard by their father into the Java Sea when the ferry on which they were traveling from London to Sulawesi caught fire on January 25, 1981.

The 375-foot *Tampomas II* sank two days later, drowning 431 of its 1,442 passengers, including the Walandau parents. Their sons, unable to swim, were likewise doomed, until intercepted by several dolphins. The animals alternately carried and pushed them along toward a lifeboat, where they were pulled aboard, exhausted, but alive. Revealingly perhaps, the dolphins did not come to the aid of any adult survivors in the water, but only rescued the three boys. Their preferential treatment hinted at dolphins' special relationship with children.

Another boy unable to swim fell from his father's boat into the Adriatic Sea in August 2000. The fourteen-year-old Davide Ceci was drowning and within minutes of death just as a dolphin abruptly pushed him to the surface.

"When I realized it was Filippo pushing me," recalls Ceci, "I grabbed on to him." Filippo was the popular name of a wild dolphin seen cavorting in the waters off the town of Manfredonia, in southeastern Italy, for the previous two years. The dolphin carried Davide directly to his boat, enabling the youth's father, Emanuele, who was unaware that his son had fallen overboard, to pull him safely on deck. Davide's mother called Filippo a hero, adding "It seems impossible that an animal could have done something like that, to feel the instinct for saving a human life."[6]

Twenty years earlier, Nick Christides was surfing off Cocos Island, in the middle of the Indian Ocean, when he was suddenly swept off his board by a large wave, then carried out to sea in the grip of strong currents. Although the boy's friends witnessed his accident and immediately raised the alarm, all efforts to find him were frustrated by high winds and steep waves. His situation worsened when he drifted into shark-invested waters. But before the predators could attack, they were warded off by a dolphin, which stayed close to Nick for the next four hours, until he was lifted into a rescue boat that had been directed to his position by an American antisubmarine aircraft flying out of Cocos Island.

In February 1989, a teenager surfing at Evans Head, south of the town of Ballina, New South Wales, Australia, was badly bitten by a large shark. The monster tore a foot-long gash in Adam Maguire's right thigh and virtually destroyed his board with the same bite "in a perfect jaw shape, and the mouthful of foam and fiberglass momentarily stopped the onslaught. Then two dolphins came up underneath me, and my friends yelled for me to get back on my board. I just stumbled back to the beach and lay there, waiting for help. The dolphins disappeared in the same direction as the shark. I'm sure they saved my life."[7]

Such rescues are still reported in the present century and can have life-changing, as well as life-saving, consequences. In February 2014, an eleven-year-old boy from Dallas, Texas, fell into the sea near Cancun, off the coast of Mexico's Yucatan Peninsula, where his family was on a fishing trip. Jimmy Lee was suddenly in the water with a school of sharks feeding on leftovers other vacationers had thrown overboard for bait. Before the sharks could reach him, they were intercepted by several dolphins, which kept them away long enough for the youngster to swim to and grasp a life preserver thrown by his uncle, who hauled him back to the boat.

"The dolphins saved my baby!" exclaimed his grateful father. "It was a really weird thing to see," Jimmy remembered. "It's like the dolphins knew I was in trouble, and came to help me. I want to study veterinary sciences when I grow up, so I can help heal the dolphins that saved my own life."[8]

Boys are mentioned more often than girls in these stories of close interaction with dolphins. Historical bias is cited by some investigators as the cause, but present-day reports are hardly less weighted in favor of male children.

Figure 17.1. Actor Luke Halpin with television's Flipper, 1964.

"People who spend a lot of time with friendly dolphins," write Cochrane and Callen, "invariably say that the creatures are prone to favoritism" extended to individuals of either sex or any age, but mostly toward the human male.[9] The accounts that do include girls are, admittedly, modern, but do not differ substantially from the accounts with boys, until the females begin to sexually mature.

An illustrative case concerns Sally Stone, who had just turned thirteen years old in the summer of 1945, when vacationing on Long Island Sound, New York. While being pulled through the water behind a sailboat, she was joined by six dolphins, which allowed the child to touch them and play with them until the boat returned to port that evening. The next morning, they were waiting for her in the same spot, and the friends resumed their fun. As these daily encounters continued throughout the season, five dolphins often swam on either side of her, with one in the lead, as though guiding them all somehow. Not surprisingly, Sally became a superior swimmer. But her dolphin companions kept urging her to swim faster and deeper, to jump and dive. Each day, as the Sun set on their aquatic merrymaking, the dolphins invariably escorted the vessel that carried her back to port, where, because of the heavy boat traffic, no dolphin had ever been seen before. Sally's unusual vacation came to a close with the end of summer, and she went home.

Autumn descended on the world. Winter was replaced by spring. A new summer arrived, and a now fourteen-year-old Miss Stone returned to Long Island Sound. Waiting for her were the same half-dozen dolphins just where she left them the previous September. As before, they frolicked together amid the chilly Atlantic waves, the girl holding onto the dorsal fin of one of her friends while he pulled her along slowly in a wide circle and his companions executed high jumps over them.

But as the weeks progressed, subtle changes occurred in the dolphins' attitude, if not behavior. They "gave her many love taps," writes Sténuit. "Becoming more and more intimate, girl and dolphins exchanged embraces and caresses."[10] These indications of affection continued to blossom as the summer of 1946 drew to a close, and Sally wisely said good-bye to her beloved companions for the last time. Her dolphin encounters came to the attention of a prominent biologist, John Clark, who, years later, urged the young woman to write about them.

Dolphins have favored other female children, such as the partiality displayed toward a young South African girl in 1953 near Capetown at Fish Hoek, by a pair of Indian Ocean bottlenose dolphins. Three years later, teenager Jill Baker was singled out for special affection by Opo, New Zealand's Opononi beach dolphin, described in chapter 15. Even so, such examples have always been outnumbered by male child versions. Precisely why is unclear, but a root cause must lie in the primeval psyche of a man's childhood. Only something that fundamental can explain the consistency of boy-dolphin relations in numerous disparate cultures over the millennia. Human female youngsters certainly love dolphins, who love them in return, but their mystical and venerable "special friendships" are instead typically with horses.

The boy-on-a-dolphin theme—not girl-on-a-dolphin—is predominant, although not exclusive, throughout classical myth, art, and coinage and occurs for reasons other than presumed male prejudice. Indeed, fully half the Greek pantheon is made up of supernaturally powerful female figures, so sexism can be ruled out as a reason for the accounts of encounters with wild dolphins skewing toward boys. Boys riding dolphins were commonly depicted in Greco-Roman art, particularly statuary and mosaics. This popular theme is exemplified in Phaenon, a handsome lad formed by the titan Prometheus and imbued with life to distract Zeus from meddling in the creation of *Homo sapiens*. Fulfilling his purpose, Phaenon sped across the sea on the back of a dolphin with the king of the Olympian gods in amorous pursuit, enabling Prometheus to steal heavenly fire, which, defying Zeus's orders, he bestowed upon Mankind.

Investigating the connection between all children and dolphins, Miller, citing the research of transformational counselor Janet Colli, says "Children are in an alpha state until they are around six years old, which explains why the dolphins are so drawn to them at petting tanks and in the wild. They are on the same wave length."[11] Perhaps so, but that does not explain why older children are at least as well favored by dolphins. Cochrane and Callen speculate that they "can relate better to children's high-pitched voices and playful nature. Children are also generally more intuitive and sensitive, and less manipulative, than most adults, which may explain why dolphins enjoy their company."[12]

Both children and dolphins live to play, and the sensitive cetaceans undoubtedly recognize that both boys and girls are generally innocent creatures without guile, naturally harmless and friendly, qualities they themselves embody. Children want nothing from them but their companionship. But among these obvious bonds may be the single most significant and potent common denominator they share: dolphins are especially attracted to children because they communicate with them—perhaps through thought transference in some instances, and far less often, through sound production, like the autistic child who accurately repeated the dolphins' complicated audio patterns, as mentioned in chapter 6.

Reciprocal transmission of information between children and dolphins is probably less *tele*pathic than *em*pathic—the sensitivity to and understanding of emotional states. As the boy matures into manhood, adult society requires that he suppress, sublimate, or otherwise control his emotions, which are henceforth expressed no longer by the free-flowing subconscious mind, but by deliberate acts of conscious thought in the formation of words. The further he undertakes this self-mastery or self-regulation, the further he distances himself from dolphins, whose communication has less to do with the literal interpretation of symbolic sounds than the shared empathy they express.

As in the case of Sally Stone, dolphins appear to sometimes initiate children into their cetacean mysteries, urging them to become more and more delphine, invitations to which boys and girls readily respond. Is there an interspecies agenda at work here? Are the dolphins interested in converting us to their point of view through our empathic offspring, or inviting us to quit the land, as we have done several times before, and join (or reunite) with them in the sea as fellow aquatic mammals?

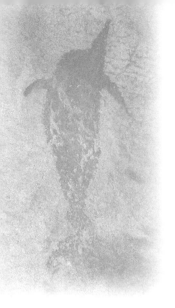

# 18

# Dolphin Connections with Cats, Dogs, and Whales

*And when the day comes that we can communicate intelligently with dolphins, they may introduce us to the concept of survival without aggression, and the true joy of living, which at present eludes us. In that circumstance, what they have to teach us would be infinitely more valuable than anything we could offer them in exchange.*

HORACE DOBBS

Sammy is the name of our cat. When Laura and I selected him from an area shelter in February 2005, we took him for a breed known as Maine coon. A few weeks later, however, we were casually paging through a newly released book about house pets and saw a photograph of a Sammy look-alike. But its caption identified the animal as a Norsk *skogkatt*, or Norwegian forest, occasionally referred to—for reasons described below—as the "mystical Norwegian forest cat."

In any case, confusing him with a Maine coon, which he closely resembles, was understandable because his ancestors jumped ship after Vikings landed a thousand years ago in Vinland—the state of Maine—

on the Eastern Seaboard of North America. Good mousers were important crewmembers aboard transatlantic longships, scouring the holds of destructive, disease-carrying vermin. Once ashore, the Norse cats mated with an unknown extinct breed, resulting in today's Maine coon. The skogkatt itself came close to extinction during World War II, was mostly unknown outside Norway until the 1970s, and was only recognized by the American Cat Fanciers Association in 1994. Today, the breed, though experiencing some popularity in New England, is still generally unknown elsewhere in the United States.

How such a rare animal found his way into a Minnesota shelter around the turn of the twenty-first century is a story only Sammy knows. His "mystical" attribution seemed no less uncertain and more apocryphal, until Laura found him hanging by his claws high on the sheer face of our basement wall. Earlier, I had been somewhat astounded to see him climb straight up the perfectly vertical plane of a smooth stone rampart. This and other unusual behaviors have earned his kind the sobriquet "Fairy Cat," as sometimes appears in old Norwegian folk stories that ascribe the skogkatt with the singular ability to scale high cliffs in search of nesting birds, together with additional talents, not all of them earthbound. I can personally testify to at least some of them, having known Sammy for more than ten years now.

On a single occasion only, after sundown one summer evening, he suddenly and excitedly demanded that the front door be opened. He flew outside without pausing, as usual, at the threshold, dashed down the front steps, and shot around the eastern side of the house. By the time I caught up with him, he was staring fixedly at something on the sidewalk. In the shadows, I could make out what appeared to be a small pile of writhing humps. On closer inspection, they belonged to a little snake never seen there before or since. Back in the house, Sammy's normal physical senses had been cut off from the outside world. He could have neither seen nor smelled the creature, and even his superb hearing ability would not have detected the smooth motion of a serpent gliding slowly across the sidewalk.

Skeptics may dismiss such anecdotal episodes as unrevealing, but anyone who lives on intimate terms with an animal for an extended period can integrate such events into the broader context of the pet's personality. While these incidents do not pass muster for strict upholders of the scientific method, they nevertheless depend upon accurate observations. I can only conclude, therefore, that Sammy accessed a form of extrasensory perception to determine the presence and whereabouts of the snake, which was otherwise unknown to him.

More remarkable than Sammy's talents at remote viewing is his concept of time, as demonstrated during our outdoor excursions. He is very sensible about them, does not run off, stays fairly close to me and mostly out of mischief, and therefore does not require a leash. If I take along some writing that needs work, listen to music on my portable player, or read, we could spend hours together "outside," a word he certainly knows. More often, my time is limited, and our walks may go on for ten or twenty minutes, though we usually take several each day.

It was at the outset of one of our first outdoor jaunts that I glanced at my watch and made a mental note to myself: "We'll go back inside the house at two thirty." For the next half hour, Sammy went about his usual business of sniffing the air, chomping grass, urinating on a territorial bush, exploring a suspicious hole in the yard, making his customary inspection of the back patio, chasing a squirrel, stalking a mole, and observing bugs and birds from a favorite vantage point. In the midst of these commonplace feline pursuits, he paused for a moment and a puzzled expression came over his face, as though he were trying to remember something, then he bolted up the front steps and demanded to be let in the door. My watch read precisely two thirty.

What first seemed a trifling coincidence progressively grew into something more significant. Over the subsequent years of our friendship, we shared and continue to share—weather permitting—daily kitty walks, which may take place from early morning to dusk, but never at the same hour. Any potential visual clues from me—conscious or not—Sammy may pick up seem unlikely, due to the entirely random

Figure 18.1. Sammy, the mystical Norwegian forest cat.
Photograph by the author.

nature of these outings. Engaged as I am in my own activity during our walks, I usually forget about the specific time I predetermined for their conclusion. Yet, he abruptly terminates about 65 percent of the walks at the explicit instant I mentally programmed before we set out. For example, in three consecutive walks, he concluded each one at the appointed minute. Moreover, whenever I mentally will him to come in from the outdoors, without having scheduled any prior cut-off, he never responds.

What could a cat possibly know about time? Even if Sammy does indeed read my mind, the hour or minute I set inside my head to end our walk is surely far beyond the limits of his feline intellect to grasp. Yet, the timeliness of his behavior is repeatedly—if not invariably—demonstrable. What it suggests is certainly outside our current understanding of interspecies communication.

As mentioned previously, Sheldrake proposes a theory in which members of a particular group are linked by self-organizing energy fields that contain a unique collective memory. These morphic fields shape patterns of behavior or adaptation. Applying his hypothesis to the animal kingdom, Sheldrake maintains that animals can communicate telepathically among themselves and with us through emotional bonding. Hence, morphic fields are channels for extrasensory perception.[1] Even if his view is correct, it may only form the basis for a greater paranormal mystery that, incredible as it might seem, connects cats with dolphins.

Since May 2012, about seven million viewers have watched a one-minute, forty-nine-second YouTube video taken in 1997 at the Theater of the Sea, a marine animal park in Islamorada, Florida.[2] It shows two bottlenose dolphins, named Shiloh and Thunder, engaging Arthur, a family cat, which, to all appearances, is thoroughly enchanted with them. There is much chummy interplay between feline and cetaceans, as the former continuously paws and nuzzles the latters' snouts. Shiloh and Thunder respond by repeatedly offering their sensitive rostrums for affection and gently tap the cat on the top of its head—remarkably, given the physical disparities between a thirteen-inch-long, eight-pound, water-hating cat and thirteen-foot-long, fourteen-hundred-pound dolphins.

One might expect Arthur to have been utterly horrified by the mere sight of such beasts, while the dolphins, for their part, should have little or no interest in the tiny landlubber. Their gentle care in petting the cat's head is astonishing. When they suddenly vanish, Arthur nervously paces back and forth, attentively searching the surface of the water for his absent friends. When they reappear, he rushes back across the gangplank to greet them again with undiminished affection.

The animals were less interested in exploring the differences in their species than in greeting each other, as though resuming a former acquaintance. They seemed to recognize each other from the start. The cat knew at once that the dolphins were not only harmless, but exceptionally desirable companions, while Shiloh and Thunder quite obviously loved Arthur. It is inexplicable that these wildly divergent species should find a commonality between themselves, much less such intimate rapport. Throughout their extraordinary encounter, eye contact was virtually unbroken.

Given dolphins' renowned telepathic abilities, as discussed in previous chapters, and those demonstrated by Sammy—who is hardly unique; many cat owners experience telepathic connections with their pets—thought transference appears to have been the medium that fashioned their amiable relationship. But what kind of information passed between them? Certainly not words, but perhaps some form of emotional knowing associated with mental imagery. Nor was the video-recorded meeting between house cat and wild dolphins a freak incident. Such unlikely get-togethers have been observed by sailors over thousands of years of seafaring, whenever their feline shipmates were visited by dolphins. Fundamentally different from each other as these animals might seem, both are notable for their curiosity, acute perception, and quick awareness, which may provide the basis for their commonality.

Perhaps the same paranormal connections account for equally close relations dolphins enjoy with dogs, likewise famous for their telepathic attributes. Sheldrake has done more than anyone to establish these canine capabilities in his highly credible and convincing book *Dogs That Know When Their Owners Are Coming Home.*[3] It was the result of five years of extensive research, during which he surveyed or interviewed more than one thousand pet owners, dog trainers, veterinarians, zookeepers, blind people with guide dogs, and pet-shop proprietors. Combining their observations with controlled testing procedures, Sheldrake made a thoroughly scientific, exceptionally plausible case for morphic fields and interspecies ESP, which appear to be the basis for mutual fondness between dolphins and dogs. Evidence of their natural friendship is most readily accessible in a number of social media presentations made by ordinary persons fortunate enough to capture the animals swimming and playing together on camera.

Although a variety of breeds appear in different circumstances, all are invariably overjoyed at first sight of the dolphins and unhesitatingly jump into the water to be with them. From the surface, dolphins are often indistinguishable from sharks, and even professional lifeguards usually need a moment or two to differentiate between them. No dogs have ever been known to deliberately swim with sharks, yet dogs properly identify dolphins instantaneously, indicating that dogs possess some form of extrasensory recognition. Although the relationship involves no conceivable advantage to benefit either species, they obviously enjoy each other's company. Even a dog brought inside a public aquarium exhibits intense interest in dolphins swimming behind their glass partition, where they make deliberate eye contact with the dog and appear similarly enthusiastic.

A particularly remarkable YouTube video documents a small gray dog named Joker that began showing up on his own around 2009 at Dolphin Reef, a ten-thousand-square-meter, horseshoe-shaped reef on the Red Sea, off the south coast of Eilat in Israel. Every morning, Joker used to stroll down the pier to gaze at dolphins cavorting near shore.

"He would sit there for hours, staring at the dolphins and, of course, the dolphins, being curious creatures themselves," according to a reporter for the Canine Club LA, "found him very interesting. After gaining some confidence, he decided to take the big plunge and join the dolphins in the water. From then on, Joker . . . decided to swim with them every day. . . . He comes to Dolphin Reef by foot each day from town, which is a few kilometers away, and spends the day at Dolphin Reef. When it's time to go home, he usually hitches a ride with one of the workers. . . . When one of the workers he recognizes comes up the stairway towards the parking lot, he joins him, and once the car doors open, he jumps in, and with a look, 'are you ready to go?'"[4]

Joker apparently feels such a compelling affinity for the dolphins that he seeks them out to spend most of his waking hours in their company, although precisely what benefit he derives from them is unknown.

In another example, after a wild female dolphin adopted Mr. and Mrs. Ashbury and their two small daughters, beginning in May 1971, Dolly, as she was locally known, enjoyed towing Puggy, the family dog, in a small plastic boat through the canals surrounding their home at the Florida Keys.

The obvious affinity between canines and cetaceans may at least partially lie in a dog's extraordinary ability to detect sounds far beyond the range of human hearing. "There have been times aboard *Calypso* [Jacques Cousteau's famous research vessel] when the sounds made by the dolphins were audible only to Ulysses, our dog. If Ulysses understood what the dolphins said, he did not tell us," Cousteau reports.[5] But if he did understand them, then something of a basis for their friendship may be understood.

Bottlenose dolphins, as mentioned above, hear sound frequencies up to 170 kilohertz, or 170,000 vibrations per second, by far the highest auditory sensitivity of any animal on Earth. Spotted dolphins may be marginally more sensitive. Dogs hear up to 44 kilohertz, while cats hear better still at 79 kilohertz. Their audio receptivity, far beyond the upper limits of human hearing, which lies between 14 and 16 kilohertz, would enable them to detect a far broader range of dolphin sounds, which they may even be able to understand. Almost certainly, if we were able to hear as many dolphin sounds as dogs and cats, progress in learning how to communicate with the cetaceans would advance beyond current scientific levels.

Another YouTube video documents a "hotel dog" at Tory Island Harbour in Ireland. The hotel dog, Ben, a yellow Labrador, trots down to the bay virtually every day to swim and play with Dukey, as local residents refer to a wild bottlenose dolphin that favors the coast.[6]

Writing for the National Geographic Society, Elizabeth Carney describes another Labrador: "It was almost like the dolphins knew that Cloud was their friend. The dolphins followed Cloud's every move. As Cloud walked up the dock, they swam along beside her in the water. When she turned back, they were still right beside her. Cloud seemed as interested in the dolphins, as they were in her. She stayed and watched them play for hours."[7]

Labradors may have a closer relationship with dolphins than other dogs because of their unique capabilities. Carney tells how Labradors are the preferred breed in rescuing distressed or endangered dolphins, pointing out that Labradors have 220 million olfactory cells, forty times more than humans, while the area of the dog's brain used to decode smells is twice as large as ours. This means that Labradors are ten thousand times better than humans at sorting out odors, so much so, they are even able to smell objects that are slightly under water.

Using her prodigious sniffer, Cloud found two ailing dolphins that had been out of sight, beneath the surface of the sea. Earlier, while in training at a marine park, her trainers discovered that she was able to distinguish between sick and healthy dolphins; a talent that enabled her to find half a dozen lost and ailing dolphins and whales, including a stranded pilot whale half a mile away.

While dolphins can smell nothing, because olfactory sensitivity does not function under water, they do share some provocative commonalities with Labradors. Both assist people suffering from autism; the dogs "help them improve social interactions and relationships, expand verbal and nonverbal communication, teach life skills, increase interest in activities, and decrease stress within the family."[8]

Like the dolphins' predecessors, Labrador ancestors passed through an aquatic phase, as evidenced by their modern descendants' oily, water-resistant coat and webbed paws. Perhaps at some stage, their evolutionary paths crossed at sea, an ancient parallel they still remember. If, as Professor Opit writes, "dolphins evolved from dog-like carnivores," then their common origins might be the root of cetacean-canine familiarity, in lieu of our proposition for a crossing of evolutionary paths between dolphin and human ancestors.[9]

In any case, the dolphins give as good as they get, returning the favor of rescuing dogs in trouble. In March 2013, Ramsay, a five-year-old cocker spaniel was pulled out to sea by rough tides at the beach in Carrickalinga, Australia. When his owner attempted to save him, she too was engulfed. "I just remember falling," explains Lynn Gitsham, a retired policewoman, "and I'm in the water, and the waves were just pounding me up against the rocks, and I could see him out there trying to get back in. I remember going under, and, coming back up, I saw a fin, and I saw him, and thought 'Oh great, it's a shark.' And then I saw another fin. Then I realized they were dolphins. These dolphins just formed this horseshoe and were guiding [Ramsay] in, pushing him in." The dolphins herded Gitsham and her dog to the safety of the shore, then swam away.[10]

On February 23, 2011, Cindy Burnett's eleven-year-old Doberman, Turbo, disappeared from their home on South Buchanan Avenue in Marco Island, Florida. Unbeknownst to anyone, Turbo had fallen into a nearby shallow canal from which he was unable to extricate himself. For the next fifteen hours, he was buoyed to the surface by several dolphins, which alerted a neighbor to Turbo's plight after daybreak by repeatedly splashing the water. "She heard a big commotion from the dolphins in the canal, and went out to see why they were so excited," writes Burnett. "That's when she saw Turbo."[11]

"Let's Be Friends" is the title of a true-life reenactment of a dog that fell off the stern of a pleasure boat into the Aegean Sea, off the Greek peninsula, and was about to be attacked by sharks, but was saved by a dolphin who carried the dog back to its vessel. This popular YouTube video is actually representative of numerous such rescues reported over time and still being documented.[12]

Figure 18.2. A still frame from the video "Let's Be Friends."

Although whales are fellow cetaceans, their differences from dolphins are nonetheless significant. Despite these important dissimilarities, whales in distress are often aided by dolphins. On March 10, 2008, two pygmy sperm whales—a female and her calf—were stranded on New Zealand's Mahia Beach. As Robson explains, "they were receiving conflicting readings on their sonar due to the maze of banks and channels in the harbor."[13]

After rescuers tried and failed to refloat them four times, Department of Conservation officers were preparing to euthanize the pair when a bottlenose dolphin familiar to local residents as Moko appeared. He vocalized at the whales, then led them 660 feet along a sandbar into the open sea.

Another incident occurred in New Zealand during September 1983, on Tokerau Beach, Doubtless Bay, Northland, where dozens of pilot whales ran aground during ebb tide. Volunteer efforts to keep the whales alive by sponging their skin and calming them until the tide came back in did little to help. Then a pod of dolphins arrived. They swam into the shallows, putting themselves at risk, and herded the pilot whales out to deep water, saving seventy-six of eighty whales. Five years earlier, a similar incident on a scale twice as large occurred at Whangarei harbor, in the northern part of North Island, New Zealand "a favorite place for whale strandings," according to Robson, "because of the shape of its estuary and the false readings this gives on the whale sonar."[14]

The sheer number of disoriented pilot whales—about 150 of them—trying to come ashore overwhelmed local rescue efforts, until a pod of dolphins came to aid.

[They] swam in amongst the whales and led them into a deeper channel, which led to an exit from the harbor. A helicopter was hovering overhead, and from there it was clear that the dolphins were leading the whales to the open sea. Some dolphins took the lead positions out in front, while others swam among the distressed whales. When set nets barred the way to freedom, the lead dolphins guided the herd around the end of the nets. When the deep channel leading to the harbor mouth was reached, the dolphins broke away. . . . The many people who took part in the rescue were adamant that the dolphins communicated continuously with the whales, and that some form of understanding and communication passed between dolphins and humans, most of whom were Fisheries Officers.[15]

This joint species operation in 1978 was the first known instance of dolphins coming to the aid of other cetaceans in the wild. It was preceded, however, by an example of intercetacean compassion and communication observed under controlled circumstances.

During the late 1960s, Bimbo, an eighteen-foot pilot whale at Florida's Marine Studio Oceanarium, stopped eating and began acting aggressively toward smaller dolphins. As a form of discipline, his trainers moved him into a small solitary tank, then drained its water level to just three feet. "Bimbo, now stranded, began to whistle piteously," writes Regina Blackstock, an Oceanarium employee at the time. "Soon, all the dolphins gathered around and comforted him with conversation, which consisted of whistles, chirps, and the usual dolphinese sounds. When the tank was again refilled, Bimbo's manners improved immediately."[16]

Nor do whales lack a sense of compassion for their fellow cetaceans. For eight days in January 2013, reports *National Geographic,* researchers observed an untypical pod of sperm whales in the vicinity of the Azores Islands, about one thousand miles from Lisbon, Portugal. In their company was a lone bottlenose dolphin with an S-shaped spinal deformity. Dolphins practice infanticide on offspring born with serious physical defects, although occasionally they are driven off instead. Apparently, one of these banished aberrations had been welcomed by a group of compassionate whales, which allowed it to travel, forage, and play with adults and their calves. When the deformed dolphin showed affection by rubbing itself against the whales, they sometimes returned the gesture.[17]

Similarly mixed cooperation, while unusual, is known to occur. In 1957, when an exhausted, frightened, and newly arrived porpoise at California's Marineland of the Pacific began emitting distress cries, it was immediately supported and comforted by a mixed group of Atlantic *Tursiops* and Pacific striped dolphins, "animals of different species and even genera," reports Lilly.[18]

During 1962, a pilot whale became badly entangled in the line of a harpoon fired into its side. "The pilot whale then began to cry as loudly as he could," states Jacques Cousteau. "Almost immediately, two other whales arrived and positioned themselves one on each side of the wounded whale. They moved their bodies against his, and, thus supported, the whale was able to free himself to swim away."[19]

Although less often, porpoises have also saved the lives of other mammals, including humans, most famously Dick Van Dyke in 2010. The eighty-four-year-old television celebrity fell asleep on an inflatable float and describes, "[I] woke up out of sight of land. I started paddling with the swells, and I started seeing fins swimming around me, and I thought, 'I'm dead!' They turned out to be porpoises, and they pushed me all the way to shore. I'm not kidding."[20]

It is not clear if Mr. Van Dyke correctly distinguished between dolphins and porpoises. In any case, it is more common to observe dolphins assisting other dolphins. According to Sténuit:

> The basic first-aid technique consists of supporting on the surface a wounded or unconscious member of the group to enable him to breathe. A single dolphin, if there is only one around, will support the injured one from beneath; if there are two, each puts one flipper under a flipper of the wounded, and will continue to hold him afloat for days at a time if necessary, working a shift system, if numbers permit, in relays of two. This system has been observed in operation hundreds of times among all species of cetaceans. They will do it not only for their own kind, but even for members of different species from different oceans.[21]

Using this method, ministering dolphins have been known to support an ailing fellow pod member "for miles with its blow-hole above the surface of the water, so that it can breathe," according to Cochrane and Callen.[22] In most species, injured animals are quickly left behind by their fellows, while helping behavior manifests only among highly intelligent and very social animals.

A case in point was observed by researchers from the Cetacean Research Institute in Ulsan, South Korea, who were following a large pod of about four hundred long-beaked common dolphins (*Delphinus capensis*) through the Sea of Japan in June 2008. The Koreans noticed about a dozen dolphins crowding around a female that was wriggling and tipping from side to side, sometimes turning upside down, because its pectoral flippers were apparently paralyzed.

The other dolphins often dove beneath their injured companion to support her from below, until, after about half an hour, they formed themselves into a living raft of their own bodies, swimming packed in, side by side, with the injured female on their backs. By keeping the female above the surface, they enabled her to breathe and avoided drowning. Most eventually realized that her rapidly declining condition was hopeless. They swam away, and she soon dropped into a vertical position. A few remaining dolphins propped her head above the water, until she stopped breathing. Five dolphins stayed with her and continued touching her body as she sank out of sight.

During the late 1960s, a young male dolphin that had been too long immobilized in a small holding basin became partially paralyzed and sank when returned to the research facility's main tank, where a pair of other dolphins immediately responded to the sufferer's distress call. They lifted his head, permitting him to breathe, but he sank after taking a single gulp of air, unable to swim. Moments after a rapid exchange of whistles between the two adults, as though they were discussing the problem, they proceeded to stroke the youngster's anal region with their dorsal fins. Stimulating this sensitive area triggered a reflex contraction of the stiffened muscles, forcing his tail in a downward thrust that pushed his head above water. For the next several hours, they took turns, regularly passing their dorsal fins over his anal region until the juvenile gradually regained all his former strength and mobility.

Dr. Lilly reports a case in which a "dolphin pup, bottle-fed on a synthetic milk, which was over-rich in lactose, was suffering so badly from wind that it was unable to swim upright. The gas in its swollen intestines was causing it to float belly up. Its struggle to straighten himself was exhausting it. At this point, an adult male approached, and, by thrusting its muzzle hard against the pup's belly, succeeded in expelling the gases through the natural orifice."[23]

The comprehension of medical problems, application of proper healing techniques, and perseverance demonstrated by dolphins and whales are practically without equal among other mammals, including humans.

# 19

## Are Mermaids Real?

*Once I sat upon a promontory and heard a mermaid on a
dolphin's back uttering such dulcet and harmonious breath
that the rude sea grew civil at her song.*

OBERON IN *A MIDSUMMER NIGHT'S DREAM*,
BY WILLIAM SHAKESPEARE, ACT 2, SCENE 1

In 1973, Gary Opit was aboard a three-hundred-ton cargo ship carrying
supplies and a few passengers along the northern coast of New Guinea.
He had been visiting the world's largest tropical island for two months,
studying regional flora and fauna with fellow biologists at the Wau
Ecology Institute, lecturing on ecology at the Lae teacher's college, and
living with indigenous tribal people, "who had never seen another white
man, or had eaten their missionaries, and still had stone axes and bam-
boo knives."[1]

On October 3, around midday, while standing near the bow of
the Papuan Explorer, he noticed something resembling a dark, round
human head floating on the sea, directly forward, but at the vessel's
approach, the object abruptly submerged. Looking over the side as the
ship passed the spot where the thing plunged under water, Opit clearly
saw a dark head attached to an elongated body diving straight down by
the use of its tail through about six feet of almost transparent water.
Although the creature was as large as a full-grown man, it appeared to

have neither arms nor fins. Opit at first presumed he had seen a dugong. On second thought, however, he realized his sighting did not match the lethargic sea-cow-like mammals, with a barrel-shaped body, forelimbs resembling flippers, and a triangular tail.

Five years earlier, he had observed these relatives of the manatee feeding in Moreton Bay, on the eastern coast of Australia, nine miles from central Brisbane, and closely examined an injured specimen washed ashore on the Sunshine Coast in Queensland. He knew they do not maintain a vertical position in the water except while feeding on sea grass. No, the slim, beardless, fast-moving creature Opit saw from the bow of the *Papuan Explorer* was not a stout, whiskered, torpid dugong, but rather unlike anything with which he was familiar.

Ten years after his chance sighting, the first scientific expedition on behalf of the unidentified animal began in June 1983. Investigators included J. Richard Greenwell (1942–2005), research coordinator for the Office of Arid Land Studies at the University of Arizona and research associate at the International Wildlife Museum in Tucson, where he was also secretary for the International Society for Cryptozoology. Cultural anthropologist Roy Wagner, Ph.D., chairman of the Department of Anthropology at the University of Virginia, was chosen team leader for his earlier fieldwork among the Daribi tribesmen of Karimui, in Simbu Province, Papua New Guinea. In the course of the expedition's numerous interviews with various tribal peoples, the Americans were surprised by the scope of native familiarity with the beast throughout Papua New Guinea, where it was most often referred to as the *Ri*.

"When Wagner asked the local people why they had not shown the animal or reported its existence to the colonial administrators and other authorities," Opit writes, "they replied, 'But you people know all about the *Ri*; you put pictures of them [mermaids] on your matchboxes and canned goods.'"[2]

On July 5, 1983, at dawn, team members sighted the same creature Opit had encountered, as it apparently hunted fish in shallow water, about one hundred feet from shore, in the Bay of Nokon, on the southeast coast of New Ireland, Papua New Guinea. For more than twenty minutes, they watched it swim rapidly, break the surface with its back, and repeatedly dive into deeper water, three hundred to four hundred feet from shore, surfacing for less than two seconds about every ten minutes in a sharp roll only an animal possessing extreme vertical flexure would be capable of executing. These behaviors do not characterize the sluggish dugong, which are physically dissimilar from the Nokon Bay creature.

As the investigators approached it within fifty feet, they saw mammalian tail flukes above the surface of the water. One week later, two members of the team found the same animal rolling at the surface in bright sunlight. They were close enough to notice that the color of its skin was tan to light green, although they did not see the head. Several photographs of the entity later published in the *International Society of Cryptozoology Journal* (volume 2, page 119) were poorly focused and made at too great a distance for identification. A slightly better shot showed what might pass for the flukes of a dolphinlike tail just above the surface of the water.

"Because of the low light conditions and the speed of the animal," the *Journal* explains, "the photographs taken by [team member Gale J.] Raymond show nothing of scientific interest."[3] After two months of further investigations, no additional sightings were made, and the expedition was concluded. Back in the United States, Wagner and his associates shared their field experiences with marine mammalogists and zoologists, who concluded that the animal was new to science. Its rapid movement, extended duration of submergence, extreme flexibility, and predatory behavior ruled out identification as a sluggish, strictly vegetarian dugong, sea cow, or species of finless dolphin. Their assessment was challenged two years later by the Ecosophical Research Association (ERA), a New Age group "dedicated to exploring the origins and actualizations of myths and legends that are pertinent to the evolution and destiny of life on this planet."[4]

Beginning in February 1985, ERA member Thomas R. Williams

led a dozen fellow enthusiasts aboard a sixty-five-foot diving vessel, the *Reef Explorer,* across a thousand nautical miles from Port Moresby, the capital of Papua New Guinea, to the island of New Ireland in search of their prey. Arriving at Nokon Bay, where Dr. Wagner and his colleagues made their earlier sighting, ERA expedition members watched a sea beast rolling on the surface of the water. Despite this decidedly un-dugong agility, Williams and his teammates declared that the animal must be an Indo-Pacific dugong, a determination emphatically embraced by conventional scholars dismissive of discoveries that tend to contradict their textbook versions of life. Henceforth, all considerations of the entity observed by Opit and others have been dismissed as make-believe or delusional by mainstream scientists, for whom the case has been finally and decidedly closed.

It was nonetheless reopened, and more publicly than ever before, on May 27, 2012, when nearly two million Americans tuned in to a television program they had been led to believe was a true-to-life documentary. *Mermaids: The Body Found* followed accredited investigators in their discovery of physical remains belonging to an aquatic human. The "scientists" were, in fact, portrayed by actors in a convincingly realistic style. Despite subsequent disclaimers by spokespersons for Animal Planet and the Discovery Channel, many—perhaps most—viewers continued to believe that the "docufiction" described an actual living creature hitherto regarded as legendary. Others—including experienced sailors, some of them U.S. Navy veterans—claimed to have seen it themselves under a variety of circumstances around the world.

While skeptics ascribe such popular reactions to mass hysteria or the power of television, a few university-trained professionals have more deeply and seriously probed the origins of a phenomenon as old as civilization and as fresh as today's news report. They find it difficult to accept that countless thousands of sightings made over the last five millennia and into modern times by culturally diverse and independent eyewitnesses around the world may be explained as the misidentification of sea cows. Some, certainly. But all? Perhaps the reverse has at least sometimes occurred, when observers mistook a genuine aquatic hominid for a common dugong, as appears to have happened when Thomas R. Williams and his fellow ERA members made their sighting in Nokon Bay.

When stopping at different villages during the course of their expedition, ERA members learned firsthand about indigenous belief in the existence of the Ri, as the beings are known in Barok, the Austronesian language of New Ireland. They are also known as *Ilkai* in the Sursurunga dialect, spoken around Nokon Bay, where several modern encounters have taken place, and Pishmary, pidgin English for "fishmary," or "fishwomen," *mary* being synonymous with *women*. Opit heard the same kind of accounts from various tribal inhabitants with whom he lived during the early 1970s. Even after his experience aboard the *Papuan Explorer*, he could not bring himself to admit that the animal he saw could have been anything more than a dugong.

But later, a native elder from a coastal hamlet near Aitape, on the north coast of Papua New Guinea, and knowledgeable concerning local fauna, described how he and a friend, while fishing not far from shore in their dugout canoe, hauled up a large, heavy, strange beast in their net. "It had a round dark head just like a person with large eyes and breasts like a woman. The rest of the body looked similar to that of a dolphin. They were so amazed at bringing such an unusual animal to the surface and concerned that it looked so human that they immediately released it back into the sea."[5] An unbelieving Opit told him the creature they caught was surely a dugong.

But the old man was insistent, Opit recalls:

It was not a dugong, because they [his people] regularly caught and ate dugongs, and that this was quite a different animal altogether. I could not believe that I was receiving a description of a mermaid. . . . [I] told him that such an animal could not possibly exist, and that he must have heard the description from a missionary, and was then pretending to have observed one himself. To my surprise, my informant became indignant. He was clearly upset that although I had been eager to hear of the animals he had encountered over his many years, I refused to believe his encounter with an aquatic animal that resembled a human. It was as if I had questioned his integrity, and I apologised to him, and described the strange animal that I had observed [between Lae and Vanimo]. I still found it hard to believe that I had encountered a mermaid.[6]

Opit's incredulity began to wane, however, when he discovered that virtually every tribe in New Guinea was familiar with the Ri or their version of it.

These island fisherman were well aware of the other marine mammals that shared their world and stated that the Ri was quite different to the dolphins, porpoises, pilot whales and dugongs, the latter known as bo narasi in Barok, meaning 'pig of the ocean,' because of its fat body, rounded, whiskery face, and vegetarian eating habits. . . . The Ri were well known long before the arrival of Europeans. . . . Like all species of animal that co-exist with [the indigenous Papuans], they hold a special place in their culture, and they have cultural stories that explain their creation. The Nakela clan on the eastern coast of New Ireland regard them as sacred animals, or *tadak*, tutelary spirits, and whenever one is killed or found dead, the Nakela hold a mortuary feast for it in their "men's house."[7]

Not all Melanesians are so solicitous of the Ri, which are still supposedly killed and devoured by the inhabitants of Lihir, Siar, and other eastern New Guinea islands. Wagner, writes Opit,

interviewed quite a number of men who had witnessed the butchering of the animals and had eaten their flesh. They commented that Ri have 'a great deal of blood, like a human being, and their body fat is yellow.' When Wagner asked whether there were vestigial leg bones in the lower extremity of the body, they replied that the skeletal structure of the tail consisted only of an elongation of the spine. An old female Ri that had been caught in a net and thrown into the back of a truck 'uttered an almost human cry of pain.' This individual and others were butchered and the meat sold at the Namatanai markets.[8]

The creatures are believed to be the offspring of human descendants, who long ago "committed mass-suicide by jumping over a high sea-cliff, and their souls turned into the Ri."[9] Papuans describe the entity "as an air-breathing marine mammal, with the head, trunk, arms and genitalia of a human, though the lower trunk was legless and terminated in a pair of lateral fins or flippers. Both sexes had long, dark, head hair. The females had obvious mammalian breasts, and the body was covered in human-like skin paler than that of the dark-skinned Melanesian people. The fingernails were long and sharp, and the palms of the hands were deeply ridged and calloused. The face was somewhat monkey-like, and the mouth was unusual and fish-like."[10]

At Nokon Bay, where Wagner and his colleagues spotted an Ilkai, the animal is said to have "a human-like upper torso and head, with the eyes set to the front of the head; the mouth protruding and peculiar. The arms were described as 'fused' to the side of the body, and the pseudo-hands serve as flippers. The legs are fused, one across the other, terminating as flippers instead of feet, which provide aquatic propulsion. Several villagers conceded that the Ilkai is really 'not man,' but 'like man,' [and lives] largely in shallow water chasing, catching and eating fish, and slept on sand bars and deserted beaches."[11] Independent sources continue to repeat similar variants of similar encounters.

Legends of mermaids have passed down through the ages and persist in mainstream society on cans of tuna and in popular Disney movies. There they are safely relegated to the status of "fairy tale." But what if there really is something to those old stories? Westerners who believe in mythic creatures are labeled unprofessional, eccentric, or worse, so it isn't often we speak of such things in polite company—yet every once in a while, the whisper of a true sighting bubbles up to the surface. Perhaps it is not simply by chance that the waters surrounding Papua New Guinea are often the focus of those tales.

"Years ago," comments a *Nexus* magazine reader in the June–July 2014 issue, "two old sea captains from the Pacific area north of New Guinea and surrounding islands (one had a group of islands named after him) often spoke with me, telling unusual stories in confidence about things that others would not understand, and would create ridicule. . . . They said that islanders in several areas talked about seeing what looked like 'dolphin people,' often on the beach and in lagoons. Several white people had told similar stories, and were ridiculed beyond belief. What if those [dolphin people] that went into the water are still there and thriving well?"[12]

# 20

# A Webfoot
# in Both Worlds

*Perhaps he [the merman] is even lounging on his coral bed
right now, fingering a rosary of cowries, ready to rise on
a midnight tide to tell his tale to the hitherto unbelieving
world.*

JANE YOLEN, FOLKLORIST

According to Opit, native accounts put the New Guinea merfolk mostly
"around the shores of the Bismarck Sea, the Solomon Sea, and the Pacific,
off the shores of the Bismarck and Solomon archipelagos. They are
particularly encountered around the central and southern shores of New
Ireland and the straits between the islands of Buka and Bougainville, in
the Northern Solomons. The Ri also exist further west, around Manus
Island, and off the north coast of New Guinea, where fisherman have
caught them in nets at Aitape."[1]

The fame of a mermaidlike mammal among various indigenous
inhabitants of Papua New Guinea suggests something more than an
oral tradition. But that the same entity should be familiar to wholly
unrelated people in the outside world defies pat explanations of myth
or misidentification and indicates instead something that continues to
endure over thousands of years because it is at least fundamentally true.

While the previous chapter described recent and highly controversial brushes with merfolk by Westerners near the island nation of Papua New Guinea, this chapter discusses the worldwide nature of this myth. Indeed, we find accounts of merfolk all across the globe, from ancient times to modern days, from the arid deserts of South Africa to the balmy shores of Greece—and almost everywhere in between.

For example, Opit tells of a Papuan village magistrate, who, while fishing, "observed a Ri rise to the surface and look at him from only about six metres [less than twenty feet] away. Its face reminded him of the face of a monkey, photos of which he had seen when he worked as a police officer in Rabaul."[2]

Similar descriptions are found throughout the western islands of Japan, where belief is still strong in the Kappa, a hairy monkey with skin webbing between his limbs. His female counterpart is the Ningyo (literally, "human fish"), a mermaid described since ancient times with the mouth of a monkey, small teeth, and a quiet voice, like that of a flute. The Kappa is said to occasionally emerge from the sea wearing a turtle shell on his back. From the top of his head grows a dish-shaped protrusion he is careful to keep wet because, if it dries out, his power is lost.

Country people in southwestern districts explain that few of the strange creatures are seen in modern times because the Kappa habitat—rivers and ponds—has suffered from agricultural pollution. Inhabitants of the Gotō Islands speak of Kappas rescuing people drowning at sea, in the manner of wild dolphins. If, as the famous scholar Joseph Campbell defined them, "private dreams are public myths," then those concerned with mermen may be subliminal memories of the aquatic phase our pre-human forebears experienced on their way to becoming *Homo sapiens*.[3] As much is implied in the Japanese Kappa—a monkey with webbed limbs.

Particularly striking is an Aesop fable, perhaps his least typical and strangest. Sometime after the turn of the sixth century BCE, he told of a storm-tossed shipwreck not far from the coast of Sunium, a promontory of Attica, in southeastern Greece, where a pet monkey was thrown into the Aegean Sea, along with his master and other passengers. A dolphin suddenly rescued the primate, which he mistook for a small man, by carrying it toward shore. "Are you an Athenian?" the dolphin asked, to which the monkey answered in the affirmative. "Then you must know Piraeus," the dolphin said.

Unaware that the sea beast referred to the main port of Athens, and assuming instead he meant a prominent Greek citizen, the monkey boasted, "He is one of my best friends." Unwilling to be in the company of such a liar, the dolphin plunged beneath the surface, leaving the monkey to fend for himself again amid the waves.[4]

Was this peculiar little tale a vague allusion to dolphins and a hominid's transition in an aquatic phase?

The classical Greeks spoke of mermen, famous for their long, flowing, green, seaweedlike hair and beards. Similar beings populate Irish myth as extremely ugly creatures, bearing pointed green teeth, piggish eyes, and a red nose; abundant green hair covers their bodies. While also hairy, the Finnish *vetehinen* is a handsome fishtailed man, powerful in ancient magic, and versed in the wisdom of the sea, his domain. He can cure illnesses, but also cause unintended harm by becoming too curious about human life. Similarly hirsute mermen were known as *marbendlar* in Icelandic folklore and Norse myth.

While traditions of merfolk are exceedingly old, they were long preceded by much earlier visual references in one of South Africa's driest regions, the Karoo Desert, the southern part of which (the Klein Karoo) was under water until about three million years ago. As the seas withdrew, they left behind a valley where mountain springs, trickling into rock pools, continue to carve out subterranean caverns, the abode of mermaids, according to local Khoi-san natives. These Hottentot Bushmen believe the creatures are primarily found at the Cango Caves, less than twenty miles outside Oudtshoorn, a town in the Western Cape province.

It was here, at the mouth of one underground chamber, that archaeologists found primitive stone tools and hearths that allowed accurate carbon dating to 80,000 years before present (BP). Near this location lies Eseljagtspoort, a large cave with its own rock pool the Khoi-san also believe is inhabited by mermaids. The walls of this cave are covered with red paintings of fishtailed humanoids. They are depicted holding staves or implements of some kind (including what appears to be dousing rods or a net), fishing on the surface of the water with spears, swimming below with dolphins, and hunted by men with bows and arrows.

"The bow and arrow is an ancient weapon," *Smithsonian* magazine reports, "going back at least 71,000 years, a study published in *Nature* suggests. Archaeologists working at South Africa's Pinnacle Point cave site [less than sixty miles from Eseljagtspoort] uncovered a collection of tiny blades, about an inch big, that resemble arrow points, likely belonging to prehistoric bow and arrows or spear-throwers."[5] Pinnacle Point is a small promontory on the southern coast, where Cave 13B yielded the first known evidence of systematic exploitation of marine resources (shellfish), together with documentation of the earliest human symbolic behavior; the heat treatment of rock for making stone tools was found at nearby Cave 5-6.

Eseljagtspoort's mermaid cave art has been tentatively dated to 50,000 BP. If correct, it predates the earliest known wall paintings—established at 35,400 years old—on the Indonesian island of Sulawesi.

Figure 20.1. Merfolk depicted swimming in the sea with dolphins and fishing on the surface at South Africa's Eseljagtspoort cave.

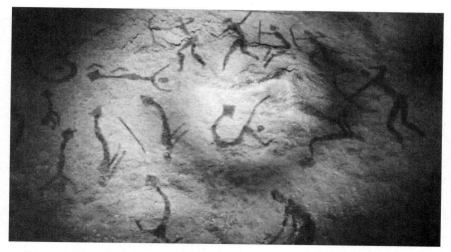

Figure 20.2. Eseljagtspoort cave's merfolk shown hunted by archers.

In view of the extreme antiquity emerging from Pinnacle Point and the Cango Caves, however, dating the Eseljagtspoort imagery earlier than the Sulawesi art by 14,600 years is not incredible.

As such, portrayals of mermaids interacting with dolphins and men may represent the oldest surviving specimens of art in the world. More to the point of our discussion, they document merfolk in a seemingly transitional, evolutionary relationship between dolphins and early humans at a period when the latter were themselves undergoing fundamental change, a phase that gave birth to art and culture (plate 13).

Merfolk were mentioned in the first written records, more than five thousand years ago, in Sumerian stories of Ea, "the god of light and wisdom, who exercised his knowledge of the healing art for the benefit of his votaries," according to twentieth-century mythologist Lewis Spence (plate 14). "From the waters of the Persian Gulf, whence he rose each morning, he brought knowledge of all manner of crafts and trades, arts and industries, for the behoof of his infant city [Eridu], even the mystic and difficult art of impressing written characters on clay."[6]

The Sumerians nurtured an already ancient belief "that humanity owed its origin to the god Ea," who "had under a fish's head another head, and also feet below, similar to those of a man, subjoined to the fish's tail. His speech, too, was articulate and human."[7] Like imagery was associated with his later Babylonian incarnation, Oannes, who was, in the words of Berosus, the third-century BCE priest of Bel Merodach, "a creature endowed with a body like that of a fish, with feet below, like those of a man, with a fish's tail. . . . There appeared other creatures like Oannes."[8]

The Vedic *Shatapatha Brahmana,* "Brahmana of One Hundred Paths," is a 2,800-year-old sacred text describing the merman Matsya, who sounded the warning about on impending deluge that would virtually destroy Mankind. Such mythic legacies are remarkable for their similarities among disparate cultures around the world, unknown to one another, and separated by impassable distances, many thousands of years, or both. They all nonetheless repeat the same description of hairy, intelligent, waterborne figures associated with human beginnings.

Amphitrite, who rode on a dolphin's back to wed Poseidon, gave birth to Triton, a merman, believed to have founded the capital of Poland in deeply ancient times. Since before the middle of the fourteenth century, Warsaw's official coat of arms has been a shield- and sword-wielding mermaid, known as the *syrenka.*

A more revealing figure from Greek myth is Glaucus, a mortal, who, after eating magical herbs, felt compelled to forever forsake the land for life in the ocean, where he changed into a merman. His transfiguration, as described by the Roman poet Ovid in his *Metamorphoses,* suggests a universally subconscious desire to reunite with our watery origins, dimly remembered in human fascination with the sea, where some hominid forebears evolved into our merfolk cousins.[9]

Although accounts of mermen go back to civilization's earliest surviving written accounts, in Sumer, the first known description of a mermaid appeared in Assyria, three thousand years ago. In relating how the goddess Atargatis transformed herself into a mermaid out of shame for accidentally killing her human lover, it repeats a motif found as far away as India, Papua New Guinea, and Brazil, namely, that sexual relations have taken place between humans and dolphins and/or dolphin-like merfolk. One of their offspring was Vatea, revered as the father of gods and humans among inhabitants of the southern Cook Islands and on Mangaia, in the South-Central Pacific, where he is depicted in myth as a half dolphin, half man.

An Indonesian story, as well known as it is profoundly old, tells how a wife, physically abused by her husband, fled from their home, down to the beach, and into the sea. While washing her bloody wounds, a compassionate dolphin changed her into a *rujung,* or mermaid, a trans-formation witnessed by her children watching from shore. They begged her to return to the land, but she could not because her legs had fused into a dolphin tail. "Take my tears," she said, "and rub them softly on your father's back without his knowledge."

"This was done," writes the encyclopedist of Pacific mythology, Jan Knappert, "and suddenly the man realized how cruel he had been, and became a loving father. He often searched for his lost wife, but in vain. In the end, he became a porpoise, but still never found his wife. He was not worth her. Dolphins' laments can still be heard."[10]

Like every myth that has achieved perennial significance among a people, this one contains eternal verities considered worth passing along from one generation to another. Among those preserved here are the dolphin's universal reputation for human compassion and its healing potential.

This theme is repeated in western Sumatra's *Minangkabau,* an epic poem of twenty-six episodes told in forty thousand lines, accumulated and repeated over the course of unknown millennia. The poem tells of the sailor Anggun Nan Tungga, who, after seeking eternal happi-ness in numerous worldly accomplishments, "goes to the seashore, sad-dened by the loss of his betrothed, plunges into the ocean and becomes a dolphin."[11]*

The most important person in the history of Tibet, Tonpa Shenrab

---

*In another tale, an Indonesian woman and man are also transfigured into aquatic mammals.

Miwoche, had webbed fingers. According to origin histories known as *chog rabs,* the Great Supreme Man of the Shen, Miwoche, created "the cradle of Tibetan culture" in the shadow of Mount Kailas, by combining local beliefs with the elevated spirituality of his people, the Mu, who had immigrated to the Himalayas many generations before his birth in 1917 BCE. In addition, he wrote a number of books detailing various aspects of the Bon religious tradition in Tibet, which he founded.[12]

Miwoche tells how a divine manifestation in anthropomorphic form appeared on Earth at the beginning of time as a handsome white man (*dkar,* literally meaning "white," signifying as well the East, his place of origin). This Sidpa Sang po married Koepa Chuchag Gyelmo, a mermaid with aquamarine skin and long, turquoise-blue hair. Their offspring—the Srid pa phi dgu and Srid pa mo dgu—were, respectively, the first men and women. Tibet's version of Genesis suggests that human ancestry lay in the crossbreeding of some godlike being with an aquatic ape or early hominid undergoing an aquatic phase.

Miwoche goes on to describe the earliest and greatest civilization as Khro ch Dmu rdzong, or the Cast-iron Fortress of the Mu, a name identical with the Motherland of Mankind, the first high culture, said to have originated in the seas around Indonesia before spreading outward to the Indian Ocean and across the Pacific, more than twelve thousand years ago. Miwoche was born 289 years before Khro ch Dmu rdzong succumbed to a natural catastrophe that dispersed its survivors throughout Asia and the Americas, in 1628 BCE.[13]

Miwoche's syndactyly may have been a personally representative trait of this people. They evolved in their archipelagic isolation through a prolonged aquatic phase that not only rendered them web-fingered and -toed, but nurtured their collective intelligence on the sea's own brain food, enabling them, over the course of generations, to develop the world's first civilization. The Mu emerged from one of Earth's greatest natural catastrophes, when the most powerful volcanic event ever known occurred in Sumatra.

Figure 20.3. Belief in mermaids is at least as old as civilization, as suggested by this seventeenth-century BCE bronze from Minoan Crete, housed at the Berlin Archaeological Museum.

*One Thousand and One Nights,* a collection of West and South Asian folk tales compiled in Arabic and first translated into English in 1706, tells of Djullanar and her fellow mermaids, who interbreed with men and give birth to children able to live under water, like themselves. As some indication of the concept's antiquity in Britain, *wasmerewif* means "mermaid" in Old English. Built by Saxon stonemasons around 1078, Durham Castle features the earliest artistic portrayal of a mermaid in England. It appears on a south-facing capital above one of the Norman chapel's original stone pillars. A chair at the Church of Saint Senara in Zennor, Cornwall, is decorated with the carving of a mermaid dated to the early fifteenth century.

"It is also in Cornwall," writes Odent, "that several families are supposed to possess mysterious powers, as a legacy of their mermaid ancestry."[14] Scottish mermaids are the pre-Christian *ceasg,* or "girls of the wave," known as *ben-varrey* at the Isle of Man. On the European Continent, they are associated with Melusine, the mermaid spirit of fresh waters in sacred springs and rivers.

Odent follows the trail of the merfolk myth across Europe and Asia, Africa and America. He tells of the "Merrimini or Meerfrun from German legends; Mermennill from Ireland; Mari Morgan from Brittany; Morfowyn from Wales. . . . These also have a lot in common with the Japanese Mujina, the Chinese mermaid who bathes in a well, the African and American Indian mermaids, and the fish-tailed divinities that appear in early Greek vase paintings."[15] A merman features as a "sea czar" in the Russian medieval epic *Sadko,* while belief in the mermaid Rusalkas is still prevalent in Ukraine, Belarus, and southern Russia after the passage of unknown centuries. Mermaids are described in an early fifteenth-century compilation of quotations from Chinese literature.

Ancient India's Suvannamaccha, or "golden mermaid," resurfaces in Cambodian and Thai versions of the fifth-century BCE Hindu epic *Ramayana.* Mermaids are known as the *jengu* in Cameroon, in the region of west Central Africa.[16] Mami Wata are mermaids venerated in western and southern Africa and, through the African diaspora, are today known throughout parts of North and South America, as well as the Caribbean. There, the native Taínos of Puerto Rico, Cuba, Jamaica, Haiti, the Dominican Republic, and Bahamas identify a mermaid they call Aycayia. Kalagan natives of the southern Philippines, near the coast, revere mermen known as the Sirena and mermaids, the Siyokoy. The waters off Java's southern beach have been regarded by generations of local natives as the realm of Nyi Roro Kidul, a mermaid queen.

These and numerous other similar traditional beliefs around the world are rooted in sightings from prehistory to the present day. Among the most famous eyewitnesses was Christopher Columbus, who in 1493 reported seeing three "female forms" that "rose high out of the sea, but were not as beautiful as they are represented," off the coast of Hispaniola—today divided between the Dominican Republic and Haiti.[17]

Another renowned explorer and navigator, Henry Hudson, tells in a posthumously published account of his voyages to the New World how, during the early evening of June 15, 1607, near Nova Zembla, an uninhabited island off Canada, "one of our company, looking overboard, saw a mermaid, and calling up some [of] the company to see her, one more of the crew came up, and by that time she was come close to the ship's side, looking earnestly on the men. A little after, [the] sea . . . overturned her. From the navel upward, her back and breast were like a woman's, as they say that saw her; her body as big as one of us, her skin very white, and long hair hanging down behind, of color black. In her going down they saw her tail, which was like the tail of a porpoise, speckled like a mackerel."[18]

Edward Teach—better remembered as the pirate Blackbeard—recorded in his logbook how he instructed his crew on several voyages to steer away from chartered waters he referred to as "enchanted" for fear of merfolk, which Blackbeard himself and members of his crew claimed to have seen. Canadian observers saw what they described as "mermaids" near Vancouver and Victoria from 1870 to 1967.[19]

As recently as February 2012, work on planned reservoirs in Zimbabwe stopped, "because mermaids have been hounding workers away, stated the country's Water Resources Minister." According to an article in London's *Daily Mail*, "Samuel Sipepa Nkomo told a Zimbabwean parliamentary committee that terrified workers are refusing to return to the sites, near the towns of Gokwe and Mutare. The senior politician said that mermaids were also present in other reservoirs. 'We even hired Whites, thinking that our boys did not want to work. But they also returned, saying they would not return to work there again,' he added."[20]

Old, deeply buried genetic memories of our own merfolk heritage—a physical legacy from a watery phase our evolutionary predecessors experienced—sometimes resurfaces today in a congenital deformity known as *sirenomelia,* or the mermaid syndrome. Occurring in approximately one out of every one hundred thousand live births, sirenomelia is a condition in which the legs are fused together, giving them the appearance of a mermaid's tail or the flukes of a dolphin. The defect is usually fatal within a day or two of birth (more than half the cases result in stillbirth) due to complications associated with abnormal kidney and urinary bladder development and function.

Akin to the humanlike dolphin embryo, the syndactyly of our webbed fingers or toes, our subcutaneous fat, our diving reflex, sebum, the gills exhibited in human fetuses, and all of the other persistent, vestigial traits inherited from our species' rite of passage through the sea, the mermaid syndrome is a rare throwback to an ancestral form, one we gradually discarded in our return to dry land. The defect manifests itself when so-far unknown factors activate a recessive gene containing data from our aquatic past in the estuaries and along the coastlines of the temperate Pliocene Epoch, less than three million years ago. Each of us carries this dormant gene, which only springs to life when triggered by some infrequently occurring stimulus. Our genetic code remembers that all of us were once mermaids or mermen.

Given the vast body of evidence pertaining to them, mermaids and mermen may have at least some basis in fact. "The legends about mermaids are mysterious," Odent writes, "because they are universal. . . . Regardless of the area, the place or the climate, all legends about mermaids are variations of the same theme."[21]

"If any narrative in the world deserves credit," write folklorists Jane Yolen and Shulamith Oppenheim, "it is this, for the merfolk were seen by so many witnesses. But was the sighting a hoax? A misunderstanding of native ceremony? A misreading of animal behavior? Or was it a true encounter with real mermen? Without scientific evidence, we cannot know. . . . It is always possible—if highly improbable—that mermen did exist and exist no more. Perhaps like the passenger pigeon, the dodo, and the saber-toothed tiger, the merman is extinct. Or perhaps, like the *coelacanth*, the merman is still waiting to be discovered by modern science."[22]

Opit arrives at similar conclusions:

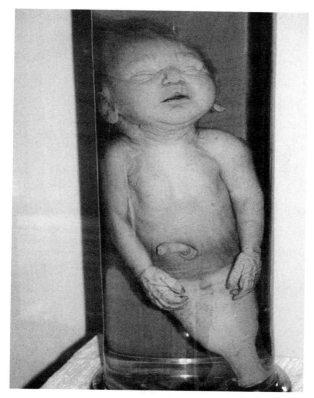

Figure 20.4. Sirenomelia specimen at the
Natural History and Anatomy Museum, Lyons, France.

From the observations of mermaids over hundreds of years, the descriptions of the animals reveal that there may have been, and perhaps still is, an aquatic species of hominid. Perhaps, like ourselves, it evolved from a chimpanzee-like species that spent so much time foraging in the water that it adapted its body to a wholly aquatic life style. On the other hand, it may well be our nearest relation, a true aquatic human, that evolved from semi-aquatic humans that gave rise to our species. Although this may sound unlikely, it must be remembered that the oceans are teeming with marine mammals, the ancestors of which were terrestrial species that adapted themselves to a marine existence.

It may well be a fact that mermaids represent a population of early human-like hominids that continued to adapt to an ever-more aquatic lifestyle. The descent of humanity may then have come from another population that moved back onto the land. We then had an advantage over other animals, in that we were able to survive both on land and in the water with a very large brain essential for survival in an aquatic environment. . . . We have almost certainly been hunting the mermaid to extinction, so that by the time records began to be kept, mermaid numbers were so reduced that observations were extremely rare, until they virtually disappeared, and have become a myth. Perhaps the last mermaid species still clings to life in the waters around New Guinea.[23]

# 21
## Sirius
## Dolphins

*If there is another answer to the Sirius mystery, it may be
even more surprising, rather than less so. It certainly will
not be trivial.*

ROBERT TEMPLE

The central plateau in the West African country of Mali is a dry
region, spread with flinty, unproductive soil. During January, the cold-
est month, high temperatures average more than 91 degrees Fahrenheit;
in April, they soar above 102 degrees. For the last five hundred years,
a tribal people known as the Dogon have inhabited this arid, uninvit-
ing territory, bisected by the Bandiagara Escarpment, a sandstone cliff
approximately 1,650 feet high and ninety miles long. Their ancestors
fled to this remote, defensible formation from the southwest, where
Islam had threatened conversion by the sword in the fifteenth century.

During the process of migration, they combined with several other
ethnic groups of diverse origins, until today half a million or more
Dogon reside south of a bend in the Niger River. They remain a pre-
modern people, fundamentally unchanged from their tribal ways, and,
therefore, attractive to European scholars interested in studying native
societies still relatively unaffected by contemporary Western influences.

During the early to mid-twentieth century, the Dogon appeared especially valuable in this respect because they were among the last indigenous sub-Saharan Africans to lose their independence before coming under French rule.

Paris anthropologists Marcel Griaule and Germaine Dieterlen spent several decades living with the Dogon in field missions ranging from several days to two months, in 1931, 1935, 1937, and 1938 until the outbreak of World War II the following year, then annually beginning in 1946 for the next ten years. Among the highlights of their research, Griaule's *Dogon Masks* "remains one of the fundamental works on the topic."[1]

But he and Dieterlen gained the confidence of tribal elders only after fifteen years of consistently amiable relations. At that time, the French scientists were introduced to a blind elder, Ogotemmêli, the keeper of secret religious traditions. In late 1946, Griaule spent thirty-three consecutive days interviewing Ogotemmêli, who disclosed spiritual signs running into the thousands, including "their own systems of astronomy and calendrical measurements, methods of calculation and extensive anatomical and physiological knowledge, as well as a systematic pharmacopoeia."[2]

Such a vast body of information sharply contrasted with the outwardly primitive folk into whose care it had been entrusted. Yet more amazing was Ogotemmêli's apparent knowledge of a star—invisible from Earth—relatively adjacent to Sirius, which is 8.6 light-years from Earth and the brightest object in the heavens after the Sun, Moon, Venus, and Jupiter. The Dogon informant went on to say that this companion star was small and extremely heavy, which accurately describes Sirius B, a white dwarf, or undersized, very dense star formed when all its central nuclear fuel has been spent. He added further that yet another small star formed a kind of stellar triad. But the existence of Sirius C, as it is referred to in the West, has not been confirmed by astronomers.

In any case, it was from this region of space by Sirius, also known as the Dog Star, that long ago, according to Ogotemmêli, the "great ark came out of the sky and came down," displacing "a pile of dust raised by the whirlwind it caused." Thereafter, the vessel was attached with lines and dragged by some kind of "quadruped" to a hollow. "When the water filled the pond, the ark floated on it like a huge pirogue [a dugout, or long, narrow canoe hewn out of a single tree trunk]."[3] From it then emerged beneficent, amphibious beings, which elevated the cultural level of humankind by sharing their high wisdom with Dogon ancestors.

Conforming to professional protocol, Griaule and Dieterlen recorded Ogotemmêli's account in the same straightforward manner with which they had already documented West Africa's native cultures, minus their opinions or interpretations of any kind. Not until twenty years after Griaule's death in 1956 was his work made known to the general public with the release of *The Sirius Mystery*. Critics dismissed the evidence presented by author Robert Temple, arguing that the Dogon must have learned about Sirius B from Jesuit missionaries. Dieterlen laughed off their speculation as "absurd" and pointed out that "Dogon artifacts hundreds of years old already depict the three stars of the Sirius system."[4]

Although unsympathetic to any "Sirius mystery," writers Lynn Picknett and Clive Prince doubt that native West Africans learned about the Dog Star from twentieth-century outsiders: "Some skeptics have attempted to explain away the Dogon's knowledge of Sirius by ascribing it to itinerant Christian missionaries, who felt that urge to pass this piece of somewhat anachronistic and highly specialist knowledge on to the Dogon. In turn, the Dogon felt compelled to add it to their religion. In fact, the first Christian mission in Mali was not established by American Protestants until 1936, when the Dogon-based religion was already deeply embedded in Dogon culture."[5] This influence occurred five years after Griaule and Dieterlen began interviewing the Dogon.

Yet, detractors continue to question the Dogon beliefs, particularly the possibility of beings able to traverse both land and water inhabiting that region of space. Robert S. Harrington of the U.S. Naval Observatory offers that, so far as current deep-space technology is able to determine, planetary orbits in the "habitable" zone around Sirius—defined as the region in which water would be liquid—are possibly too unstable for any amphibious beings living on planets in the Sirius system today.[6]

A more formidable challenge was made in 1991 by W. E. A. van Beek, who led a team of fellow anthropologists to central Mali for the specific purpose of confirming Griaule's research there. They found, as alternative investigator Philip Coppens reports:

> absolutely no trace of the detailed Sirius lore reported by the French anthropologists. Griaule had stated that about fifteen percent of the Dogon tribe knew about this secret knowledge, but Van Beek could, in a decade of research with the Dogon, find not a single trace of this knowledge. Van Beek was initially keen to find evidence for Griaule's claims, but had to admit that there may have been a major problem with Griaule's claims.
>
> Van Beek actually spoke to the original informants of Griaule. . . . Though they do speak about *sigu tolo* [interpreted by Griaule as their name for Sirius], they disagree completely with each other as to which star is meant; for some, it is an invisible star that should rise to announce the sigu [festival], for another it is Venus that through a different position appears as *sigu tolo*. All agree, however, that they learned about the star from Griaule. So whatever knowledge they possessed, it was knowledge coming from Griaule, not knowledge native to the Dogon tribe. All agree, however, that they learned about the star from Griaule.[7]

In short, van Beek uncovered no evidence that the Dogon regarded Sirius as a double star or that astronomy was particularly important in their belief system. He accused Griaule of misinterpreting and influencing his own results. While skeptics were satisfied, these revelations are less convincing than they seemed at first glance. Griaule supposedly led on tribal elders by showing them star maps; he was an enthusiastic amateur astronomer, detractors insisted, anxious to give greater knowledge of the heavens to the Dogon. Yet, one of the concluding statements in his report is at odds with this characterization: "The question has not been solved, nor even asked, of how men with no instruments at their disposal could know the movements and certain characteristics of stars which are scarcely visible."[8]

In fact, Temple, himself a fellow of London's Royal Astronomical Society, points out in 1976 that Sirius B "is totally invisible, and was only discovered in the last century with the use of the telescope. . . . But in even saying this, the anthropologists [Griaule and Dieterlen] were indicating their own lack of astronomical expertise."[9]

"As for his alleged training in astronomy," writes Griaule's daughter, Genevieve Calame-Griaule, herself an accredited and respected anthropologist until her death in 2013, "he had no notion at all of astronomy, and it was the Dogon who just began telling him about the stars. If he later displayed charts of the heavens, it was for his own use, and not to instruct the Dogon. As for the satellite of Sirius, he was completely ignorant of its existence until the Dogon spoke to him of a 'companion,' at which point he consulted the astronomers of the Paris Observatory, and found them as surprised as he was."[10]

Van Beek went on to suggest that Griaule's assistant, Germaine Dieterlen, aided and abetted him in his concoction of an astronomical hoax. In a personal e-mail, Temple states, "You would had to have met and talked with Dieterlen to know how totally and completely ignorant of astronomy she was, and how impossible it would have been for her to carry out any such 'hoax.'"[11] He writes in his book how Griaule and his colleagues had to wait fifteen years before the Dogon allowed "four of their head priests, after a special priestly conference among the tribe and a 'policy decision' to make their secrets known to Marcel Griaule, the first outsider in their history to inspire their confidence."[12]

Van Beek admits that he and his colleagues did not pass through this same long process of initiation. As Temple explains, "Van Beek claimed that he could not find the priests who informed Griaule and Dieterlen when he went to Mali decades later, but that was because they were dead! I should point out that it is obvious that sudden and casual visitors to the Dogon are not going to be told anything esoteric, because there is such a thing as needing to gain the confidence of people, which appears to be a wholly unknown concept to certain types of hatchet, pseudo-investigators with an agenda to discredit honest reports."[13]

Temple is seconded by Calame-Griaule, who asserts that van Beek "had not gone through the appropriate steps for acquiring knowledge [from the Dogon]." His criticism was merely "misguided speculation rooted in an apparent ignorance of esoteric tradition," she continues, while his unnamed tribal informants likely feared that he had been "sent by the political and administrative authorities to test the Dogon's Muslim orthodoxy," and therefore denied all original knowledge of Sirius.[14] As a people, they mostly rejected and resisted Islam, which is practiced by a minority of Dogon. More than two-thirds of the tribe follow their traditional religion, Christianity, or a synthesis of both. Mali's Muslim government unquestionably has a chilling effect on any potentially unorthodox statements the Dogon may make, especially to Western infidels.

Genevieve's father, of course, was not alive to defend his professional reputation from van Beek and other critics, but his rather eminent professional background seems strangely at odds with the skepticism leveled against his work. In 1927, Marcel Griaule received a degree from the École nationale des langues orientales (National School of Oriental Languages), specializing in the languages of Amharic and Gueze. In 1938, after his first nine years studying the Dogon, he produced his dissertation and received a doctorate based on his Dogon research, in the course of which he pioneered the use of aerial photography over the Bandiagara Escarpment. Following the close of World War II, Griaule served as the first chair of anthropology at the University of Paris–Sorbonne.

His colleague, Germaine Dieterlen, "made pioneering contributions to the study of myths, initiations, techniques, graphic systems, objects, classifications, ritual and social structure."[15] She was the director of studies at École pratique des hautes études (School for Advanced Studies), at the Sorbonne, Paris; a founding member of the Centre national de la recherche scientifique (French National Center for Scientific Research); and president of the Committee on Ethnographic Film. "No one ever questioned the integrity of Griaule and Dieterlen in Paris to my knowledge," says Temple, "and all the people of their acquaintance whom I knew praised their indefatigable work and professional expertise."[16]

That either or both of these outstanding and important scientists would have fudged evidence to support their claims or misinterpreted them through incompetence, seems unlikely, to say the least. Moreover, their report about Dogon beliefs languished unknown to the outside world in only a few published copies of the scholarly *Journal de la société des africainistes* (Journal for the Society of African Artifacts) for sixteen years before it was translated and republished by Temple. "It is also essential to remember," he states, "that the key article appeared in an obscure French anthropological journal in 1950 and neither she [Dieterlen] nor any of her acquaintance made the slightest effort to call anyone's attention to it for more than twenty-six years outside the narrow circle of their anthropological colleagues. I was the one who dug it out by dint of hard research, and had it translated into English at my own expense."[17]

Genevieve Calame-Griaule personally attended the French expeditions to Mali. "I also witnessed," she states, "along with Germaine Dieterlen and Solonge de Ganay [an ethnologist from the Musée du Trocadéro] my father's return from his interviews [with Ogotemmêli] night after night with wonderful accounts of the discoveries of the day. . . . Van Beek's article contains so many misreadings that it is impossible to correct them all in limited space. . . . It would take a whole article to refute all the errors in his 'restudy' point by point."[18]

Nor are the Dogon the only West Africans who preserve oral

accounts of visitors from the sky. Three related tribes hold "as their most secret religious tradition a body of knowledge concerning the system of the star Sirius, including specific information about that star system, which it should be impossible for any primitive tribe to know," Calame-Griaule points out.[19]

The white dwarf of Sirius B is ten thousand times less bright than its companion Dog Star, the luminosity of which is approximately thirty-five times greater than our Sun. "The Dogon insisted that they themselves had *not* been visited by beings from the system of the star Sirius," Temple states. "What the Dogon were meticulous about pointing out was that their ancestors, who lived in a different location, had been visited in the very remote past, and that this knowledge had come down to them and been preserved by them over a very great period of time."[20]

The criticisms of Griaule and his colleagues, along with the skepticism directed at his native informants, are exceptionally weak, failing to hold up against either common sense or cultural evidence. With the collapse of solid evidence to debunk the Dogon version, we are logically left with its essential veracity, although many questions remain. Why, for example, would representatives from a civilization more highly advanced than anything ever developed on Earth care to interact with a pre-Stone Age ethnic group? The Dogon themselves may have provided an answer in their description of the heavenly vessel's landing, which more resembled a crash: "The violence of the impact roughened the ground. . . . It skidded on the ground."[21]

Given this description, it appears that the arrival of technologically sophisticated beings from another world may have occurred in prehistoric Mali more by accident than design. Just when it took place is uncertain, as the oldest known images found on Dogon ritual objects referring to the encounter date back, as Dieterlen states, five centuries. Ogotemmêli and his fellow tribal elders spoke with greater sureness about the occupants of the "ark." These were the Nommos, portrayed in Dogon folk art as creatures the size of an adult human male, with a humanoid upper torso and a fishlike lower body, with the legs fused into a fishlike tail. A Nommo appears "a good deal like a dolphin with arms and hands," writes Temple. "The tradition known to us of the mermaid expresses this state of affairs quite well."[22]

That the Nommos were either dolphins or merfolk was indicated by their plunge into the artificial reservoir or "pond" excavated immediately after landing among the Dogon, who stated that the visitors from Sirius required an aquatic environment in which to live. Their leader, O Nommo, took up "his seat in the waters of the Earth." He and his kind had "many descendants and will always be present in the fresh 'male' water of the brooks, rivers, ponds and wells, and also the 'female' sea water."[23] Could this be a reference to river dolphins and ocean dolphins?

"In fact," Temple observes, "the Dogon have a tradition that their Nommos breathed through their clavicles," or collar bones.[24] While dolphins use a blowhole at the top of their heads, such minor errors of detail accrue in retelling an oral account over generations. Far more significant is that the utterly landlocked Dogon, who reside more than nine hundred miles from the sea and are personally unfamiliar with marine mammals, should venerate cetaceanlike creatures at the core of their traditional belief system. This tends to affirm that the ancestors of this isolated tribe did indeed witness the arrival of entities wholly removed from anything resembling life at the desiccated Bandiagara Escarpment. If the Dogon account is true, what are the implications of that encounter? Does the story suggest that today's dolphins are the descendants of extraterrestrial beings? And what of the mermaids and mermen examined in our previous chapter? Could they be the Nommos?

These questions may seem too fantastic for serious consideration, but they neither begin nor end in West Africa. The Dogon, for example, are not the only sub-Saharan Africans with traditions of dolphin-like or merfolklike culture-bearers descending out of the sky long ago from another world. The Zulus are a Bantu ethnic group, the largest in South Africa, with some eleven million people, whose shamans treasure a large green stone of unknown origins, inscribed with a no less inscrutable text and configured to resemble a dolphin holding a golden tablet in its mouth. The sacred icon is worn on a ceremonial necklace to represent Hlengeto, Zulu for dolphin, "the one who saves," who brought the Golden Tablet of the Law in the ancient past.[25] In chapter 17, we learned that Ganga is a Hindu goddess who descended out of the heavens heralded by dolphins, the *makara*, one of which she rode through the Indus Valley, spreading the arts, sciences, and social order.

Around 350 BCE, the Greek philosopher and scientist Aristotle composed his *History of Animals*, in Book 8 of which he tells how "the dolphin actually disappears at the time of the Dog Star for about thirty days."[26] Twenty-four centuries later, during the 1980s, while on his way to Denpasar, in Bali, author Timothy Wyllie learned "of millions— *literally millions*—of dolphins congregating in a small area of sea in the Straits of Lombok. By all accounts, they gather for three or four days at a time when the Dog Star, Sirius, is directly overhead . . . every year in May."[27]

Wyllie's informant did not exaggerate. During several expeditions undertaken by Professor Busnel, cited in chapter 3, he encountered packed masses of dolphins stretching thirty-five to forty miles across. "Once," writes Jacques Cousteau, "en route to Dakar, his [Busnel's] ship was completely surrounded by dolphins, with the animals spaced out so that there was only one dolphin to every twenty square yards of surface. He estimates that some of these schools comprised several million dolphins."[28]

Lying between the Indonesian islands of Bali and Lombok, the thirty-seven-mile-long Lombok Strait, or Selat Lombok, connects the Java Sea to the Indian Ocean. "Each spring, on exactly the same dates," Dr. DeMares writes, "millions of dolphins are said to converge in a huge, spiraling super pod at a certain location in the tepid waters of Indonesia. No human knows the reason for the dolphins' four-day convocation, or understands the mechanism behind its precise timing."[29]

Dr. Lilly agrees, but hints at a link with Sirius:

We know nothing about how certain species move accurately over literally thousands of miles of open ocean. They may possibly use the Moon and stars and the Sun as visual aids to navigation. . . . If one goes under with a face mask and looks back up at the surface, most of the surface looks like a distorted, shimmering mirror, except for an area directly above one's head. . . . It may be that they have learned to solve the mirror problem at the surface of the water and come up and look around at the stars, Moon, Sun, etc., in order to navigate. Their vision in air, as well as in water, is excellent; how they see so well without a face mask is still a puzzle.[30]

Dolphin migration has been recognized since Aristotle's time and before. "This writer learned from Greeks from Marmara," reports Denis Diderot, a prominent figure of the Enlightenment during the mid-eighteenth century, in his *A Rational Dictionary of the Sciences, Arts, and Industries,* "that dolphins migrate, going from the Mediterranean northward in the seas of the Hellespont and the Marmara. They remain for a while in the Black Sea, and then return to their starting point."[31]

But their patterns are as mysterious now as they have ever been, and similarly massive gatherings—although not as immense as the Lombok Strait assemblies—occur elsewhere. "We know that in late summer and fall, all the porpoises [sic] from the lee side of Hawaii seem to gather in a sort of 'Porpoise [sic] National Convention,' usually off Keāhole Point," according to dolphin trainer Kenneth S. Norris.*

Keāhole Point is the westernmost point of the island of Hawaii. "Many young appear at that time, but birth seems clearly not restricted to such a short time, but is instead spread over most or all of the year," Norris continues.[32]

---

*Until as recently as the 1960s, when he conducted his research, dolphins were often called "porpoises," even by cetologists like Norris, as in the subtitle of his own book—*The Life & Times of the Spinner Dolphin, The Porpoise Watcher.*

Yet, the dolphins' choice of Selat Lombok as the site for their largest annual meeting could not be more significant. It was in this part of the world that the Great Bottleneck happened, when the global population of two million humans abruptly shrank to perhaps as few as one thousand breeding pairs, approximately 75,000 years ago. Our species had been driven to the brink of extinction by the most powerful supervolcanic event in Earth's history: Sumatra's Mount Toba eruption, with the power equivalent to one hundred thousand atomic bombs of the magnitude that destroyed Hiroshima at the end of World War II.

About 670 cubic miles of material, including six thousand million tons of poisonous sulphur dioxide, were released into the atmosphere, causing a planetwide winter that drastically reduced temperatures and killed off plant life. Out of this natural cataclysm only the most adaptive, mentally alert, and physically strong survivors emerged, advancing the species from *Homo sapiens* to *Homo sapiens sapiens*. In short, that single catastrophic event brought about our transformation from anthropomorphic apes to modern humans.

In time, their success in coping with a radically altered, more challenging environment led to expanding populations, and the resulting social cooperation prompted their first step from savagery to civilization. These changes took place in only a few generations after Mount Toba erupted, in the temperate paradise of Indonesia, Man's real Garden of Eden. Here, the earliest high culture arose appropriately as Mu, the "Motherland," subsequently referred to around the world in variants of the name Lemuria. Lemuria's inventions of agriculture, city planning, religion, arts, and sciences developed, proliferated, and prospered over seventy centuries.

But in 1628 BCE, a series of monster tsunamis, far larger and more devastating than those that struck the Indian Ocean in 2004 or northern Japan seven years later, scoured civilization from the islands and archipelagoes so long occupied by the Lemurians. More than a thousand years later, their passing was still commemorated in ancient Rome by a major ceremony known as the Lemuria.

During its annual observance, celebrants walked barefooted, as though fleeing from disaster, going from room to room of their homes casting black beans behind them nine times; black beans were symbolic of earthbound human souls (i.e., ghosts), while nine was a sacred numeral signifying birth (after nine months of pregnancy). The ritual's objective was to honor and exorcise any unhappy spirits that may haunt a house. The period set aside for its annual celebration—May 9–13—coincided with the days of the Lemurian destruction. These dates remarkably correspond to Timothy Wyllie's statement that millions of dolphins congregate at the Lombok Strait "for three or four days at a time when the Dog Star, Sirius, is directly overhead . . . every year in May."[33]

It seems beyond all possibilities of belief that these nonhuman creatures could be celebrating the Roman Lemuria, but what else could account for their appearance in massive numbers at the very place where our ancestors became modern humans, where our species created its first civilization, and where those early *Homo sapiens sapiens* bore witness to its final destruction? Nor are dolphin connections with the lost Motherland confined to Selat Lombok.

Limu is among the 175 islands that run through five hundred miles of the South Pacific Tonga archipelago. Its evocative name has been highlighted by the local discovery of artifacts from the Lapita culture, including obsidian tools and distinctive pottery stamped with geometric designs.

Dating of these objects to circa 1600 BCE coincides with the final destruction of Lemuria, after which survivors arriving in the Tonga archipelago referred to the island of their refuge as Limu—just as early British immigrants during colonial times began refering to the eastern seaboard of North America as New England. Additional cultural references echo in the Tongan calendrical periods—still used today—of Lihamui and Lihamu'a. No less cogent to our investigation, the most popular myth repeated throughout Limu recounts how four hundred maidens escaped otherwise inevitable death long ago by throwing themselves into the sea, where they changed into dolphins.

Takiti-Mu, "the ancestral vessel from Mu," carried the first Ngati Kahungunu settlers from their sunken homeland—after which it had been named—to New Zealand, not far from a location then known as Ahuriri, today's Napier. "The dolphins were the frequent companions of the people," according to Maori folklorist Te Rina Sullivan-Meads. "For the ancient Maori, and those who still nurture the ancient knowledge today, the dolphin is their *aumakua,* or *katikati,* their protection relation, their family member in the sea, their sign of good luck and safety . . . believed to be the manifestation of an early ancestor, one of those who landed from the ancestral canoe at Ahuriri. The guardian spirit in the form of a living dolphin is believed to be in the sea near Ahuriri."[34]

On the other side of the Pacific Ocean, Chumash Indians residing on the Southern California coast likewise spoke of Limu, their ancestral homeland across the sea. It was there, they believe, that the first humans were created by Hutash, the Earth goddess. Over the course of many generations, they flourished, creating with her a splendid paradise. But their prosperity eventually resulted in overcrowding, with all its attendant social evils, so Hutash made a rainbow extending to the California mainland. Over this light bridge could cross whoever wished to leave Limu, she said, but they must never look down.

Most people obeyed her instructions, and their migration proceeded successfully; they stepped down in what is now Los Angeles County to become the ancestors of the Chumash. But some people could not avoid looking down from the dizzying perspective of the high rainbow, lost their balance, and fell into the sea. Rather than allowing them to drown, Earth Mother changed them into the first dolphins.

This Native American mythic tradition associates Lemuria with the creation of dolphins from humans, just as the Tongan tale connects Lemuria with human transfiguration into the same creatures. Both accounts perhaps represent folkish memories of the Lemurian Garden of Eden, where our beginnings as a modern species were forged in the epic conflagration of Mount Toba and nurtured over the next seventy centuries in the Indo-Pacific bosom of the Motherland, a seminal process

Figure 21.1. According to the oral tradition of the Chumash Indians,
their ancestors arrived from Limu on the California coast
above Malibu near Los Angeles at Point Dume,
an ancient ceremonial site for dolphin worship.

intimately accompanied in some mysterious way with dolphins. Yet, this
interpretation, however credible and correct as it may be, could comprise
only a small part of a vaster history almost too bizarre for comprehension. For what are we to make of the Dogons' dolphinlike Nommos from
Sirius, the same star Aristotle said signaled the dolphins' disappearance
from his part of the world because they were gathering "in the millions"
at Java's Lombok Strait, just as the Dog Star rose directly over head?

The mystery does not appear to have been restricted to the
Lemurian sphere of influence. Fifty-five miles into the Atlantic Ocean
from Miami, Florida, lies the uninhabited Bahaman island of East
Bimini, featuring some ten to twelve effigy earthworks, mostly depicting various animals, among them a few geometric designs.

All had been skillfully configured by heaping up white sand into various shapes and hedging them in with rocky barriers and, wherever necessary, larger boulders. Indistinguishable hillocks at ground level, the huge figures are recognizable only from the perspective of several thousand feet directly above. But who went to the self-evidently colossal labor of forming these gigantic terraglyphs in this remote place, when, and for what purpose utterly baffles archaeologists.

Among the island's illustrated menagerie is the world's largest image of a dolphin, 525 feet in length, according to leading Bimini researcher William Donato. Since the 1990s, he has undertaken joint archaeological investigations in the Bahamas with Virginia's Association for Research and Enlightenment (ARE). The ARE's website describes "a series of effigy sand mounds shaped like a shark, dolphin and alligator within the Bimini mangrove swamps. The mounds align primarily with the stars Sirius, Rigel, Vega, and Capella, in about A.D. 1000."[35] Their celestial orientation previously occurred around 1600 BCE (plus or minus fifty years), when the natural cataclysm that destroyed Lemuria was survived by a better-known civilization, Atlantis.

Bimini itself is more famous for the so-called road lying in nineteen feet of water off the north shore. Donato believes it is probably the remnant of a prehistoric harbor facility.

The ARE was founded by Edgar Cayce, "thought by many to have been the greatest clairvoyant and prophet since the days of apostolic revelation," according to Brad Steiger, author of *Atlantis Rising*.[36] In several "life readings," he described Bimini as an outpost of Atlantis decades before the discovery of its underwater structure or colossal dolphin mound aligned with the Dog Star. The East Bimini bioglyphs are part of a deeply ancient, unthinkably mysterious relationship—between humans and cetaceans—spanning the globe from West Africa to Greece, Indonesia, Polynesia, California, and the Bahamas. Although Cayce never mentioned dolphins in any of his life readings, he repeatedly placed the Atlantean outpost of Poseidia at a small island fifty-five miles east of Miami, Florida.

Thirty years after Cayce's death in 1945, an aerial survey of uninhabited East Bimini revealed a dozen effigy mounds depicting various animals and geometric shapes. Although a dolphin effigy is in otherwise good condition, natural erosion has partially obliterated its rostrum, or snout, which is additionally obscured by a broadly spreading palm tree. In any case, the appearance of the foremost dolphin representation at a location associated with Atlantis decades before the dolphin bioglyph's discovery must give us pause.

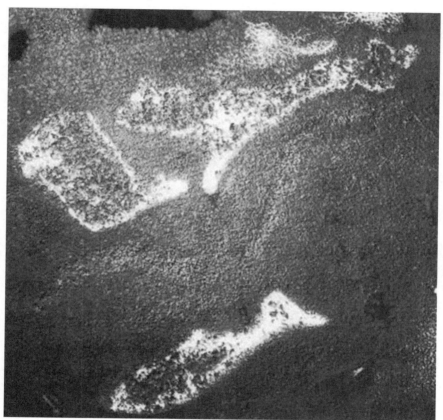

Figure 21.2. Aerial view from twelve thousand feet above the East Bimini earthworks. Although the cat and dolphin bioglyphs are clearly discernible, the elongated structure, far right, is thickly covered with vegetation, obscuring its surface details. Core-sample research continues at the square feature, a possible platform or temple mound. Photograph taken by the late Raymond Leigh Jr., a professional surveyor and photographer.

# 22

# The Dolphins
# of Atlantis

*The so-called myths of the ancients were based on solid
facts of observation, and not, as has hitherto been supposed,
on the imaginings of mythmakers.*

ASHLEY MONTAGU

While our ancestors huddled around campfires listening to their favorite storytellers, our current generation sits in the glow of a television or computer screen. And like all great myths retold over time—occasionally after thousands of years—the story of Atlantis has its modern twist. Today's version of repetitious myth is the rerun, a case in point being *Man from Atlantis,* originally an NBC series popular during the 1977–1978 broadcast season, but now aired on cable channels and YouTube.

Its title character was played by Patrick Duffy, who starred in the role of a lone survivor from the lost civilization. Following a terrible storm far out at sea, his half-dead body was accidentally found by rescuers, who gave him a cover name, "Mark Harris," to conceal his bizarre identity. Restored to good health, he is able to swim under water like a dolphin, aided by webs of skin growing between his fingers. Harris postpones the resumption of his former aquatic existence after several encounters with terrestrial humans because, as he says, "I have not yet learned enough."[1]

That he was depicted with syndactylic hands seven years before Elaine Morgan popularized the aquatic ape theory mirrors the precognitive insightfulness of myth, just as his cetacean swimming technique foreshadowed our own investigation into suggestive human connections with dolphins. His Atlantean origins are no less appropriate in light of Edgar Cayce's anthropomorphic beings, which were genetically altered to serve the power elite of Atlantis.

A few remarks about Edgar Cayce's life story will help put this significant psychic in perspective. In March 1900, severe laryngitis robbed the young Kentuckian of his ability to speak. While undergoing hypnosis therapy the following year, he not only recovered the use of his voice, but uttered statements about subjects far beyond a twenty-four-year-old apprentice photographer's experience, including information concerning the sunken kingdom. Over the subsequent course of many hundreds of life readings, until his death at sixty-seven years of age in 1945, Cayce consistently described the prehistoric Atlanteans as early practitioners of sophisticated technology whose material achievements preceded and sometimes excelled those of the modern industrial world.

Among these extraordinary examples of applied science were human hybrids modified to perform mundane tasks. "They were in the form of—and acted in the capacity of—servants," according to Cayce. Experimental versions of these "things" were created—occasionally resulting in dangerous anomalies—Cayce explains, even unto the last days of Atlantis: "Some brought monstrosities, as those of its (the entity's) association by its projection with its association with beasts of various characters. Hence, those of the . . . sea, or mermaid. . . . Many [merfolk] existed in the [Atlantean] period."[2] Perhaps some of these creatures, as presented in chapter 18, have survived into modern times.

Cayce's life readings do not comprise the only source of information about genetic experimentation in Atlantis. During the 1960s, the Center for Soviet-American Dialogue, sponsored Dr. John Lilly and seventeen other prominent U.S. scholars, toured Russia's Black Sea water-birthing and dolphin research facilities, founded and operated by Dr. Igor Tcharkovsky, previously described. Among the American guests was Athena Neeley, a registered nurse, particularly interested in discovering local cultural traditions pertinent to the subject at hand, especially those unfamiliar outside the Iron Curtain.

"In Russian lore," she learned from her Soviet hosts, "there is the story of people working in Atlantis, trying to develop mutations, experimenting with humans, to get them back to the sea, so that they could live in the sea like the dolphins. The experiments weren't accomplished in time to save the Atlanteans, although some did go back to being dolphins. Eons and eons ago, they were half human, half fish—like mermaids. There were also half humans and half dolphins, and these are shown in the tapestries that we saw in Leningrad [Saint Petersburg], in the museum called the Hermitage."[3]

Although Cayce never mentioned dolphins in any of his life readings, he repeatedly placed the Atlantean outpost of Poseidia at the Bahamian island of Bimini, where we find the world's largest dolphin image (described in the previous chapter), a location associated with Atlantis decades before the bioglyph's discovery.

Dolphins in Atlantis themselves were cited by the early fourth-century BCE Greek philosopher and mathematician Plato, perhaps the single most influential thinker in the history of Western civilization. He also composed the earliest, most complete account of its kind in two dialogues, the *Timaeus* and *Kritias*. Together, they tell of a vast pre-Classical empire stretching from the "opposite continent" of America in the west across the sea and the British Isles to Africa and Europe in the east. The splendid capital of this ancient imperial enterprise was headquartered on a large island (*nesos*) in the mid-Atlantic Ocean, which derived its name from "the sacred city," laid out in concentric circles of alternating moats and land rings.

Near the center of the smallest, innermost artificial island stood the Temple of Poseidon, 600 feet long, 300 feet across, and 150 feet high. "The outside of it," Plato writes, "was covered overall with silver, except for the figures on the pediment, which were covered with gold. Inside, the roof was ivory picked out with gold, silver and orichalc [high-grade copper], and all the walls, pillars and floor were covered with orichalc. It contained gold statues of the god [Poseidon] standing in a chariot drawn by six winged horses, so tall that his head touched the roof, and around him, riding on dolphins, a hundred Nereids."[4]

These were the female spirits of oceanic waters, patrons of sailors in trouble and friendly to fishermen, and may have more epitomized the dolphins themselves than distinct mythic figures. As much has been suggested by the names of some Nereids, like Pherusa, for "carrying" rescued seafarers; Polynoe, "rich of mind"; Sao of the "safe passage"; Eumolpe, the "fine singer"; or Doto, "giving" a secure voyage or generous catch. The names of other Nereids seem related to the first lady of Atlantis, Leukippe, or White Mare, mentioned by Plato in the *Kritias* and analogous to the waves of the sea. These Nereids are: Hipponoe, "who knows about horses"; Hippothoe, "of the swift waves"; and Menippe, "strong horses." Nereids were sometimes portrayed on Greek and Roman gemstones as mermaids. They were the children of Nereus, a merman, and the sea nymph Doris, aunt to Atlas, the titan whose island and city—Atlantis—literally means the daughter of Atlas.*

The Greeks referred to dolphins as *hieros ichthys,* or sacred fish, because the Sun god was said to have appeared before a group of Cretan businessmen at sea, declaring, "Behold, I am Apollo Delphinus!" Assuming the form of a dolphin, he guided their ship into the Gulf of Corinth and toward Mount Parnassus, at the summit of which he founded his famous oracle. The name Delphi derives from the Greek *delphís,* for dolphin, itself a play on the word *delphys,* or womb. No other animal was so deeply revered by the Greeks, who honored the uniquely mystical, spiritual relationship between dolphins and themselves.

Delphi, or Delphoi, was known as "the navel of the world," or

---

*Atlantis was the birthplace of astronomy and astrology; hence, Atlas's depiction in Greek myth as a giant supporting the Zodiac on his shoulders.

Figure 22.1. The Temple of Apollo at Delphi. Photograph by the author.

*omphalos,* a sacred stone signifying the Cosmic Egg from which all life sprang at the beginning of time. The oracle at Delphi was governed by a *hoisioi,* or "college" of priests required to trace their family lineage to Deucalion before taking office, because he was believed to have brought the principles of divination to Delphi from a former Golden Age overwhelmed by the Deluge. Deucalion and his wife, Pyrrha, were the only survivors of a catastrophic inundation that otherwise exterminated all Mankind. The myth tells that the human race is descended from this pair, a way of expressing the Atlantean heritage of every Greek born thereafter, because Deucalion's uncle was none other than Atlas himself.

The Deucalion Flood belongs to a major but not the final geologic upheaval that beset Atlantis in 1628 BCE—the same global cataclysm that overwhelmed Lemuria—after which some survivors arrived as culture bearers in the Eastern Mediterranean. The Sumerian scholar Neil Zimmerer associates the coming of Deucalion with a natural catastrophe around 1700 BCE. Deucalion's "ark" was said to have come to rest on Mount Parnassus—itself consecrated to Poseidon, the sea god of Atlantis—where the most important religious center of the classical world, Delphi, was established.[5]

Cult practitioners from the lost civilization appear to have arrived along the shores of the Gulf of Corinth, where they reestablished the antediluvian spiritual center no later than the late third millennium BCE. They were refugees fleeing a global natural catastrophe that preceded Deucalian's flood and the ultimate destruction of Atlantis by fifteen and nineteen centuries, respectively. Initiation into the Delphic mysteries may have included mind-melding with dolphins in telepathic exchanges that enabled hoisioi adepts to avail themselves of the creatures' immense psychic and paranormal mental capacities. Aristophanes (448–380 BCE) hinted as much when he wrote in his play *The Frogs* how the dolphin "races here and oracles there." How else might we account for Delphi's unequaled and long-lived prestige throughout the classical world?

Before the omphalos was installed atop Mount Parnassus, according to alternative myth, it had been enshrined at Delos, a small island at virtually the geographic center of the Cyclades Islands, in the Eastern Mediterranean. Delos became the cultural and spiritual hub of early Aegean civilization from around 1600 BCE—immediately following the third Atlantis catastrophe and the mass migration of survivors in 1628 BCE—until one thousand years later, when the growing threat of piracy necessitated the navel stone's relocation to mainland Greece.

The Atlantean identity of Delos emerges through its repetition of the fifth and sixth numerals as they were likewise incorporated in the sacred architecture and religious ceremonies of Atlantis, "thereby showing equal respect to both odd and even numbers," according to Plato.[6] On Delos, six columns fronted the supremely important Temple of Apollo, behind which were positioned five *oikoi,* or treasuries, each with five pillars. Also in Delos, the Monument of the Bulls—animals associated with kingship in Atlantis—had six columns, the same number found at the Portico of Antigonos in the Temple to Artemis and at the Portico of Poseidon. So, too, the Delia was a festival held every five years at Delos.

The images of dolphins appear more often than any other creatures here, as they once did at Delphi. A pair prominently adorn the threshold to the House of Masks, and a perfectly preserved red, white, and black mosaic depicting a dolphin with an anchor (the symbolic significance of this image is discussed in chapter 7) may still be found on the floor at the House of Triaina. Red (tufa), white (pumice), and black (lava) were, according to Plato, the Atlanteans' preferred construction colors and building stones.

Especially revealing at Delos is the House of the Dolphins. On its floor lies a large polychrome mosaic representing an aerial view of Atlantis itself, complete with concentric rings of alternating moats and artificial islands in the proper sequence of Atlantean sacred numbers. Spaced equidistantly beyond the outermost ring dolphins are depicted in four pairs, each ridden by a winged human male figure; together, they demarcate the cardinal directions, thereby defining Atlantis at their center as the original Navel of the World and home of the omphalos. Nearby, no less intriguing is the so-called House with the Mosaic Floor of the Mermaids.[7]

The Sumerian merman, Ea, was described in chapter 21, but his Atlantean origins were not addressed. As the Lord of the Waters, he presented the secrets of a high civilization to the early inhabitants of Mesopotamia following a great flood. Ea's identity is confirmed by his portrayal on a cylinder seal in which he bids farewell to a central Atlaslike figure, Enlil, referred to as the Great Mountain, who held up the sky. Enlil was famous as the conqueror of Tiamat, the ocean, just as Atlantis dominated the seas. In the *Epic of Gilgamesh,* where he is known as Bel, Enlil is responsible for the Deluge.

Ea warns Utnapishtim, the flood hero, by telling him, "Oh, reed

Figure 22.2. Delos mosaic in the House of the Dolphins depicting Atlantis. Photograph by the author.

hut, reed hut! Oh, wall, wall! Oh, reed hut, listen!"[8] In the North American Pima Indian deluge story, its flood hero survived by enclosing himself in a reed "tube," which, like the Babylonian "hut," was metaphorical for a contained space or vessel of some kind, no different from the biblical ark.[9] A Navajo version recounts that the survivors made their escape through giant reeds. The implications of these folk memories with regard to the Atlantean catastrophe are unmistakable.[10]

In a later Babylonian incarnation, Ea, now known as Oannes, carried the Tablets of Civilization from his kingdom in the sea to the Near East. The Maya preserved an almost identical tradition of Oa-ana, "he who has his residence in the water."[11] Like his Mesopotamian counterpart, he was considered an early culture bearer who sparked Mesoamerican civilization after arriving with great wisdom from across the Atlantic Ocean. Both Oannes and Oa-ana are suggestive of Atlanteans landing on either side of the world.

In chapter 15, the mid-second-century Greek geographer Pausanias testified to the existence of Periander's monument at Cape Tainaron, at the southernmost point of the Greek peninsula, where the dolphin that saved Arion's life was honorably entombed. A similar structure came to light around the turn of the twenty-first century, near the east coast of Florida, on the south bank of the Miami River, which empties into Biscayne Bay and the Atlantic Ocean. There, a thirty-eight-foot-wide circle had been cut four feet down into bedrock to form a perfectly circular platform. Around its perimeter, in twenty-four uniformly spaced oval apertures from six to twelve inches wide, originally stood posts oriented to noteworthy positions of the Sun, Moon, Venus, Jupiter, certain constellations, and various celestial phenomena; hence, the site is popularly known as "Florida's Stonehenge," a reference to the more famous Neolithic observatory at Britain's Salisbury Plain.

While conventional archaeologists guess local Indians built it maybe 2,500 years ago, the presence of copper from the Great Lakes region, mined between 3000 BCE and 1200 BCE, together with trace elements, push the Miami location much deeper into prehistory and away from any speculation of construction by hunter-gatherer engineers. Due to its colossal mining enterprise during pre-Columbian times, Michigan's Upper Peninsula has long been associated by researchers with Atlantean monopolies on copper procurement and bronze production, the sources, according to Plato, of the oceanic kingdom's great wealth.[12] But the Florida site is unique in America for more than its untypical design because it featured the bones of an adult bottlenose dolphin.

"The remains were also buried, instead of just tossed on the ground," explains Robert Carr of the State Archaeological and Historical Conservancy, "adding to the belief that they were not simply remnants from a discarded meal."[13]

In fact, the skeleton had been originally and carefully laid out at the precise center of the circle's east-west axis, underscoring the limestone structure's orientation to the cardinal directions. According to local archaeologist Alison Elgart-Berry, who spent three weeks painstakingly reassembling the animal's skull and part of its rostrum, "cut marks and pieces missing at the top of the dome suggest the cranium may have been used as a mask."[14] If so, the prehistoric Floridians perhaps recognized their fundamental commonality with dolphins and endeavored to meld with them through ritual behavior.

In addition to parallels with Periander's dolphin monument in Greece, we find parallels on the other side of the world at another ancient site, 6,890 miles away from Florida's Stonehenge, in northern Japan. Hokkaido's Mawaki circle is a cross between the Miami circle and Wyoming's Bighorn Medicine Wheel. Although similar to other Stonehenge-like sites around the world, this Japanese counterpart is the only structure of its kind in Asia, "remarkable for the hundreds of dolphin skulls arranged in a special way, suggesting a cult place for the Early Jomon Period [4000–2500 BCE]."[15] Although time parameters for the Florida and Japan sites are roughly complementary, any direct relationship with Atlantis is less clear, given the Mawaki circle's position in the Pacific Ocean. Even so, the sunken city is generally regarded as the former capital of a global civilization.

While Periander ruled over Corinth during the early sixth century BCE, the monument he is said to have built has roots going farther back into the Atlantean Bronze Age. Arion, for example, was a son of Poseidon, the sea god of Atlantis, and Ino, a sea nymph, whose name was changed after her death to Leukothea, the "white goddess," reminiscent of Leukippe, the "white mare" cited by Plato.[16]

Nor was Plato the only prominent scholar of the classical world to mention the role played by dolphins in Atlantis. Claudius Aelianus, better remembered as Aelian, was an early third-century CE Roman teacher of rhetoric and author of *De natura animalium* (*The Nature of Animals*), in which he reports, "The inhabitants of the shores of the Ocean tell that in former times the kings of Atlantis, descendants of Poseidon, wore on their heads, as a mark of power, the fillet of the male sea-ram, and that their wives, the queens, wore, as a sign of their power, fillets of the female sea-rams."*[17]

---

*A *fillet* is a band or ribbon worn around the head, especially for binding one's hair.

The dolphin was commonly referred to as a "sea ram" for its rostrum, or snout, beginning in the Roman era to at least the mid-sixteenth century, when the animal was known in France as the *oye,* or *bec d'oye,* meaning the goose or goose's beak. An early Greek nickname commonly applied to a dolphin was Simo, meaning "snub-nosed." A Hawaiian term for dolphin is *mano ihu wa'a,* or "mano with a beak like the prow of a canoe." *Mano* in Hawaiian means "shark."

Aelian learned about Atlantis in Lusitania, Rome's Portuguese colony, where local traditions were rife with tales of the sunken civilization—naturally enough, if only because the capital's name, Lisbon, is a derivation of Elasippos, mentioned by Plato as the Atlantean king of Portugal. In his first-century *History of the Gauls*—a Keltic people who then occupied the Iberian Peninsula—Timagenes, a Greek historian from Alexandria, Egypt, related the Gauls' belief that their ancestral ruling class originated at the "Isle of Glass Towers," or *Turris Vitrea* in Latin.[18] This Turris Vitrea was formerly a splendid island before it disappeared during a natural disaster in the North Atlantic Ocean. Survivors were said to have landed at the mouth of the Douro River on the Iberian Peninsula, where they built their first town, the harbor city of Porto. From there, they migrated throughout Iberia and France, where they were the first chiefs of the Gauls.

In fact, a Keltic settlement on the Douro natives referred to as Porto Galli, or "Port of the Gauls," developed over time into the Roman Portus Cale, from which the whole Lusitanian province eventually derived its modern name, Portugal. In Greek myth, the Titan Iberus, after whom the entire Spanish peninsula was named, was the brother of Atlas, the eponymous figure of Plato's sunken city. Aware of these mythic-historic connections, the Romans referred to all Iberians as "children of Atlantis."[19]

Since it was the chief city of a transatlantic empire, the kingdom's impact was felt and recorded across the Northern Hemisphere. Among those surviving documents is the *Leabhar Gabhata* (Book of Invasions), the earliest known history of Ireland "from before the Flood."[20] It tells of a series of immigrations as a result of natural catastrophes that rocked the ancient world. The last of these Late Bronze Age invaders were the Milesians, led by Eremon, who became the first king of all Ireland. His name is a Gaelic variation of Euaemon, the fourth king of Atlantis in Plato's *Kritias*. The *Book of Invasions* goes on to tell how *suire,* or dolphins, accompanied and played around the Milesian ships as they sailed from drowned Atlantis and approached Irish shores.

Today's dolphins may remember all this, and much more, in view of their long association with the lost civilization. Cetologists have learned that they do indeed pass along cultural information from one generation to the next. If so, they might possess an "oral" history of Earth's oceans—more incentive for researchers to finally make that long-sought-for breakthrough in interspecies communication. That achieved, what might the dolphins tell us about Atlantis? Perhaps even the precise whereabouts of its ruins? Such a monumental discovery— the Holy Grail of archaeology—may not only connect us with the most dramatic episode in our development as civilized beings, but simultaneously reveal a closer relationship with our cousins in the sea than we ever imagined.

# 23
## Planet Earth
## or SeaWorld?

*Don't any of you be surprised in future if land beasts change places with dolphins and go to live in their salty pastures, and get to like the sounding waves of the sea more than the land.*
ARCHILOCHUS, GREEK POET, CIRCA 680–645 BCE

Of all the enigmas Jacques Cousteau observed during almost seven decades of underwater exploration, perhaps his most bizarre encounter took place sixty years ago, off a reef in the middle of the Indian Ocean. In the process of gathering material for his now classic film *The Silent World,* he "saw a dolphin rise to the surface to breathe, and then let himself sink down into the water again, without swimming." This sighting followed several days of other unusual delphine behavior, specifically, "every morning at about ten o'clock" a small pod of dolphins swam by his anchored research vessel. Intrigued, Cousteau and a fellow diver slipped into the sea. Cousteau recalls the event:

To this day, I have not forgiven myself for not taking a camera. The sight that greeted us was one that we have never seen again. There were about fifteen dolphins—probably the school that we had seen going past *Calypso* every morning—in the crystal-clear water, on the side of the reef. They were *sitting* on the bottom, in a group, as though they were holding a conference. I say "sitting"; I mean that they were literally poised on their tails.

They remained where they were, stirring a bit and looking at one another. Then they continued with their meeting. But when we tried to move in closer to them, they swam away immediately. It was a unique and extraordinarily impressive sight. The truth is that I still have no idea what they were doing.[1]

Telepathically communicating with each other, most likely. Cousteau himself writes that their "meeting" suggested "an underwater congress."

More intriguing still, about what did they confer? Given their proximity to *Calypso,* they were probably discussing the unusual presence of anthropomorphic divers in an otherwise unvisited area of the vast Indian Ocean; what could have brought the strangers there, how the pod should regard them, and related issues of the moment. The dolphins sat together, as humans do, yet another comparison between both species—like lanugo; eye similarity; the soft spot at the top of our head corresponding to the dolphin's blow hole; humanlike fingers, hands, thighs, knees, feet, and toes in the dolphin embryo; and many more—indicating a shared evolution of some kind.

Can all this mean that we were once dolphins before our ancestors returned to dry land, where primate attributes are more useful? If so, do the dolphins still preserve a cultural or collective memory of our aquatic past and regard us on account of it as their mammalian relatives? Is *that* the real basis for their demonstrable love of Mankind? Given their immense intellect, they may know much more—everything, in fact, that there is to understand concerning the illimitable bounty of the sea. What they might teach us about it could mean the difference between our annihilation or survival in an age of extinction.

And what are we to make of their much larger "underwater

congress" in Indonesia during the ancient Roman festival of Lemuria? Is their gathering at the Lombok Strait an annual remembrance of the lost Motherland, where they may have played a crucial role in our civilized beginnings? Tragically, the magnitude of loss there is appalling. In the mid-twentieth century, millions of dolphins congregated there every May, but their numbers have since fallen to a few hundred.[2] Japan's wholesale slaughter of the animals has assumed international notoriety, but even more devastating is the progressive poisoning of the planet's water resources.

Just how far rising levels of toxicity have already gone to reduce dolphin population is difficult to determine. But cetologists do know that a dolphin mother's first birth dies from all the human toxins it ingests, while a second birth usually survives because its immediate predecessor absorbed most of the toxins. This process, even if it continues at present levels—which, of course, it won't—must result in at least cutting the dolphin population in half.

"The growing presence of toxic chemicals in the marine environment presents a crisis unlike any ever faced on this planet," warns BlueVoice, an ocean conservation organization founded in 2000. The group continues:

> Vast quantities of toxic chemicals enter the waterways and oceans of the world each day and accumulate, then bio-magnify in the marine food chain. In a time when we have reduced the number of large pelagic fish by ninety percent and the bio-mass of the oceans by seventy percent, we are poisoning much of the living marine resources that remain. This has staggering global implications for ocean life and human health. A level of one hundred parts per million of mercury has been found in a bottlenose dolphin killed for food in Japan—a level more than one hundred times that accepted by Japanese health authorities. . . . Dolphins, toothed whales, large tuna and swordfish are among the marine creatures with highest levels of contamination, because they feed at the apex of the food chain.[3]

Whenever greed and self-interest are at work, Man's indifference to the suffering and extermination of his fellow creatures—even if their plight endangers himself—is human nature. As such, it cannot be eradicated by education or legislation, but will only disappear with Man himself. This is what Jacques Cousteau, Jacques Mayol, John Lilly, and other scientists came to realize and share in the last century. In the words of Cousteau:

> Gravity is the original sin. . . . The sea, the great unifier, is man's only hope. . . . We must plant the sea and herd its animals using the sea as farmers instead of hunters. That is what civilization is all about—farming replacing hunting. . . . If we go on the way we have, the fault is our greed, and if we are not willing to change, we will disappear from the face of the globe, to be replaced by the insect. If we were logical, the future would be bleak, indeed. But we are more than logical. We are human beings, and we have faith, and we have hope, and we can work.[4]

That work, as he envisioned it, is to gradually return to our aquatic origins in the baptism of a new species, to wash away the original sin of our all-too-human nature. Nor is the prospect as fantastic as it may seem. Some human populations living in an intimate relationship with the sea are already developing marine mammal characteristics, like the blubbery bodies of Polynesians or the duck-footed Agaiumba pygmies of Papua New Guinea. As embodied in the physical evolution of these examples, some peoples experienced aquatic transformation more recently or proceed through this evolutionary process more often than others.

The long-term habitation of sub-Saharan Africans in a regional arid climate necessitated flared nostrils less suitable for swimming than the narrower Indo-European nose, which guides moving water away from the nasal cavities. So too, the Indo-European mother's hair grows fuller than usual throughout pregnancy and for months after she gives birth, just as the scalp during this period becomes stronger, allowing a newborn, in bouyant conditions, to instinctively grasp her long tresses missing from the Sub-Saharan mother's much shorter hair, which is less suitable for grasping. These relative comparisons demonstrate human adaptability to aquatic challenges—their retention or rejection over time—and our ready response to them during the past, even currently.

Projecting what we have learned or suspect about such transformational potentials and our own aquatic origins into some inconceivably distant future, we can imagine an Earth entirely restored to its original pristine condition. All its creatures would roam free—unhunted, unexploited, and unharmed, save by natural predators, as part of the eternal balance of life—through an unpolluted environment of worldwide fresh air and water.

The wheel of organic existence would run on undisturbed, because no trace would be found of the viral species that formerly dominated this exquisitely beautiful planet, save among the last vestiges of its overgrown and crumbling cities. Their former inhabitants would be gone, for the good of the world and themselves. Nor would the descendants of this lost race be found among the deserted, disintegrating ruins because they would have—all of them—reunited with their brother and sister dolphins in the sea.

# A Dolphin Fulfills
# the Mayan Prophecy

*The Earth may continue to sprout seeds, yet one day it too*
*must end. . . . When will that destructive strike threaten to*
*tear the world apart?*
                   RICHARD WAGNER, *THE FLYING DUTCHMAN*

The Mayan Calendar came to an end on December 21, 2012, but not its Prophecy. Doomsayers were disappointed and their critics felt vindicated when the world did not end on that winter solstice, because neither the scaremongers nor the skeptics got it right. I first learned of the controversy long before prognostications for global catastrophe became popular around the turn of the last century.

During my first research trip to Mexico in 1986, I was fortunate enough to meet with several Mayan elders, who shared with me a traditional and authentic version of their Prophecy, as they had orally received it from their ancestors, intact, over the last 120 generations. While such a feat of preservation seems unbelievable by modern standards of recordkeeping, history vouches for the technique among earlier, highly advanced peoples, such as the classical bards hired by Greek and Roman aristocracy for their ability to recite the *Illiad* and *Odyssey* by rote. Western Europe's Keltic Druids regarded the written word—

used by commercial bureaucrats—as too profane for the transmission of sacred wisdom, but were capable of astounding performances of memory, as personally witnessed by Julius Caesar, who lauded them in *The Conquest of Gaul,* his account of Rome's military campaigns in Western Europe.[1] Seventeen centuries later, Captain James Cook was presented to a native "speaker" capable of reeling off the entire royal lineage and history of preconquest Hawaii in an unbroken recitation that took more than three hours to complete.

The Maya were and still are no less skillful in preserving those folk memories most important to them, including the so-called Mayan Prophecy. I had inadvertently won the elders' trust when one of them asked me what I thought of the Pyramid of the Magician towering over the ruins of Uxmal, a ceremonial city in western Yucatán. We were conversing near the foot of this enormous, aesthetically appealing stone structure, 105 feet high, with its base measuring 207 feet by 147 feet.

"The Magician," I said, "is a reference to Itzamna, husband of Ixchel—known as Lady Rainbow, or White Face—both of them survivors from an island city across the sea, 'where the sun rises'—a reference to the Atlantic Ocean. That city was called Tutulxiu, or the Bountiful Land. Long ago, a flood engulfed Tutulxiu and most of its inhabitants. From the many gifts—art, architecture, science, government, weaving, etc.—that Itzamna and Ixchel shared with Uxmal's native people eventually grew Mayan civilization, a hybrid culture from local Yucatán and foreign Tutulxiu influences. For this, Itzamna and Ixchel were worshipped as creation deities."

The elders added that Itzamna also salvaged from Tutulxiu's destruction his sacred almanac, known in our time as the Mayan Calendar. Its Long Count of 1,872,000 days, which began on August 11, 3114 BCE, was set to terminate when the southern end of our galaxy's Dark Rift perfectly aligned with a midpoint in the Milky Way, as seen in the Northern Hemisphere on the morning of December 21, 2012. This precision and its moral significance, they said, are based on the recognition that all forms of energy interface. Just as natural energies

Figure E.1. Uxmal's Pyramid of the Magician.

impact human life, so human behavior may affect natural processes. In this, the ancients foreshadowed modern physicists, who have determined that the mere presence of an experimenter influences the outcome of his or her experiment. The cosmos strives for harmony, but when an imbalance upsets the equilibrium of life, Nature responds with corrective measures to restore universal stability.

When applied to Man, so long as he lives at least fundamentally in accord with the greater totality of existence, he prospers. But if human society runs counter to Creation, it sets in motion those natural, restorative forces that ultimately redound to its destruction. The Mayan Calendar depicts four such civilization-killing events in the deep past. Exactly 5,126 years following the last such cataclysm—the Great Deluge that overwhelmed Tutulxiu in 3114 BCE—another global catastrophe will begin after the winter solstice of 2012 CE, but only if by then humans and Nature are still at odds with each other. If so, Itzamna's calendar will end with 4-Ollin, otherwise known as a Rebellion of the Earth.

This view is not exclusive to the Maya, but known to many pre-Columbian peoples throughout the Americas. Even today, the Hopi Indians define such a world crisis as *Koyaanisqatsi*—"life disintegrating, or out of balance," a state of being that calls for another way of living.[2] "If, however, our species has at least begun to reassert its proper relationship with the cosmos," the Mayan elders said, "2012 will mean the beginning of a new golden age thereafter for the whole Earth."

In other words, the longest night of that year was a shadow through which we time traveled, a demarcation signifying the difference between human destruction and renewal. As such, 4-Ahau 3-Kankin, as the Maya expressed December 21, 2012, was never understood as "Doomsday," the end of the world. It represented instead a symbolic threshold—signified by the longest night contrasting with the shortest day—with possibilities for either the dominance of an eternal night—that is, annihilation—or the beginning of a new day, with continued existence and positive development. Having crossed it, we find no middle path, but must follow the fast track to a Dark Age or Golden Age—toward either extinction or expansion.

Uxmal's native elders never specified any particulars concerning the former possibility, save to define it as the total obliteration of our civilization, and possibly our species, although not of the planet itself. They did, however, characterize the potential cataclysm as a consequence of humankind's fatal interface and Nature. A Rebellion of the Earth—4-Ollin—would be triggered by Bolon Yokte, a Mayan demon of absolute destructiveness, falling out of the sky. Nothing more was related by either the ancients or their twentieth-century descendants. But if we are to give their Prophecy any credence—and perhaps we should, in view of its uncanny relevance to our modern world's precarious condition—we must ask ourselves: Are we worth surviving, or will our planet be purged of the human virus?

While the Mayan record is silent concerning our generation's eligibility for continued existence or final extermination, actions may speak louder than the absence of these words. On February 15, 2013, almost two months after the apparently uneventful, anticlimactic passing of the Mayan Calendar, a sixty-five-foot-wide meteor heavier than the Eiffel Tower of Paris entered Siberian air space. Falling at fifty times the speed of sound, the massive object detonated 97,000 feet above the ground in a blinding flash that momentarily blotted out the Sun with an explosive force more powerful than the atomic bomb that destroyed another civilian population center—Hiroshima—sixty-eight years earlier. Shock waves from the five-hundred-kiloton blast encircled the planet several times in the greatest sonic booms ever recorded by the United Nations' monitoring system. They damaged 7,200 buildings in Chelyabinsk, plus five other cities, knocking out both electrical grid and cell phone networks, collapsing the two-thousand-square-foot roof of a zinc factory, and injuring about 1,500 residents with flying shards of broken glass.

An incomprehensibly greater, but entirely harmless (to us) burst lit up the night sky seven months and one day later, when "a new star

Figure E.2. The Chelyabinsk meteor.

explosion" was observed for the first time by Koichi Itagaki of Yamagata, Japan. Using a CCD camera attached to a seven-inch reflecting telescope, the amateur astronomer documented his discovery of Nova Delphini 2013, a powerful eruption in the constellation Delphinus, the dolphin.

According to Joe Rao, an instructor and guest lecturer at New York's Hayden Planetarium:

> The new nova was not present in a photo taken by Itagaki on Tuesday (August 13), when he observed stars down to a magnitude +13, so overnight it had brightened at least three hundred-fold. More likely, however, it initially was much dimmer—perhaps as faint as magnitude +17, implying that in less than twenty-four hours it may have increased in brightness by more than ten thousand times! . . . What we see as a nova is believed to originate from the surface of a white dwarf star in a binary system. If these two stars are close enough, material from one star can be pulled off the companion star's surface and onto the white dwarf, producing an extremely bright outburst of light. When the outburst has subsided, the white dwarf usually reverts back to its original state. This likely is the case for the nova discovered in Delphinus.[3]

Bright, naked-eye novas are infrequent but not all that rare, appearing about once or twice per decade.

To almost all of us living in the early twenty-first century, the Mayan Calendar's galactic alignment, Siberia's meteor, and Nova Delphini 2013 were three intriguing but unrelated celestial occurrences of nothing more than passing interest to astronomers. For the civilizers of pre-Columbian Mexico and their modern descendants, however, these events were far more significant. The ancients were less concerned with predicting obvious phenomena—like a global catastrophe in 2012—than with the subtleties that generated them, a viewpoint that allowed the Maya to clearly and instantly grasp the

Figure E.3. Nova Delphini 2013 at its maximum radiance.

ultimate explanation and final fulfillment of their Prophecy. They were left in no uncertainty concerning its meaning, which was not open to various contrary metaphysical interpretations, but unambiguously spelled out in simple mathematics, a system they used as the cosmic language of the universe to communicate with the gods and future generations across time.

The Maya believed numbers were not invented by humans, but discovered by them while observing relationships between celestial bodies. As such, numbers were naturally encoded among the stars. Therefore, tracing the interconnections joining our three outstanding astronomical events should enable us to decode them.

Fifty-six days after the Long Count of the Mayan Calendar ended with 2012's winter solstice, a 13,000-ton meteor exploded less than nineteen miles above Siberia, shortly after sunrise, around 9:15 in the morning. Appropriately enough, fifty-six is a number of particular astronomical and metaphysical significance. A periodic "broom star," more familiar to us as Halley's comet, was observed for fifty-six days by Chinese astronomers beginning December 22, 841 CE and reappeared for the same length of time during the last century.

For fifty-six days, the Sun still casts a moving shadow across a five-turn, counter clockwise spiral—fifteen by sixteen inches wide—engraved circa 1100 CE on a volcanic boulder at the east entrance of Picture Canyon, part of Northern Arizona University's Centennial Forest, in northeastern Flagstaff. The effect is created by a nearby, pointed rock projecting its silhouette diagonally over the petroglyph at sunrise. A shadow line moves across the spiral, right to left, between the first day of spring and mid-May (the optimum period for planting in the area), then repeats itself, going left to right between high summer (late July) and the fall equinox. A thousand years ago, the American Southwest was dominated by Anasazi astronomers renowned for such seasonally oriented rock art.

"The full moon at the northern minimum lunar standstill position," writes Arizona archaeologist Gerald Snow, "will also cast a shadow line tangent to the left side of the [Picture Canyon] spiral."[4] Its lunar aspects were incorporated on the other side of the world at England's Stonehenge, where "Aubrey holes" (named after their seventeenth-century discoverer, John Aubrey) surround the monument in fifty-six chalk pits. These held as many wood posts during the late fourth millennium BCE for calculating the Metonic cycle of 18.6 years ($3 \times 18.6 = 55.8$, or, 18.6 equates, for all practical purposes, to one-third of 56), thereby enabling Neolithic observers to synchronize relative positions of the Sun, Moon, and Earth in their own fifty-six-year cycle, determine tidal motions, and predict eclipses.

An eclipse, classical Greek for "failure," is a celestial event, like the appearance of comets, believed to herald catastrophe: hence, so many traditionally dire associations with fifty-six. In the Hebrew *Kabbalah*, for example, the number is regarded as "lunar" and "unfortunate."[5] "The law of the number fifty-six," stated French philosopher, Louis Claude de Saint-Martin (1743–1803), is a "terrifying law, dreadful for those who are exposed to it," because it embodies "a perverse being grappling with the principles of Nature and surrendering to his own justice."[6] Saint-Martin's characterization manifested itself some two centuries later with the detonation of America's first atomic bomb in the New Mexico desert on July 16, 1945, followed precisely fifty-six years, fifty-six days later by New York City's World Trade Center terrorist attack of September 11, 2001.

Economist David McMinn points out that "a 9/56-year cycle has been established in trends of U.S. and Western European financial crises" since the mid-eighteenth century. "Clearly, many major financial crises are precipitated by some mechanism, as they tend to occur preferentially in patterns of the 9/56-year cycle and not as random events . . . the 9/56-year cycle was found to correlate very closely with cycles of the Sun and Moon. . . . The two cycles of 9.0 and 56.0 tropical years result in alternating full/new moons every 111.5 and 692.5 synodic months, respectively. . . . It is hypothesized that tidal harmonics [as calculated by Stonehenge's fifty-six Aubrey hole posts] involving Moon-Sun cycles activate cycles of financial distress."[7]

These astrological, astronomical, and transcendental qualities repeatedly define fifty-six as a negative, cosmically hazardous number appropriate in the extreme for the Siberian meteor's 2013 appearance. Fifty-six days separating the end of the Mayan Calendar from the Chelyabinsk fireball represented more than a near miss. Had it impacted or air burst at a lower altitude, far more than the city's 1.1 million inhabitants would have been vaporized. At the time, Chelyabinsk was used as a storage area for chemical and bacteriological weapons manufactured during the Soviet era. They had been collected from all over Russia for future demobilization. Had this immense arsenal of mass-destructiveness been ignited by the incoming superbolide, it would have unleashed clouds of lethal agents into Earth's atmosphere on a scale many times more murderous than the combined disasters at Chernobyl in 1986 and the Fukushima Daiichi nuclear plant, twenty-five years later. Millions of agonizing deaths around the globe would have resulted in social dislocation not unlike that suffered by Europeans during the Black Plague. How, in its present condition, the world economy would have survived an early twenty-first-century version of such a catastrophe, care of an impact at Chelyabinsk, is difficult to imagine. Had the meteor exploded a nanosecond later, we would be living in a different world.

In another transient occurrence of astronomical significance, 183 days following Siberia's incoming superbolide, a nova swelled to its maximum radiance in the Dolphin constellation. But the stellar detonation in Delphinus was something of an illusion. What amateur astronomer Koichi Itagaki saw for the first time during mid-August 2013 had actually occurred early in the previous century: light traveling $570{,}214{,}482 \times 104$ miles from the constellation required ninety-seven years to reach his eye. The nova had actually erupted in 1916, when its earthly counterpart conflagration was exploding into World War I. Both were events of massive self-destruction, simultaneously paralleling each other and the Mayan Calendar Prophecy. Its Long Count began 5,032 years before the Delphinus nova with an earlier celestial event on August 11, 3114 BCE, when the planet Venus transited directly over the Pyramid of the Moon at the Valley of Mexico's greatest pre-Columbian site, the ceremonial metropolis of Teotihuacán, "where men become gods."[8]

The Morning Star, or Venus, was identified with Kukulcan—a Classic Period (250–900 CE) variation of the earlier Itzamna—remembered as the Feathered Serpent for his insignia, which resembles the ancient Egyptian *ur-uatchti*. This was a winged Sun disc flanked on either side by a pair of *uraei,* or protective goddesses in serpent form, and commonly placed over temple entrances. The sacred emblem appears to have originated in Atlantis, from whence royal or priestly survivors carried it eastward into the Nile valley, where it was known as the ur-uatchti, and westward into the Valley of Mexico. There, the symbol was so increasingly associated with its Atlantean culture bearer that it became his title. The Feathered Serpent was symbolized by Venus, because he and the planet arose in the East and disappeared in the West. After running afoul of the natives, his myth tells, Kukulcan vanished over the Pacific Ocean.

Figure E.4. Teotihuacán's Pyramid of the Moon.

Figure E.5. Kukulcan, the feathered serpent, at Teotihuacán's
Temple of the Feathered Serpent.

Figure E.6. Dolphins of Kukulcan at Chichén Itzá's Venus Platform.

His totem animal was the dolphin, because it led him, his family, and his followers from their sunken homeland to the shores of Yucatán, and later escorted him to his exile across the western sea. These events are depicted at the Maya's most famous city, in Chichén Itzá's central plaza, where sculpted dolphins surround a representation of Kukulcan. He and the dolphins are portrayed on the Venus Platform, named after its numerous references to the Feathered Serpent's planet.

As the delphine theme extends outward from Chichén Itzá's Venus Platform into space and time, the three astronomical events mentioned above connect in noteworthy synchronicity. For example, the 183 days separating Siberia's fireball from the Delphinus constellation's nova correspond to the same number of days in a mythic account of Ixchel, mentioned above, as the founder, along with her husband, of Mesoamerican civilization. Before Tutulxiu, their Bountiful Land across the sea, was engulfed by catastrophe, Itzamna won her heart when he appeared in his highest aspect as Kinich Ajaw, the god of light. But their union was vigorously opposed by her grandfather, a storm god, who, enraged by the girl's defiance, killed Lady Rainbow with a thunderbolt, rather than allow her to marry the despised "Face of the Sun."

Itzamna-Kinich Ajaw took his lover's body to a secret location, where, as the divine patron of healing, he commanded dragonflies to hover and sing over the corpse. After 183 days, Ixchel was restored to life, and the reunited couple entered Tutulxiu's Palace of the Sun. Among the Maya, the dragonfly symbolized regeneration: as the insect completes its nymphal stage, an adult emerges from the *exuviae*—the remains of its exoskeleton—which is left behind like a dead shell. In temple hieroglyphics, Kinich Ajaw regulates the *k'in,* or the day unit, of the Mayan Calendar, defining him as its master and inventor.

The 183 days he needed to revive Ixchel were neither meaningless nor randomly chosen; they comprise exactly one-half of the Mayan solar year, over which he presided in its entirety. Applying this ancient story of rebirth to the 183 days from 2013's Chelyabinsk meteor to Delphinus's nova maximum, a transcendental inference is self-evident: our species will survive all threats and crises to fulfill a divine destiny. Like Ixchel, our descendants will emerge godlike from Death's exuviae to enter a Palace of the Sun. As such, the same number of days connecting 2013's outstanding astronomical events are perfectly paralleled in a myth thousands of years old.

Near Delphinus is the similarly small and dim constellation of Sagitta, the arrow; its tip pointed directly at the August 16, 2013 nova. This impossibly significant alignment was no less novel than 2012's winter solstice relationship between our galaxy's Dark Rift and a midpoint in the Milky Way, a once-only orientation that exactly dovetailed with the closing date of the Mayan Calendar. And how astonishing that a potential killer-meteor should have terminated its existence on our relatively submicroscopic world in the illimitable vastness of the cosmos at such an infinitely precise moment after surviving a wandering odyssey through space for the previous 4.5 billion years, just when the Earth itself was born!

Statistical probabilities for an accidental coincidence of this incomprehensible magnitude are beyond every category of thought, exceeding all conceivable realms of material possibility, leaving only a metaphysical explanation. Had the Siberian fireball ignited Russia's bacteriological warfare arsenal, the Mayan Prophecy's darkest possibilities might have been fulfilled in the agonizing deaths of untold millions, potentially of our whole species, as a pathogenic cloud poisoned Earth's atmosphere. Fortunately, the meteoric air burst caused no fatalities, although fifteen hundred people in need of medical attention and time to heal their injuries signify that civilization may suffer from the fundamental purging it requires, but *Homo sapiens sapiens* will recover. So too, damage caused by the meteor, while severe (exceeding a billion rubles, more than $33 million), was not permanent, just as the coming Great Cleansing may pulverize our material culture, but leave sufficient debris for future generations to rebuild something different and better.

The fifty-six days separating 2012's winter solstice date for the end of the Mayan Calendar from the exquisitely close call with a flaming superbolide (the personification of Bolon Yokte, if ever there was one!) at Chelyabinsk's genocidal germ warfare arsenal can only mean that Mankind escaped a guilty verdict. The following 183 days—coinciding with the beginning of Ixchel's new life—climaxed with "a new star explosion" in the Delphinus constellation.

These exceptional celestial relationships imply that we are not doomed, despite challenges historically unprecedented for their magnitude. The dolphin has never been a harbinger of death, but always was and is our savior, the bringer of life and hope—from our early shared evolution, to Atlantis and the Feathered Serpent, to modern instances of human rescue and a felicitous white dwarf event in the constellation Delphinus. For all our terrible transgressions against ourselves and against our fellow creatures with which we share our much-abused world, at least enough of us have somehow convinced the Universal Consciousness that we deserve to live.

Four event horizons are of note—the transit of Venus over Mexico's Pyramid of the Moon at Teotihuacán, "where men become gods," on August 11, 3114 BCE, coinciding with the beginning of the Mayan Calendar's Long Count; the Calendar's conclusion on December 21, 2012, just as our galaxy's Dark Rift aligned with a midpoint in the

Milky Way; Chelyabinsk's near miss fifty-six, cosmically significant days later, followed by the Delphinus nova's appearance in the same number of days Ixchel required for her rebirth. Combined and viewed together in sequence, these events bespeak an otherworldly mechanism we may recognize and even understand, but we may never know what or who set it in motion.

# Notes

## INTRODUCTION. THE EYE OF THE DOLPHIN

1. Haldane, *Possible Worlds and Other Essays*, 12.
2. Cousteau, *Dolphins*, 127.
3. Titelman, *Dictionary of Popular Proverbs and Sayings*, s.v. "Les yeux sont le miroir de l'dme," 17.
4. Cochrane and Callen, *Dolphins and Their Power to Heal*, 49.
5. Cousteau, *Dolphins*, 153.
6. Sténuit, *Dolphin, Cousin to Man*, 115.
7. Cousteau, *Dolphins*, 182.
8. Dobbs, *Dolphin Healing*, 55.
9. Lilly, *Lilly on Dolphins*, 201.
10. Devine, and Clark, *Dolphin Smile*, 143.

## 1. WE ARE AQUATIC APES

1. Ben Richmond, "How the Aquatic Ape Theory Keeps Floating On," VICE, May 10, 2013, www.vice.com/read/how-the-aquatic-ape-theory-keeps-floating-on.
2. Elizabeth Armstrong Moore, "How Deadly Flies Spurred Remarkable Evolution," FOX News, June 3, 2014, www.foxnews.com/science/2014/06/03/how-deadly-flies-spurred-remarkable-evolution/.
3. Wyllie, *Dolphins, Telepathy and Underwater Birthing*, 186.
4. Opit, *Australian Cryptozoology*, 44.
5. Odent, *Water and Sexuality*, 110.
6. Ibid.
7. Darwin, *Origin Of Species*, 237.
8. Odent, *Water and Sexuality*, 117.
9. Cousteau, *Dolphins*, 193.
10. Cochrane and Callen, *Dolphins and Their Power to Heal*, 159.

## 2. OUR SEA-MAMMAL HERITAGE

1. Morris, *Naked Ape*, 87.
2. Opit, *Australian Cryptozoology*, 17.
3. Zuckerman, "Sold Gras," 33.
4. Paula Peterson, "Dolphin-Human-Ape," Earthcode International Network, http://paulapeterson.com/dolphin_human_connection.html.
5. Cochrane and Callen, *Dolphins and Their Power to Heal*, 182.
6. "Michel Odent," *The Lancet*, 764.
7. Odent, *Water and Sexuality*, 121.
8. Ibid., 121.
9. Ibid., 121.
10. Ibid., 122.
11. Opit, *Australian Cryptozoology*, 49.
12. Ibid., 49.
13. Odent, *Water and Sexuality*, 130.
14. Ibid., 130.
15. Cochrane and Callen, *Dolphins and Their Power to Heal*, 198.
16. Ibid., 198.
17. Odent, *Water and Sexuality*, 57.
18. Opit, *Australian Cryptozoology*, 53.
19. Odent, *Water and Sexuality*, 39.

## 3. HOMO DELPHINUS

1. Sophocles, *Antigone*, 16.
2. Lovelock, *Vanishing Face of Gaia*, 218.
3. Lilly, *Man and Dolphin*, 177.
4. Nietzsche, *Beyond Good and Evil*, 161.
5. Goethe, *Faust*, 48.
6. Williams, *Night of the Iguana*, act 1, scene 7.
7. Goodall, *In the Shadow of Man*, 66.
8. Opit, *Australian Cryptozoology*, 47.
9. Lilly, *Man and Dolphin*, 222.
10. Gibson, *Reenchanted World*, 54.
11. Dobbs, *Magic of Dolphins*, 136.
12. William L. Newmeyer III, "History of the Jornal of Hand Surgery: 1976–1999, *Journal of Hand Surgery*, September 30, 1999, www.jhandsurg.org/article/S0363-5023(00)95804-0/abstract.
13. Dobbs, *Follow the Wild Dolphins*, 118.
14. Cousteau, *Dolphins*, 146.

15. Odent, *Water and Sexuality,* 119.
16. Sténuit, *Dolphin, Cousin to Man,* 172.
17. Mead and Gold, *Whales and Dolphins in Question,* 93.
18. Jean Charles Genet, "Dolphins and Children with Autism Communicate the Same Way," Decrypted Matrix, July 27, 2011, decryptedmatrix.com/live/dolphins-andchildren-with-autism-the-connection/.
19. Sanderson, *Animal Treasure,* 91.

## 4. THE MIND IN THE SEA

1. Wyllie, *Dolphins, Telepathy and Underwater Birthing,* 174,
2. Dobbs, *Magic of Dolphins,* 12
3. Seema Kumar, "Humans Genes Closer to Dolphins' Than Any Land Animals," *Discovery Channel Online News,* January 9, 1998, www.aquacranial.com/Home.html.
4. Ibid.
5. Ibid.
6. Lilly, *Mind of the Dolphin, A Non-Human Intelligence,* 38.
7. Opit, *Australian Cryptozoology,* 22.
8. Michael Crawford, "Seafood Human Evolution and Health with Professor MA Crawford," YouTube, July 3, 2008, www.youtube.com/watch?v=TUpuhXbUX64.
9. Dobbs, *Tale of Two Dolphins,* 36.
10. Quoted in Lohn, *Historical Dictionary of Competitive Swimming,* 86.
11. Gibson, *Reenchanted World,* 11.
12. Oppian, *Halieuticks,* 31.
13. Odent, *Water and Sexuality,* 50.
14. Thomas White, "A Primer on Non-Human Personhood and Cetacean Rights," Whale and Dolphin Conservation (WDC), us.whales.org/issues/primer-on-non-human-personhood-and-cetacean-rights.
15. de Bergerac, *Dolphin Within,* 79.
16. Sténuit, *Dolphin, Cousin to Man,* 204.
17. Cochrane and Callen, *Dolphins and Their Power to Heal,* 184.
18. Lilly, *Communication between Man and Dolphin,* 138.
19. Edwards, *Shark,* 45.
20. Cochrane and Callen, *Dolphins and Their Power to Heal,* 64.
21. Oppian, *Halieuticks,* 21.

## 5. THE OTHER HUMANS

1. Cochrane and Callen, *Dolphins and Their Power to Heal,* 188.

2. Reiss, *Dolphin in the Mirror*, 109.

3. Ibid., 109.

4. Béder Chávez, "Stories from the River," www.virtualexplorers.org/ard/peo ple/myth.htm.

5. Jeanna Bryner, "In Photos: The World's Oldest Cave Art," LiveScience, October 8, 2014, www.livescience.com/48199-worlds-oldest-cave-art-photos.html.

6. Wikipedia, s.v. "Cave Painting," https://en.wikipedia.org/wiki/Cave_painting.

7. Sténuit, *Dolphin, Cousin to Man*, 211.

8. Aelian, *Historical Miscellany*, 101.

9. Jebb, *Bacchylides*, 42.

10. Odent, *Water and Sexuality*, 126.

11. Stewart and Knox, *Earthquake America Forgot*, 52.

12. Douglas G. Nuelle, M.D., personal correspondence with author, June 12, 2014.

## 6. FROM EXTINCTION TO REBIRTH

1. Louis Burke, "Swimmers: Body Fat Mystery!" Australian Institute of Sport, November 16, 1997, www.sportsci.org/news/compeat/fat.html.

2. Cousteau, *The Living Sea*, 174.

3. Ibid., 174.

4. Mircea, *Shamanism*, 93.

5. Wyllie, *Dolphins, Telepathy and Underwater Birthing*, 137.

6. Odent, *Water and Sexuality*, 84.

7. Nietzsche, *Thus Spake Zarathustra*, "Zarathustra's Prelude."

## 7. ARE DOLPHINS THE MOST INTELLIGENT CREATURES IN THE WORLD?

1. Morgan, *Aquatic Ape*, 128.

2. Odent, *Water and Sexuality*, 33.

3. Betsy Querna, "Dolphins Recognize, Admire Themselves in Mirrors, Study Finds," National Geographic, May 2, 2001, http://news.nationalgeographic.com/news/2001/05/0502_dolphinvanity.html.

4. Cochrane and Callen, *Dolphins and Their Power to Heal*, 189.

5. Jeremy Manier, "Dolphins Keep Lifelong Social Memories, Longest in a Non-human Species," *U Chicago News*, University of Chicago, August 6, 2013, http://news.uchicago.edu/article/2013/08/06/dolphins-keep-lifelong-social-memories-longest-non-human-species.

6. Jennifer Viegas, "Dolphins May Be Math Geniuses," *Discovery,* July 17, 2012, http://news.discovery.com/animals/whales-dolphins/dolphins-math-geniuses-120717.htm.

7. Ibid.

8. Ibid.

9. Sténuit, *Dolphin, Cousin to Man,* 114.

10. Roberta Goodmam, "Eye of the Dolphin Hurricane," Wild Dolphin Swims Hawaii with Roberta Goodman, June 10, 2012, http://robertagoodman. blogspot.com/2012/06/eye-of-dolphin-hurricane.html.

11. Miller, *Call of the Dolphins,* 120.

12. Goodman, "Eye of the Dolphin Hurricane."

13. Cochrane and Callen, *Dolphins and Their Power to Heal,* 123.

14. Robson, *Pictures in the Dolphin Mind,* 145.

15. The Asking Sea, Instagram, www.instagram24.com/tag/cetaceanconsciousness.

16. Odent, *Water and Sexuality,* 61.

17. Senegoid, "Do Animals have a Sense of Humor?" Straight Dope Message Board, December 4, 2012, http://boards.straightdope.com/sdmb/archive/ index.php/t-674345.html.

18. Wyllie, *Dolphins, Telepathy and Underwater Birthing,* 149.

19. Dobbs, *The Magic of Dolphins,* 84.

20. Lilly, *Man and Dolphin,* 202.

21. Keith Cooper, "Dolphins, Aliens, and the Search for Intelligent Life," *Astrobiology Magazine,* August, 29, 2011, www.astrobio.net/news-exclusive/ dolphins-aliens-and-the-search-for-intelligent-life/.

22. Adams, *Hitchhiker's Guide to the Galaxy,* 189.

## 8. THE HOLOGRAPHIC DOLPHIN

1. U.S. Constitution, preamble, www.law.cornell.edu/constitution/preamble.

2. Miller, *Call of the Dolphins,* 113.

3. de Bergerac, *Dolphin Within,* 120.

4. Lilly, *Man and Dolphin,* 224.

5. Odent, *Water and Sexuality,* 111.

6. Jacobs, Morgane, and Glezer, "Comparative and Evolutionary Anatomy."

7. Paula Peterson, www.paulapeterson.com/ITP/InterspeciesTelepathicProject. html.

8. Odent, *Water and Sexuality,* 112.

9. A. Stuckey, "Misguided, Dated by about 30 Years," review of *Are Dolphins Really Smart,* Amazon.com, January 10, 2014, www.amazon.com/ Are-Dolphins-Really-Smart-mammal/product-reviews/019966045X.

10. Sténuit, *Dolphin, Cousin to Man*, 221.
11. Miller, *Call of the Dolphins*, 66.
12. Dobbs, *The Magic of Dolphins*, 39.
13. Kirby, *Death At Seaworld*, 12.
14. Science News, quoted in David Kirby, "Can Dolphins Really 'Hear' Human Tumors?" Takepart, May 17, 2013, www.takepart.com/article/2013/05/16/can-dolphins-detect-cancer-in-humans.
15. Cochrane and Callen, *Dolphins and Their Power to Heal*, 174.
16. Odent, *Water and Sexuality*, 19.
17. Miller. op. cit., 112.
18. Cousteau, *Call of the Dolphins*, 197.

## 9. TELEPATHIC DOLPHINS

1. Ric O'Barry, "Human Rapport with Dolphins," Dolphin Project, http://dolphinproject.org/.
2. Cochrane and Callen, *Dolphins and Their Power to Heal*, 214.
3. Sténuit, *Dolphin, Cousin to Man*, 134.
4. Robson, *Pictures in the Dolphin Mind*, 152.
5. Ibid., 83.
6. Herzing, *Dolphin Diaries*, 136.
7. *Phylarchus, Phylarchi Historiarum Reliquiae*, 10.
8. Pliny, *Natural History*, Volume I, Books 1–2, 52.
9. Cousteau, *Dolphins*, 144.
10. Hogel, *Symeon Metaphrastes*, 14.
11. Nick Bramhill, "Dolphins Kept Vigil on Irishman's Body," *Irish Times*, June 18, 2011, www.irishtimes.com/news/dolphins-kept-vigil-on-irishmans-body-1.599602.
12. Herzing, *Dolphin Diaries*, 221.
13. Kevin Costa, "The Dolphin Connection Aquatic Telepathy," ParaNexus Association of Anomalous Researchers, March 15, 2010, http://paranexus.org/index.php?action=blog&bact=memberart&member=15&blogid=15&article=77&where=Member_Article.
14. Cousteau, *Dolphins*, 132.
15. Wyllie, *Dolphins, Telepathy and Underwater Birthing*, 84.
16. Ibid., 84.
17. Dobbs, *Dolphin Healing*, 149.
18. de Bergerac, *Dolphin Within*, 101.
19. Burr, *Blueprint for Immortality*, 124.
20. Sheldrake, *Morphic Resonance*, 77.

21. SETI Institute, "Our Mission," www.seti.org/about-us.

22. David Strege, "Dolphin Makes Rare Discovery: A 130-year-old Torpedo," GrindTV, May 21, 2013, www.grindtv.com/outdoor/nature/post/navy-dolphin-makes-rare-find-a-130-year-old-torpedo/.

## 10. THE ORDER OF THE DOLPHIN

1. Sagan, *Cosmic Connection*, 189.

2. Herzing, *Dolphin Diaries*, 97.

3. Aristotle, *History of Animals*, 12.

4. Llano, *Airmen against the Sea*, 207.

5. Lilly, *Man and Dolphin*, 239.

6. Jeff Brent, "The Whistling Language of La Gomera," http://silbo-gomero.com/silbohome.html.

7. Busnel, *Animal Sonar Systems*, 19.

8. Cousteau, *Dolphins*, 164.

9. Ibid., 164.

10. Sténuit, *Dolphin, Cousin to Man*, 42.

11. Lori Marino, "Does Dolphin Intelligence Hint at Possible Type of ET Life?" The Daily Galaxy, September 7, 2011, www.dailygalaxy.com/my_weblog/2011/09/does-dolphin-intelligence-hint-at-possible-type-of-et-life.html

12. Reiss, *Dolphin in the Mirror*, 58.

13. Marino, "Does Dolphin Intelligence Hint at Possible Type of ET Life?"

14. Paula Peterson, www.paulapeterson.com/ITP/InterspeciesTelepathicProject.html.

15. Sténuit, *Dolphin, Cousin to Man*, 82.

16. Jacobs, Morgane, and Glezer, "Comparative and Evolutionary Anatomy."

## 11. HEALING DOLPHINS

1. David Kirby, "Can Dolphins Really 'Hear' Human Tumors?" Takepart, May, 17, 2013, www.takepart.com/article/2013/05/16/can-dolphins-detect-cancer-in-humans.

2. Ibid.

3. DeMares, *Dolphins, Myths and Transformation*, 92.

4. Taylor, *Souls in the Sea*, 69.

5. Quoted in Michael T. Hyson, "Dolphins, Therapy and Autism," www.planetpuna.com/dolphin-paper/Dolphin%20Paper%20HTML/Dolphin-Paper-Final.htm.

6. Wyllie, *Dolphins, Telepathy and Underwater Birthing*, 164.

7. Marino, Lori. "Dolphins Are Not Healers." August 7, 2015. www.dolphin-way.com/2015/08/dolphins-are-not-healers/#axzz3rtJxAmSk.

8. Cochrane and Callen, *Dolphins and Their Power to Heal,* 57.

9. Miller, *Call of the Dolphins,* 129.

10. Ibid., 129.

11. Jennifer Welsh, "Miraculous! Dolphin Healing Powers May Help Humans," LiveScience, July 21, 2011, www.livescience.com/15150-dolphin-recovery-human-healing.html.

12. Ibid.

13. Ibid.

14. Cochrane and Callen, *Dolphins and Their Power to Heal,* 193.

15. Ibid., 193.

16. Thomas Rogers, "Grandin on the Autism Surge," Salon, April 24, 2012, www.salon.com/2012/04/24/grandin_on_the_autism_surge/.

17. Alice Park, "Autism Rises: More Children than Ever Have Autism, but Is the Increase Real?" Time, March 29, 2012, http://healthland.time.com/2012/03/29/autism-rises-more-u-s-children-than-ever-have-autism-is-the-increase-real/.

18. Rogers, "Grandin on the Autism Surge."

19. Hyson, "Dolphins, Therapy and Autism."

20. Dobbs. *The Magic of Dolphins,* 43.

21. Ibid., 43.

22. Lilly, *Man and Dolphin,* 242.

23. Miller, *Call of the Dolphins,* 88.

24. Nomura, Higuchi, Yu, et al., "Slow-wave Photic Stimulation Relieves Patient Discomfort during Esophagogastroduodenoscopy."

25. Ptolemy, *Tetrabiblos,* 12.

26. Nomura, Higuchi, Yu, et al., "Slow-wave Photic Stimulation Relieves Patient Discomfort during Esophagogastroduodenoscopy."

27. Cochrane and Callen, *Dolphins and Their Power to Heal,* 158.

28. Ajit Vadakayil, "Vishnu First Matsya Avatar, Dolphins and 7.38 Hertz Frequency of Hindi King Mantra Om," http://ajitvadakayil.blogspot.com/2013/05/vishnu-first-matsya-avatar-dolphins-and.html.

## 12. PSYCHIATRISTS AT SEA

1. Jaime Licauco, "The Amazing Power of Alpha Brain Waves," *Philippine Daily Inquirer,* August 21, 2012, http://lifestyle.inquirer.net/62828/the-amazing-power-of-alpha-brain-waves.

2. Cochrane and Callen, *Dolphins and Their Power to Heal,* 205.

3. Dobbs, *The Magic of Dolphins,* 33.
4. Ibid., 33.
5. Ibid., 33.
6. Ibid., 33.
7. Cochrane and Callen, *Dolphins and Their Power to Heal,* 198.
8. Dobbs, *The Magic of Dolphins,* 61.
9. Dolphinspedia, "Your Therapist Today Is—A Dolphin," http://dol phinspedia.com/dolphin-therapy/your-therapist-today-is-a-dolphin/#.VD9NqIvF_e4yy.
10. David M. Cole, "Dolphin Therapy," *Cerebral Palsy Network,* http://thecpnetwork.org/dolphintherapy.html.

## 13. THEY OWE THEIR LIVES TO DOLPHINS

1. Mike Celizic, "Dolphins Save Surfer from Becoming Shark's Bait," Today News, November 8, 2007, www.today.com/id/21689083/ns/today-today_news/t/dolphins-save-surferbecoming-sharks-bait/#.VD9TDYvF_e4.
2. Daily Mail, "Dolphins Saved Swimmers from Killer Shark Attack," November 24, 2004, www.dailymail.co.uk/news/article-328242/Dolphins-saved-swimmers-killer-shark-attack.html.
3. Ibid.

## 14. MUSICAL DOLPHINS

1. Pausanias, *Guide to Greece,* 32.
2. Dobbs, *The Magic of Dolphins,* 83.
3. Payne, "Songs of Humpback Whales," 19.
4. Oppian, *Halieuticks,* 12.
5. Odent, *Water and Sexuality,* 13.
6. Kristin L. Stewart, "Dolphins," in *Encyclopedia of Environment and Society,* SAGE, September 25, 2007, www.sage-ereference.com/view/environment/n308.xml.
7. Devine and Clark, *Dolphin Smile,* 108.
8. Sophocles, *Electra,* 17.
9. Pliny, *Natural History,* 42.
10. Cochrane and Callen, *Dolphins and Their Power to Heal,* 175.
11. Randall, *The Metropolitan Museum of Art Cloisters Bestiary,* 11.
12. Dobbs, *Dolphin Healing,* 126.
13. Cousteau, *Dolphins,* 168.
14. de Bergerac, *Dolphin Within,* 115.

15. Dobbs, *Dolphin Healing,* 127.
16. Ibid., 127.
17. Reiss, *Dolphin in the Mirror,* 112.
18. de Bergerac, *Dolphin Within,* 148.
19. Lilly, *Man and Dolphin,* 232.
20. Matthew Edlund, "Do Dolphins Sing Like Whales as They Sleep?" The Rest Doctor, January 30, 2012, http://therestdoctor.wordpress.com/2012/01/30/do-dolphins-sing-like-whales-as-they-sleep-13012/.
21. Dobbs, *Dolphin Healing,* 55.
22. Ibid., 55.

## 15. DOLPHINS AND MEN

1. Cavan Sieczkowski, "Divers Rescue Dolphin after It 'Asks' For Help," *Huffington Post,* March 14, 2014, www.huffingtonpost.com/2013/01/23/dolphin-asks-divers-for-help-caught-in-fishing-line_n_2534674.html.
2. Sténuit, *Dolphin, Cousin to Man,* 119.
3. Ibid., 119.
4. Dobbs, *The Magic of Dolphins,* 63.
5. Mead, *People of the Land,* 13.
6. Pliny, *Natural History,* 34.
7. Oppian, *Halieuticks,* 41.
8. Dobbs, *Follow the Wild Dolphins,* 45.
9. Sténuit, *Dolphin, Cousin to Man,* 173.
10. Ibid., 173
11. Chase, *Narrative of the Most Extraordinary and Distressing Shipwreck.*
12. Cirlot, *Dictionary of Symbols,* 273.

## 16. DOLPHINS AND WOMEN

1. Amy B. Bond, "Three Stories of Dolphin Saviors," Care2, August 25, 2008, www.care2.com/greenliving/3-stories-of-dolphin-saviors.html.
2. Tanya Lewis, "Dolphins May Detect Pregnant Women's Growing Fetuses," Fox News, July 11, 2013, www.foxnews.com/health/2013/07/11/dolphins-may-see-pregnant-women-fetuses/.
3. Cochrane and Callen, *Dolphins and Their Power to Heal,* 182.
4. Odent, *Water and Sexuality,* 12.
5. Cochrane and Callen, *Dolphins and Their Power to Heal,* 184.
6. Lilly, *Man and Dolphini,* 262.
7. Hawkes, *Atlas of Early Man,* 117.
8. Lilly, *Man and Dolphin,* 265.

9. DeMares, *Dolphins, Myths and Transformation*, 193.
10. Ibid., 193.
11. Knappert, *Indian Mythology*, 116.
12. Deena Budd, "Encantado (Dolphin Men)," BellaOnline, www.bellaonline .com/articles/art45516.asp.
13. "Various African Images," DolphinTale, http://dolphintale.com/A3Africa. html#.
14. Jorge Amado, *Bahia de Todos os Santos*, translated by Sabrina Gledhill, http://dolphintale.com/A3Africa.html#.
15. Cochrane and Callen, *Dolphins and Their Power to Heal*, 137.
16. Ibid., 137.
17. Alister McGeorge, "Dolphin Sex: Everything You Need to Know about the Girl Who Talked to Dolphins," *Daily Mirror*, July 17, 2014, www.mirror. co.uk/tv/tv-previews/dolphin-sex-everything-you-need-3709225.
18. Lilly, *Lilly on Dolphins*, 209.
19. Ibid., 209.
20. Sténuit, *Dolphin, Cousin to Man*, 141.
21. Lilly, *Dolphin in History*.

## 17. DOLPHINS AND CHILDREN

1. Pliny, *Natural History*, 31.
2. Pausanius, *Guide to Greece*, 46.
3. Aristotle, *History of Animals*, 37.
4. Dobbs, *Dolphin Healing*, 183.
5. Sténuit, *Dolphin, Cousin to Man*, 104.
6. "Dolphin Saves Boy's Life," *Daily Record*, August 30, 2000, www.eurocbc .org/page158.html.
7. Associated Press, "Dolphins Save Youth from Shark Attack," January 4, 1989, www.apnewsarchive.com/1989/Dolphins-Save-Youth-From-Shark-Attack/ id-e850a14822e5b2f5f2e47a43a4aae754.
8. Bob Flanagan, "Boy's Life Saved by Dolphins," World News Daily Report, June 26, 2014, http://worldnewsdailyreport.com/ boys-life-saved-by-dolphins/.
9. Cochrane and Callen, *Dolphins and Their Power to Heal*, 159.
10. Sténuit, *Dolphin, Cousin to Man*, 107.
11. Miller, *Call of the Dolphins*, 133.
12. Cochrane and Callen, *Dolphins and Their Power to Heal*, 174.

## 18. DOLPHIN CONNECTIONS WITH CATS, DOGS AND WHALES

1. Sheldrake, *Morphic Resonance,* 12.
2. "Cat and Dolphins Playing Together," YouTube, March 6, 2011, www.you tube.com/watch?v=rynvewVe21Y.
3. Sheldrake, *Dogs That Know When Their Owners Are Coming Home.*
4. "Joker and the Dolphins," Animal Liberation Front, www.animalliberation front.com/News/AnimalPhotos/Animals_211-220/218DogDolphins.htm.
5. Cousteau, *Dolphins,* 49.
6. "Dog and Dolphin," YouTube, November 17, 2008, www.youtube.com/watch?v=2D6aAKW-lE4.
7. Carney, *Dog Finds Lost Dolphins,* 15.
8. Ibid., 15.
9. Opit, *Australian Cryptozoology,* 49.
10. Salvatore Cardoni, "Dolphin Pod Saves Policewoman and Her Dog from Drowning," Takepart, March 6, 2013, www.takepart.com/arti cle/2013/03/06/dolphin-pod-plays-lifeguards-saves-policewoman-and-her-dog-drowning-video.
11. "Dolphins Save Dog," YouTube, February 24, 2011, www.youtube.com/watch?v=YEHVJL3lOHQ.
12. "Dolphin and Dog—Let's Be Friends," YouTube, January 7, 2011, www.you tube.com/watch?v=WT69H5ZEoto.
13. Robson, *Pictures in the Dolphin Mind,* 122.
14. Ibid., 122.
15. Ibid., 122.
16. Regina Blackstock, "Dolphin and Man, Equals?" May 1970, www.little townmart.com/dolphins/.
17. Linda Poon, "Deformed Dolphin Accepted into New Family," National Geographic News, January 23, 2013, http://news.nationalgeographic.com/news/2013/130123-sperm-whale-dolphin-adopted-animal-science/.
18. Lilly, *Lilly on Dolphins,* 122.
19. Cousteau, *Dolphins,* 122.
20. Xan Brooks, "Porpoises Rescue Dick Van Dyke," *The Guardian,* November 11, 2010, www.theguardian.com/film/2010/nov/11/dick-van-dyke-porpoises-rescue.
21. Sténuit, *Dolphin, Cousin to Man,* 217.
22. Cochrane and Callen, *Dolphins and Their Power to Heal,* 108.
23. Lilly, *Man and Dolphin,* 194.

## 19. ARE MERMAIDS REAL?

1. Opit, *Australian Cryptozoology,* 20.
2. Ibid., 20.
3. Wagner, "The Ri, Unidentified Aquatic Animal of New Ireland, Papua New Guinea," 19.
4. The Ecosophical Research Association, http://caw.org/content/?q=era.
5. Opit, *Australian Cryptozoology,* 36.
6. Ibid., 38.
7. Ibid., 39.
8. Ibid., 40.
9. Ibid., 43.
10. Ibid., 44.
11. Wagner, "The Ri, unidentified Aquatic Animal of New Ireland, Papua New Guinea," 38.
12. Gil, "Dolphin People Sightings."

## 20. A WEBFOOT IN BOTH WORLDS

1. Opit, *Australian Cryptozoology,* 58.
2. Ibid., 58.
3. Campbell, *Hero with a Thousand Faces,* 272.
4. Aesop, *Aesop's Fables,* 51.
5. Erin Wayman, "Early Bow and Arrows Offer Insight Into Origins of Human Intellect," Smithsonian, November 7, 2012, www.smithsonianmag.com/science-nature/early-bow-and-arrows-offer-insight-into-origins-of-human-intellect.
6. Spence, *Myths & Legends of Babylonia & Assyria,* 158.
7. Ibid., 158.
8. Ibid., 159.
9. Ovid. *Metamorphoses,* 139.
11. Pauka, *Theater and Martial Arts In West Sumatra,* 33.
12. Norbu, *Drung, Deu and Boen,* 147.
13. Ibid., 147.
14. Odent, *Water and Sexuality,* 131.
15. Ibid., 131.
16. Courlander, *Treasury of African Folklore,* 355.
17. Markham, *Journal of Christopher Columbus,* 52.
18. Hunter, *Half Moon,* 207.
19. Perry, *Blackbeard,* 184.
20. Dan Newling, "Reason for Zimbabwe Reservoir Delays: Mermaids Have Been Hounding Workers Away," *Daily Mail,* February 6, 2012, www.dailymail

.co.uk/news/article-2097218/Reason-Zimbabwe-reservoir-delays-mermaids-hounding-workers-away.html.

21. Odent, *Water and Sexuality,* 154.

22. Yolen and Oppenheim, *Fish Prince and Other Stories,* 188.

23. Opit, *Australian Cryptozoology,* 126.

## 21. SIRIUS DOLPHINS

1. Temple, *Sirius Mystery,* 111.

2. Ibid., 111.

3. Ibid., 111.

4. Wikipedia, s.v. "Germaine Dieterlen," http://en.wikipedia.org/wiki/Germaine_Dieterlen.

5. Picknett and Prince, *Stargate Conspiracy,* 59.

6. Harrington, "Planetary Orbits in Binary Stars," 753.

7. Phillip Coppens, "Dogon Shame," www.philipcoppens.com/dogonshame.html.

8. Temple, *Sirius Mystery,* 112.

9. Ibid., 112.

10. Calame-Griaule, "On the Dogon Restudied."

11. Robert Temple, e-mail message to author, September 9, 2014.

12. Ibid.

13. Ibid.

14. Calame-Griaule, "On the Dogon Restudied."

15. Wikipedia, s.v. "Germaine Dieterlen," http://en.wikipedia.org/wiki/Germaine_Dieterlen.

16. Robert Temple, e-mail message to author, September 9, 2014.

17. Ibid.

18. Calame-Griaule, "On the Dogon Restudied."

19. Robert Temple, e-mail message to author, September 9, 2014.

20. Ibid.

21. Temple, *Sirius Mystery.*

22. Robert Temple, e-mail message to author, September 9, 2014.

23. Temple, *Sirius Mystery,* 179.

24. Ibid., 179.

25. "Dolphins," Ian Somerhalder Foundation, www.africa4isf.com/dolphins.html.

26. Aristotle, *History of Animals,* 55.

27. Wyllie, *Dolphins, Telepathy and Underwater Birthing,* 209.

28. Cousteau, *Dolphins,* 200.

29. DeMares, *Dolphins, Myths and Transformation*, 82.
30. Lilly, *Man and Dolphin*, 190.
31. Diderot, *Pictorial Encyclopedia of Trades and Industry*, 388.
32. Norris, *Dolphin Days*, 55.
33. Wyllie, *Dolphins, Telepathy and Underwater Birthing*, 38.
34. Mead, *People of the Land*.
35. "Update on Research on Cayce's Three Hall of Records," EdgarCayce, www.edgarcayce.org/_AncientMysteriesTemp/hallofrecordsupd.html.
36. Steiger, *Atlantis Rising*, 32.

## 22. THE DOLPHINS OF ATLANTIS

1. Woodley, *Man from Atlantis*, 7.
2. Cayce, *Atlantis*, 203.
3. Miller, *Call of the Dolphins*, 25.
4. Plato, *Timaeus and Critias*, 102.
5. Zimmerer, *Chronology of Genesis*, 109.
6. Plato, *Timaeus and Critias*.
7. Zaphiropoulou, *Delos, Monuments and Museum*, 71.
8. Sanders, *Epic of Gilgamesh*, 59.
9. Shaw, *Pima Indian Legends*, 183.
10. O'Bryan, *Navaho Indian Myths*, 105.
11. Ganeri, *Mesoamerican Myth*, 272.
12. Plato, *Timaeus and Critias*, 102.
13. Powell, "Miami Dolphin," 41.
14. Ibid., 41.
15. Naumann, *Japanese Prehistory*, 337.
16. Plato, *Timaeus and Critias*, 102.
17. Aelian, *On Animals*, 71.
18. Kelly, *Ammianus Marcellinus*, 59.
19. Joseph, *Survivors of Atlantis*, 132.
20. Slavin, *Ancient Books of Ireland*, 104.

## 23. PLANET EARTH OR SEAWORLD?

1. Cousteau, *Dolphins*, 251.
2. Risa Roe, "If I Had to Swim between the Gili Islands, Would I Get Eaten by a Shark?" August 4, 2009, http://risaroe.wordpress.com/2009/08/04/if-i-had-to-swim-between-the-gili-islands-would-i-get-eaten-by-a-shark/.
3. "A Shared Fate," BlueVoice, www.bluevoice.org/news_sharedfate.php.
4. Cousteau, *Living Sea*, 252.

## EPILOGUE.
## A DOLPHIN FULFILLS THE MAYAN PROPHESY

1. Caesar, *Conquest of Gaul*, 89.
2. Waters, *Book of the Hopi*, 196.
3. Joe Rao, "New 'Nova' Star Explosion Spotted in Night Sky," www.space .com/22389-nova-star-explosion-delphinus-discovery.html.
4. Gerald Snow, "A Possible Calendric Spiral Petroglyph in Picture Canyon, Flagstaff, AZ," Society for Cultural Astronomy in the American Southwest 2009, www.scaas.org/2009conference.
5. Kozminsky, *Numbers*, 64.
6. de Saint-Martin, *Man*, 152.
7. David McMinn, "The Moon, the Sun and the 9/56-Year Panic Cycle," www.davidmcminn.com/pages/smnum56.htm.
8. Cowgill, *Ancient Teotihuacan*, 5.

# Bibliography

Adams, Douglas. *The Hitchhiker's Guide to the Galaxy*. New York: Del Rey, 1995. First published in 1979.

Aelian. *Historical Miscellany*. Loeb Classical Library, No. 486. Cambridge, Mass.: Harvard University Press, 1997.

———. *On Animals*. Vol. 1., Books 1–5, Cambridge, Mass.: Harvard University Press, 1958.

Aesop. *Aesop's Fables: Complete, Original Translation from Greek*. New York: Forgotten Books, 2007.

Allendy, René. *Le Symbolisme des nombres*. Paris: LeClerc, 1921.

Aristotle. *The History of Animals*. Books 7–10. Loeb Classical Library, No. 439. Cambridge, Mass.: Harvard University Press, 1991.

Au, W. W. L. "The Dolphin Echolocation System." *Journal of the Acoustic Society of America* 102, no. 5 (1997): 3077.

Bastian, J., C. Wall, and C. L. Anderson. "Further Investigation of the Transmission of Arbitrary Environmental Information between Bottlenose Dolphins." Naval Undersea Warfare Center. Report TP 109. 1968.

Beck, Horace. *Folklore and the Sea*. Mystic, Conn.: Mystic Seaport Museum, 1970.

Bielec, P. E., D. S. Gallagher, J. E. Womack, and D. L. Busbee. "Homologies between Human and Dolphin Chromosomes Detected by Heterologous Chromosome Painting." *Cytogenetics and Cell Genetics* 81, no. 1 (1998):18–25, http://tinyurl.com/jwh8ubn.

Buck, William (retold by). *Ramayana*. Oakland: University of California Press, 2012.

Budker, Paul. *Encyclopedie Alha*. Paris: Maison d'édition LeClerc, 1973.

Burr, Harold Saxton. *Blueprint for Immortality: The Electric Patterns of Life*. London: Neville Spearman, 1972.

Busnel, Rene-Guy. *Animal Sonar Systems: Biology and Bionics.* Vols. 1–2. Paris: Laboratoire de Physiologie Acoustique, 1967.

Caesar, Julius. *The Conquest of Gaul.* New York: Penguin Classics, 1983.

Calame-Griaule, Genevieve. "On the Dogon Restudied." *Current Anthropology* 32, no. 5 (December 1991): 77–79.

Campbell, Joseph. *The Hero with a Thousand Faces.* Princeton, N.J.: Princeton University Press, 1972.

Carney, Elizabeth. *Dog Finds Lost Dolphins: And More True Stories of Amazing Animal Heroes.* Washington, D.C.: National Geographic Children's Books, 2012.

Carrington, R. *Mermaids and Mastodons: A Book of Natural and Unnatural History.* London: Chatto and Windus, 1957.

Cayce, Edgar. *Atlantis.* Vol. 22 of *The Edgar Cayce Readings.* Virginia Beach, Va.: Association for Research and Enlightenment, 1987.

Chase, Owen. *The Narrative of the Most Extraordinary and Distressing Shipwreck of the Whale-Ship Essex.* San Diego, Calif.: Harcourt Brace, 1999.

Cirlot, J. E. *A Dictionary of Symbols.* New York: Philosophical Library, 1962.

Cochrane, Amanda, and Karena Callen. *Dolphins and Their Power to Heal.* Rochester, Vt.: Healing Arts Press, 1992.

Cole, D. M. "Electroencephalographic Results of Human-Dolphin Interaction: A Sonophoresis Model." In *Proceedings of the 2nd International Symposium on Dolphin Assisted Therapy.* Cancun, 1996.

Cooper, Keith. "Dolphins, Aliens, and the Search for Intelligent Life." *Astrobiology Magazine,* August 29, 2011, www.astrobio.net/news-exclusive/dolphins-aliens-and-the-search-for-intelligent-life/.

Courlander, Harold. *A Treasury of African Folklore.* New York: Marlowe and Co., 1995.

Cousteau, Jacques-Yves. *Dolphins.* New York: Doubleday, 1975.

———. *The Living Sea.* San Francisco, Calif.: HarperCollins, 1963.

———. *The Ocean World.* New York: Harry N. Abrams, 1985.

Cowgill, George L. *Ancient Teotihuacan.* Cambridge, UK: Cambridge University Press, 2015.

Curtis, L. "The Amazon Dolphin, *Inia geoffrensis,* at the Fort Worth Zoological Park." *International Zoological Yearbook* 4 (1962): 7–9.

Darwin, Charles. *The Origin of Species: 150th Anniversary.* New York: Signet Classics, 2003. First published in 1859.

de Bergerac, Olivia. *The Dolphin Within.* Cammeray, Australia: Simon and Schuster Australia, 1998.

de Saint-Martin, Louis Claude. *Man: His True Nature and Ministry.* County Durham, England: Aziloth Books, 2011.

DeMares, Ryan. *Dolphins, Myths and Transformation.* Boulder, Colo.: Dolphin Institute Press, 2003.

Devine, Eleanor, and Martha Clark. *The Dolphin Smile.* New York: Macmillan, 1967.

Diderot, Denis. *Pictorial Encyclopedia of Trades and Industry.* Vol. 2. New York: Dover, 1993.

Dobbs, Horace. *Dolphin Healing.* London: Judy Piatkus, 2000.

———. *Follow the Wild Dolphins.* New York: St. Martin's Press, 1987.

———. *The Magic of Dolphins.* New York: Sheridan House, 1990.

———. *Tale of Two Dolphins.* New York: Jonathan Cape, 1988.

Edelstein, S. "An Alternative Paradigm for Hominoid Evolution." *Human Evolution* 2, no. 169 (1987): 24–35.

Edwards, Hugh. *The Remarkable Dolphins of Monkey Mia.* Melbourne, Australia: Edwards, 1989.

———. *Shark: The Shadow Below.* San Francisco, Calif.: HarperCollins, 1998.

Eliade, Mircea. *Shamanism: Archaic Techniques of Ecstasy.* Princeton, N.J.: Princeton University Press, 2004.

Ganeri, Anita. *Mesoamerican Myth: A Treasury of Central American Legends, Art, and History.* London: Chartwell Books, 2000.

Gibson, James William. *A Reenchanted World: The Quest for a New Kinship with Nature.* New York: Picador, 2010.

Goethe, Johann Wolfgang von. "Zwei Seelen wohnen, ach!, in meiner Brust, Die eine will sich von der andern trennen." Chap. 5 in *Faust.* Translated by Peter Salm. New York: Bantam Books, 1988. Reprint. Goodall, Jane. *In the Shadow of Man.* New York: Mariner Books, 2010.

Griaule, Marcel. *Dogon Masks.* New Haven, Conn.: Human Relations Area Files, 1986.

Haldane, J. B. S. *Possible Worlds and Other Essays.* London: Chatto and Windus, 1932.

Hardy, A. "Has Man an Aquatic Past?" *The Listener* 2, no. 5 (May 12, 1960): 10–15.

Harrington, Robert S. "Planetary Orbits in Binary Stars." *Astronomical Journal* 82, no. 9 (September 1977): 753–756.

Hawkes, Jacquetta. *The Atlas of Early Man: Concurrent Developments across the Ancient World, 35,000 B.C.–A.D. 500.* New York: St. Martin's Press, 1976.

Herman, L. M., A. A. Pack, and M. Hoffmann-Kuhnt. "Seeing through Sound: Dolphins (*Tursiops truncatus*) Perceive the Spatial Structure of Objects

Through Echolocation." *Journal of Comparative Psychology* 112 (1998): 292–305.

Herman, L. M., A. A. Pack, and A. M. Wood. "Bottlenose Dolphins Can Generalize Rules and Develop Abstract Concepts." *Marine Mammal Science* 10, no. 1 (1994): 70–80.

Herman, L. M., D. G. Richards, and J. P. Wolz. "Comprehension of Sentences by Bottlenosed Dolphins." *Cognition* 16 (1984): 129–219.

Herzing, Denise L. *Dolphin Diaries: My 25 Years with Spotted Dolphins in the Bahamas.* New York: St. Martin's Press, 2011.

Hindley, M. Patricia. Human/Animal Communication: Cetacean Roles in Human Therapeutic Situations. Paper presented at the IWC Non-Consumptive Utilization of Cetacean Resources Conference, Boston, 1983.

Hogel, Christian. *Symeon Metaphrastes: Rewriting and Canonization, Opuscula Graecolatina.* Copenhagen, Denmark: Museum Tusculanum Press, 2002.

Hoyt, Erich. *Orca: The Whale Called Killer.* Toronto, Ontario: Firefly Books, 2013.

Hunter, Douglas. *Half Moon: Henry Hudson and the Voyage That Redrew the Map of the New World.* London: Bloomsbury Press, 2009.

Iikura Y., Y. Sakamoto, T. Imai, L. Akai, T. Matsuoka, K. Sugihara, M. Utumi, and M. Tomikawa. "Dolphin-Assisted Seawater Therapy for Severe Atopic Dermatitis: An Immunological and Psychological Study." *International Archives of Allergy and Immunology* 1, no. 3 (2001): 389–90.

Jacobs, Myron, Peter J. Morgane, and Ilya I. Glezer. "Comparative and Evolutionary Anatomy of the Visual Cortex of the Dolphin." *Cerebral Cortex* 8B (1990): 215–62, http://link.springer.com/chapter/10.1007/978-1-4615-3824-0_4.

Janik, V. M., G. Dehnhardt, and D. Todt. "Signature Whistle Variation in a Bottlenosed Dolphin, *Tursiops truncatus.*" *Behavioural Ecology and Sociobiology* 35, no. 2 (1994): 243–48.

Jebb, Richard. *Bacchylides: The Poems and Fragments.* Cambridge, Mass.: Cambridge University Press, 1905.

Joseph, Frank, *Before Atlantis.* Rochester, Vt.: Bear & Company, 2013.

———. *Survivors of Atlantis* Rochester, Vt.: Bear & Company, 2004.

Kelly, Gavin. *Ammianus Marcellinus: The Allusive Historian.* Cambridge, UK: Cambridge University Press, 2008.

Kirby, David. *Death at SeaWorld.* New York: St. Martin's Griffin, 2013.

Knappert, Jan. *Indian Mythology: An Encyclopedia of Myth and Legend.* London: Diamond Books, 1995.

Kozminsky, Isodore. *Numbers, Their Meaning and Magic.* New York: Samuel Weiser, 1912.

Lang, T. G., and H. A. P. Smith. "Communication between Dolphins in Separate Tanks by Way of an Electronic Acoustic Link." *Science* 150, no. 5 (1965): 1,839–44.

Lilly, John Cunningham. *Communication between Man and Dolphin: The Possibilities of Talking with Other Species.* New York: Crown, 1978.

———. "Distress Call of the Bottlenose Dolphin: Stimuli and Evoked Behavioral Responses." *Science* 139, no. 7 (1965): 116–18.

———. The Dolphin in History. Papers delivered by Ashley Montagu and John C. Lilly at a symposium at the William Andrews Clark Memorial Library, Los Angeles, 1962 and 1963. www.archive.org/stream/dolphininhistory 00mont/dolphininhistory00mont_djvu.txt.

———. *Lilly on Dolphins.* New York: Anchor Press, 1975.

———. *Man and Dolphin.* New York: Doubleday, 1961.

———. *The Mind of the Dolphin: A Non-Human Intelligence.* New York: Avon Books, 1967.

———. "Vocal Mimicry in Tursiops: Ability to Match Numbers and Durations of Human Vocal Bursts." *Science* 147, no. 9 (1965): 300–301.

Lilly, J. C., and A. M. Miller. "Sounds Emitted by the Bottlenose Dolphin." *Science* 133, no. 8 (1961): 1689–93.

Llano, George Albert. *Airmen against the Sea: An Analysis of Sea Survival Experiences.* Honolulu, Hawaii: University Press of the Pacific, 2002.

Lohn, John P. *Historical Dictionary of Competitive Swimming.* Lanham, Md.: Scarecrow Press, 2010.

Lovelock, James. *The Vanishing Face of Gaia: A Final Warning.* New York: Basic Books, 2010.

Gil, M. "Dolphin People Sightings." *Nexus* 21, no. 4 (June–July): 214.

Mackay, R. P. *Searching for Hidden Animals.* London: Cadogan Books, 1981.

Mackenzie, Donald A. *Mythology of the Babylonian People.* London: Gresham, 1915.

Markham, Clements, R., trans. *The Journal of Christopher Columbus (during His First Voyage, 1492–93).* Boston, Mass.: Adamant Media Corporation, 2001.

Mayol, Jacques. *L'homo delphinus* [*Homo Delphinus: L'Uomo, Questo Anfibio Sconosciuto*]. Translated by Renato Caporali Mayol. Milan: Giunti Martello, 1983.

Mead, James G., and Joy Gold. *Whales and Dolphins in Question.* Washington, D.C. : Smithsonian Institution Press, 2002.

Mead, Te Rina. *People of the Land: Images and Maori Proverbs of Aoteroa New Zealand.* Honolulu: University of Hawaii Press, 2010.

"Michel Odent." *The Lancet* 353, no. 9154 (February 27, 1999): 764.

Miller, Greg. "Is a Dolphin a Person?" *Science Magazine*, February 21, 2010, http://news.sciencemag.org/brain-behavior/2010/02/dolphin-person.

Miller, Lana. *Call of the Dolphins*. Portland, Ore.: Rainbow Bridge, 1989.

Morgan, Elaine. *The Aquatic Ape*. New York: Stein and Day, 1982.

Morris, Desmond. *The Naked Ape: A Zoologist's Study of the Human Animal*. New York: Delta, 1999.

Morton, Alexandra. *Listening to Whales: What the Orcas Have Taught Us*. New York: Ballantine Books, 2004.

Mutwa, Credo Vusamazulu. *Song of the Stars: The Lore of a Zulu Shaman*. New York: Institute for Publishing Arts, 1996.

Nathanson, David E. "Long Term Effectiveness of Dolphin Assisted Therapy for Children with Severe Disabilities." *Anthrozoos* 11, no. 1 (1989): 22–32.

Nathanson, David E., and S. D. Faria. "Cognitive Improvement of Children in Water with and without Dolphins." *Anthrozoos* 6, no. 1 (1993): 17–29.

Nathanson, David E., D. de Castro, H. Friend, and M. McMahon. "Effectiveness of Short-term Dolphin-assisted Therapy for Children with Severe Disabilities." *Anthrozoos* 10, no. 2–3 (1997): 90–100.

Naumann, Nelly. *Japanese Prehistory: The Material and Spiritual Culture of the Jōmon Period*. Munich, Germany: Harrassowitz Verlag, 2000.

Nietzsche, Friedrich. *Beyond Good and Evil*. New York: Tribeca Books, 2013. First published in 1886.

———. *Thus Spake Zarathustra*. Translated by R. J. Hollingdale. New York: Penguin Classics, 1961.

Nollman, Jim. *Dolphin Dreamtime: The Art and Science of Interspecies Communication*. New York: Bantam, 1987.

Nomura, T., K. Higuchi, H. Yu, S. Sasaki, S. Kimura, H. Itoh, M. Taniguchi, T. Arakawa, and K. Kawai. "Slow-wave Photic Stimulation Relieves Patient Discomfort during Esophagogastroduodenoscopy." *Journal of Gastroenterol Hepatol* 21, no. 1, part 1 (2006): 54–58.

Norbu, Namkhai. *Drung, Deu and Boen: Narrations, Symbolic Languages and the Bien Tradition in Ancient Tibet*. Translated by Adriano Clemente and Andrew Lukianowicz. New York: Library of Tibetan Works and Archives, 1998.

Norris, Frank. *Dolphin Days: The Life and Times of the Spinner Dolphin*. New York: W. W. Norton, 1991.

O'Bryan, Aileen. *Navaho Indian Myths*. New York: Dover, 1993.

Odent, Michel. *Water and Sexuality*. London: Arkana, 1990.

Opit, Gary. *Australian Cryptozoology*. Sydney, Australia. Australia Equilateral Enterprise, 2009.

Oppian. *Halieuticks*. Memphis, Tenn.: The Classics.us, 2013.

Ovid. *Metamorphoses*. Translated by Rolfe Humphries. Indianapolis, Indiana University Press, 1960.

Pauka, Kirstin. *Theater and Martial Arts in West Sumatra: Randai and Silek of the Minangkabau*. Cleveland: Ohio University Press, 1999.

Pausanias. *Guide to Greece*. Vol. 2, *Southern Greece*. New York: Penguin Classics, 1984.

Payne, Roger S. "Humpbacks: Their Mysterious Songs." *National Geographic*, January 1979: 18–25.

———. "Songs of Humpback Whales." *Science* 173, no. 5 (1971): 107.

Pennick, Nigel. *Secrets of King's College Chapel*. London: Aeon Books, 2012.

Picknett, Lynn, and Clive Prince. *The Stargate Conspiracy: The Truth about Extraterrestrial Life and the Mysteries of Ancient Egypt*. New York: Berkeley Books, 1999.

Perry, Dan. *Blackbeard: The Real Pirate of the Caribbean*. New York: Basic Books, 2006.

Phylarchus. *Phylarchi Historiarum Reliquiae*. Whitefish, Mont.: Kessinger, 2009. First published in 1839.

Plato. *Timaeus and Critias*. Translated by Desmond Lee. New York: Penguin Classics, 1969.

Pliny. *Natural History*. Vol. 1, books 1–2. Loeb Classical Library, No. 330. Translated by H. Rackham. Cambridge, Mass: Harvard University Press, 1938.

Powell, Eric A. "Miami Dolphin." *Archeology* 55, no. 2 (March–April 2002): 14.

Ptolemy. *Tetrabiblos*. Loeb Classical Library, No. 435. Translated by F. E. Robbins. Cambridge, Mass: Harvard University Press, 1940.

Randall, Richard H., Jr. *The Metropolitan Museum of Art Cloisters Bestiary*. New York: Metropolitan Museum of Art, 1960.

Reiss, Diana. *The Dolphin in the Mirror: Exploring Dolphin Minds and Saving Dolphin Lives*. Boston, Mass..: Houghton Mifflin Harcourt, 2011.

Ridgway, Sam. *The Dolphin Doctor: A Pioneering Veterinarian Remembers the Extraordinary Dolphin That Inspired His Career*. Windsor, Conn.: Yankee Books, 1987.

Robson, Frank. *Pictures in the Dolphin Mind*. New York: Sheridan House, 1988.

Sagan, Carl. *The Cosmic Connection: An Extraterrestrial Perspective*. Cambridge, Mass.: Cambridge University Press, 2000.

Sandars, N. K., trans. *The Epic of Gilgamesh*. New York: Penguin Classics, 1960.

Sanderson, Ivan. *Animal Treasure: A Naturalist in Search of Strange Creatures*. New York: Viking Press, 1937.

Schopenhauer, Arthur. *The World as Will and Representation*. Vol. 1. Translated by E. F. J. Payne. New York: Dover, 1966.

Shaw, Anna Moore. *Pima Indian Legends*. Tucson: University of Arizona Press, 1968.

Sheldrake, Rupert. *Dogs That Know When Their Owners Are Coming Home*. New York: Broadway Books, 2011.

———. *Morphic Resonance: The Nature of Formative Causation*. Rochester, Vt.: Park Street Press, 2009.

Slavin, Michael. *The Ancient Books of Ireland*. Montreal, Quebec: McGill-Queens University Press, 2005.

Sophocles. *Antigone*. Boston, Mass.: Focus/R. Pullins, 1998.

———. *Electra*. Translated by Sir George Young. New York: Dover, 1995.

Spence, Lewis. *Myths and Legends of Babylonia and Assyria*. London: George G. Harrap, 1916.

Steiger, Brad. *Atlantis Rising*. New York: Dell, 1973.

Sténuit, Robert. *The Dolphin, Cousin to Man*. New York: Sterling, 1968.

Stewart, David. "Our Father, Who Art in . . . Water?" *Simply Living Magazine* (Sydney, Australia) 11 (1980): 44.

———. "The Wading Ape." *Simply Living Magazine* (Sydney, Australia) 14 (1981): 37.

Stewart, David, and Ray Knox. *The Earthquake America Forgot*. St. Louis, Mo.: Gutenberg-Richter, 2005.

Taylor, Scott. *Souls in the Sea: Dolphins, Whales, and Human Destiny*. Berkeley, Calif.: Frog Books, 2003.

Temple, Robert. *The Sirius Mystery*. Rochester, Vt.: Destiny Books, 1998.

Thompson, P. M. "Evidence of Infanticide in Bottlenose Dolphins: An Explanation for Violent Interactions with Harbour Porpoises?" *Proceedings of the Royal Society London* 265 (1998): 1167–70.

Titelman, Gregory Y. *Dictionary of Popular Proverbs and Sayings*. New York: Random House, 1996.

Viegas, Jennifer. "Did a Dolphin Really Say 'Sargassum'?" *Discovery*, March 31, 2014, http://news.discovery.com/animals/whales-dolphins/did-a-dolphin-really-say-sargassum-140331.htm.

Wagner, R. "The Ri, Unidentified Aquatic Animal of New Ireland, Papua New Guinea." *Cryptozoology, the Interdisciplinary Journal of the International Society of Cryptozoology* 1, no. 7 (1982): 33–39.

Waters, Frank. *Book of the Hopi*. New York: Penguin Books, 1977.

Williams, Tennessee. *Night of the Iguana*. New York: New Directions, 2009.

Woodley, Richard. *Man from Atlantis*. New York: Dell, 1977.

Wyllie, Timothy. *Dolphins, Telepathy and Underwater Birthing.* Santa Fe, N.M.: Bear & Company, 1993.

Yolen, Jane and Shulamith L. Oppenheim, *The Fish Prince and Other Stories: Merman Folk Tales.* New York: Interlink Books, 2001

Zaphiropoulou, Photini. *Delos, Monuments and Museum.* Translated by H. L. Turner. Athens, Greece: Krene Editions, 1983.

Zimmerer, Neil. *The Chronology of Genesis.* Kempton, Ill.: Adventures Unlimited Press, 2003.

Zuckerman, Catherine. "Sold Gras." *National Geographic* 225, no. 2 (February 2014): 54–55.

# Index

Numbers in *italics* preceded by *pl.* indicate colored plate numbers.

# BOOKS OF RELATED INTEREST

**Before Atlantis**
20 Million Years of Human and Pre-Human Cultures
*by Frank Joseph*

**Atlantis and the Coming Ice Age**
The Lost Civilization—A Mirror of Our World
*by Frank Joseph*

**Advanced Civilizations of Prehistoric America**
The Lost Kingdoms of the Adena, Hopewell,
Mississippians, and Anasazi
*by Frank Joseph*

**Animal Voices**
Telepathic Communication in the Web of Life
*by Dawn Baumann Brunke*

**Animal Messengers**
An A–Z Guide to Signs and Omens in the Natural World
*by Regula Meyer*

**Dolphins, ETs & Angels**
Adventures Among Spiritual Intelligences
*by Timothy Wyllie*

**Psychic Communication with Animals for Health and Healing**
*by Laila del Monte*

**Dolphins and Their Power to Heal**
*by Amanda Cochrane and Karena Callen*

INNER TRADITIONS • BEAR & COMPANY
P.O. Box 388
Rochester, VT 05767
1-800-246-8648
www.InnerTraditions.com

Or contact your local bookseller